network linking computer research centers at colleges and universities. E-mail within a computer network was made possible by the creation of a file-transfer program in 1972. There was a problem, however; it was not possible to send e-mail that was created on one network to a computer on a different network. This problem was solved the following year when Vinton Cerf and Robert Kahn created a software framework known as TCP/IP (Transmission Control Protocol/Internet Protocol). Launched in 1973, this cross-network protocol paved the way for a "network of networks," and the **Internet** was born.

The ability to exchange e-mail messages on the Internet had a revolutionary impact on society, as technology guru Stewart Brand noted in the late 1980s:

> Marshall McLuhan used to remark, "Gutenberg made everybody a reader. Xerox made everybody a publisher." Personal computers are making everybody an author. E-mail, word processing programs that make revising as easy as thinking, and laser printers collapse the whole writing–publishing–distributing process into one event controlled entirely by the individual. If, as alleged, the only real freedom of the press is to own one, the fullest realization of the First Amendment is being accomplished by technology, not politics.[3]

"There are certain limitations that are part of the network, and we are struggling with that. We're worried that in the zeal to address localization that people will not be able to communicate any more. If someone gives you a business card with the e-mail address in Chinese, what are you to do?"[6]

Vinton G. Cerf, Internet pioneer and former chairman of ICANN

Of course, the Internet revolution did not end with the advent of e-mail. More hardware and software innovations were yet to come. As America Online cofounder Steve Case has noted, the "first wave" of the Internet revolution began in the mid-1980s as companies such as Cisco Systems and Xilinx created the core technologies (e.g., routers) that were the infrastructure or "on ramps" to the Internet.[4]

In 1990, a software consultant named Tim Berners-Lee invented the **Uniform Resource Locator (URL)**, an Internet site's address on the World Wide Web; **Hypertext Markup Language (HTML)**, a format language that controls the appearance of Web pages; and **Hypertext Transfer Protocol (HTTP)**, which enables hypertext files to be transferred across the Internet.[5] These innovations allowed Web sites to be linked and visually rich content to be posted and accessed. In short, Berners-Lee is the father of the **World Wide Web** (see Exhibit 15-2).

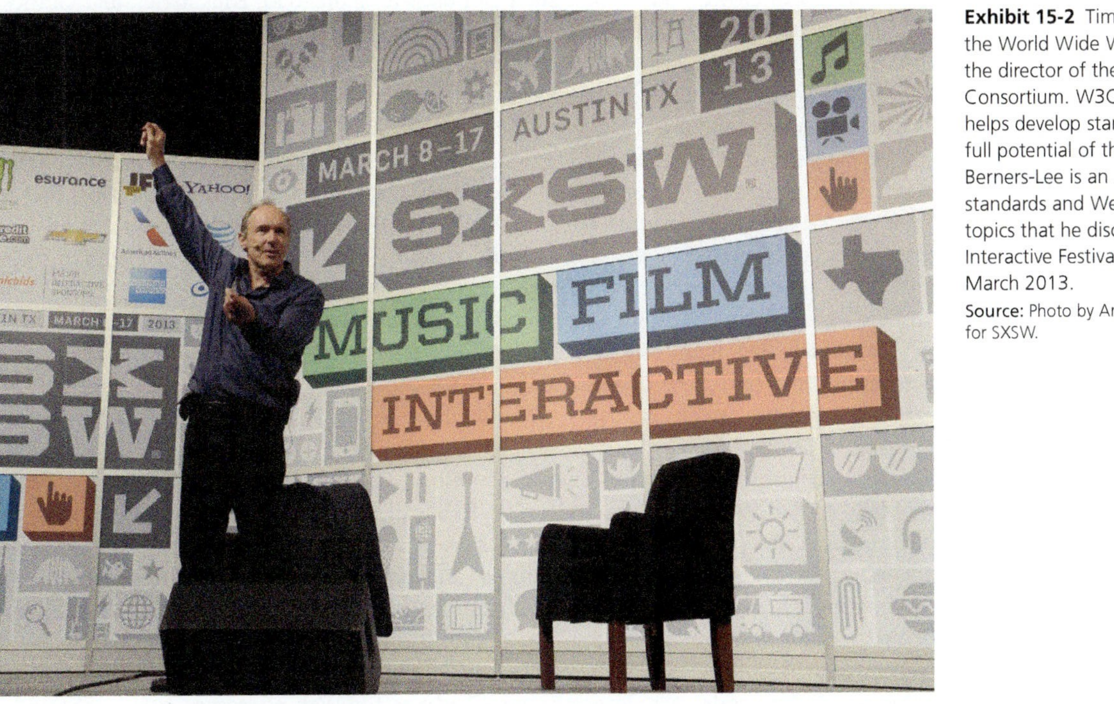


**Exhibit 15-2** Tim Berners-Lee invented the World Wide Web, and today he is the director of the World Wide Web Consortium. W3C is a foundation that helps develop standards that allow the full potential of the Web to be realized. Berners-Lee is an advocate for open standards and Web neutrality, two topics that he discussed at the SXSW Interactive Festival in Austin, Texas, in March 2013.

**Source:** Photo by Amy E. Price/Getty Images for SXSW.

[3]Stewart Brand, *The Media Lab: Inventing the Future at MIT* (New York: Penguin Books, 1988), p. 253.
[4]Steve Case, "Pardon the Disruption: Steve Case on Entrepreneurs." Keynote address presented at SXSW Music, Film, and Interactive, March 14, 2015. See also Nick Summers, "Steve Case's Second Life," *Bloomberg Businessweek* (August 26, 2013), pp. 52–57.
[5]Hypertext is any text that contains links to other documents.
[6]John Markoff, "Control the Internet? A Futile Pursuit, Some Say," *The New York Times* (November 24, 2005), p. C4.

In 1992, the U.S. government authorized the use of the Internet for commercial purposes. At the time, however, it was believed that programmers and scientists would be the heaviest users. In the mid-1990s, a computer scientist at the University of Illinois named Marc Andreessen developed a Web browser; called Mosaic, it combined images and words together on the same screen and allowed users to search for and view resources on the Web. Andreessen joined forces with Jim Clark, one of the founders of Silicon Graphics, to form Mosaic Communications. Renamed Netscape Communications, the company became one of the brightest stars in the dot-com era as commercial demand for the Netscape browser software exploded. As Thomas L. Friedman notes, "Marc Andreessen did not invent the Internet, but he did as much as any single person to bring it alive and popularize it."[7]

Within five years of the Web's debut, the user base increased from 600,000 to 40 million. Although computer makers were slow to add modems to PCs, fledgling online services such as America Online (AOL) were exhibiting robust subscriber growth. Thanks in part to a direct-mail marketing campaign during which millions of software discs were sent to prospective customers, AOL grew from 5 million subscribers in 1996 to 20 million subscribers in 1999. And, of course, the company's iconic sign-on greeting, "You've got mail," has become a part of popular culture.

During the second wave of the Internet revolution, which Case describes as running from 2000 to 2014, the focus shifted from building the Internet to building on top of it. Search engines such as Yahoo! and Google emerged and encryption and security features were built into the Web. Social media companies, including Facebook, YouTube, and Twitter, exploded on the scene, and the iPhone launched the "app economy."

Case envisions the third wave as a time when the Internet is seamlessly integrated into everyday life. He also anticipates a period of reinvention and disruption in key economic sectors, with major changes in health care, education, financial services, and transportation. Some of this integration and disruption is already occurring, as evidenced by the popularity of ride-sharing services such as Uber and Lyft. And, as the controversy over Uber demonstrates, the third wave is likely to be characterized by an ongoing dialog between attackers and defenders of disruption and revolution.

Case foresees four trends during the third wave. Case describes the first trend as "capital for all," with global crowdfunding sites such GoFundMe, Indiegogo, Kickstarter, and Quirky growing in importance. Second will be the reemergence of partnerships; whether in health care or education, *who* a company partners with will be just as important as what the company does. A third trend will be the emergence of the social enterprise that links profit and purpose. Warby Parker, Tesla, and TOMS are three examples. Case dubs the fourth trend the "rise of the rest," as the globalization of entrepreneurship gains traction on a regional basis, far from startup hotbeds such as Silicon Valley.

Today, almost 3 billion people—nearly half of the world's population—are using the Internet. As noted in Chapter 10, because residents in developing countries lag in terms of Internet access, Google is working to build wireless networks in areas, especially outside large cities, that are beyond the reach of wired networks (see Exhibit 15-3).[8]

However, the technology's powerful capabilities and increasing importance have resulted in a backlash that manifests itself in various ways. For example, the Chinese government, alarmed by the free flow of information across the Internet, closely monitors the content on Web sites that its citizens access. Facebook, Twitter, and numerous other social media sites are blocked in China.

Who controls the Internet? Good question! The first Internet Governance Forum (IGF) was held in Athens, Greece, in 2006. The IGF will guide "the development and application by governments, the private sector, and civil society, in their respective roles, of shared principles, norms, rules, decision-making procedures, and programs that shape the evolution and use of the Internet." Some people in the global Internet community are concerned about the inclusion of the word "governments" in this statement. The nonprofit Internet Corporation for Assigned Names and Numbers (ICANN) is based in Marina del Ray, California. ICANN maintains a database of Web addresses, approves new suffixes for Web addresses (e.g., .info and .tv), and performs other behind-the-scenes procedures that are critical for keeping the Internet functioning properly. ICANN's advisory body includes international members, but the U.S. Department of Commerce retains veto power over all decisions. For example, after ICANN tentatively

[7]Thomas L. Friedman, *The World Is Flat* (New York: Farrar, Straus and Giroux, 2005), p. 58.

[8]Amir Efrati, "Google Pushes into Emerging Markets," *The Wall Street Journal* (May 25–26, 2013), pp. B1, B2.

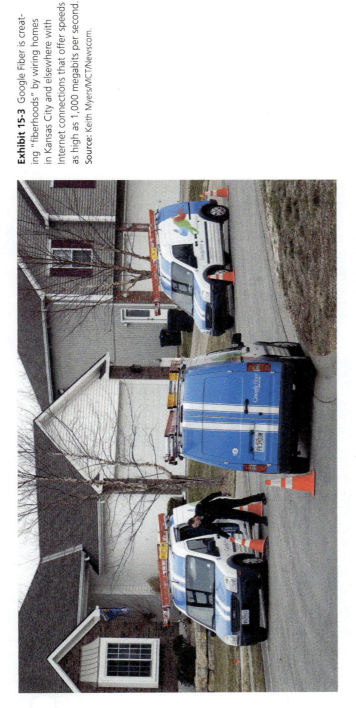

**Exhibit 15-3** Google Fiber is creating "fiberhoods" by wiring homes in Kansas City and elsewhere with Internet connections that offer speeds as high as 1,000 megabits per second.
Source: Keith Myers/MCT/Newscom.

approved the domain name .xxx for pornography sites, the U.S. Department of Commerce blocked the decision.

Policymakers in some countries are concerned about U.S. control of the Internet. For example, China, India, Brazil, and the European Union (EU) have taken the position that, because the Internet is global, no single country should be in control of it. Accordingly, these nations have sought to have the United Nations assume a role in Internet governance.[9] Privacy is another issue. As companies become more adept at using the Internet to gather, store, and access information about customers, privacy issues are becoming a focal point of concern among policymakers and the general public. In the EU, for example, a privacy protection directive was established in 1995; in 2002, the EU adopted a privacy and electronic communications directive.

## 15-2 Convergence

The digital revolution is causing dramatic, disruptive changes in industry structures. Writing in *The New York Times* at the beginning of 2010, columnist Jon Pareles summarized some of these changes as follows:

> The 2000s were the broadband decade, the disintermediation decade, the file-sharing decade, the digital recording (and image) decade, the iPod decade, the long-tail decade, the blog decade, the user-generated decade, the on-demand decade, the all-access decade. Inaugurating the new millennium, the Internet swallowed culture whole and delivered it back—cheaper, faster, and smaller—to everyone who can get online.[10]

**Convergence** is a term that refers to the coming together of previously separate industries and product categories (see Figure 15-1). New technologies affect the business sector(s) in which a company competes. What business is Sony in? Originally, Sony was a consumer electronics company best known for innovative products such as transistor radios, Trinitron televisions, VCRs, stereo components, and the Walkman line of personal music players. Then, Sony entered new businesses by acquiring CBS Records and Columbia Motion Pictures. These acquisitions themselves did not represent convergence, however, because they occurred in the early days of the digital revolution, when motion pictures, recorded music, and consumer electronics were still separate industries.

[9]Christopher Rhoads, "EU, Developing Nations Challenge U.S. Control of Internet," *The Wall Street Journal* (October 25, 2005), pp. B1, B2. See also "A Free Internet," *Financial Times* (November 14, 2003), p. 15.
[10]Jon Pareles, "A World of Megabeats and Megabytes," *The New York Times* (January 3, 2010), p. AR1.

## INNOVATION, ENTREPRENEURSHIP, AND THE GLOBAL STARTUP

### Jack Ma, Alibaba

SYNC • THINK • LEARN

MyMarketingLab

Jack Ma is an entrepreneur. He has developed several innovative products and services, created new brands, and started companies to market his creations. By applying the basic tools and principles of modern marketing, Ma has achieved remarkable success. As is true with many of today's entrepreneurs, Ma's key innovation was based on his insights into the possibilities and opportunities provided by the Internet. Today, about 80 percent of China's e-commerce is channeled through Alibaba, the company Ma founded in 1999. Not surprisingly, Ma is a billionaire many times over; he is also the richest man in China (see Exhibit 15-4).

| | |
|---|---|
| 600 million | Number of registered Alibaba users, 2014 |
| 100 million | Number of online shoppers using Alibaba every day |
| $200 billion | Value of goods handled by Alibaba in 2013 |

After teaching himself English and working as a tour guide, Ma graduated from Hangzhou Teacher's Institute on China's eastern coast. In the mid-1990s, he started his own translation business. On a trip to the United States, he discovered the Internet, an innovation whose existence China's state-run media did not acknowledge. Returning home, he started China Pages, an online directory connecting Chinese businesses with customers abroad. Ma lost control of his startup when he was forced to enter into a joint venture with the government-owned Hangzhou Telecom.

Later, as an employee of the Ministry of Foreign Trade and Economic Cooperation, Ma had a serendipitous assignment: escorting Yahoo founder Jerry Yang on a tour of the Great Wall. Soon after that encounter, in 1999, Ma and a group of friends created Alibaba. The new company was a Web service that allowed small and midsized Chinese companies to find global customers.

In 2003, Ma launched a consumer site called Taobao (Chinese for "search for treasure") as an alternative to eBay. At the time, eBay and its Chinese partner, EachNet, dominated the market. Undeterred, Ma famously remarked at the time, "EBay is a shark in the ocean, we are a crocodile in the Yantze River. If we fight in the ocean we will lose but if we fight in the river we will win."

Initially, Taobao set itself apart from eBay by not charging sales commissions or listing fees. Ma was convinced that global Internet companies entering China were making three kinds of mistakes. First, they underestimated the differences between China and the U.S. market. Second, they incurred higher costs than local Chinese operators. Finally, they went global too quickly. Ma's instincts were correct. In less than five years, eBay's share of the Chinese market was down to single digits, while Taobao dominated the market with an 85 percent share. Another service, Tmall, is a mass-market shopping site for Chinese consumers.

In 2005, Yahoo paid $1 billion for a 40 percent share of Alibaba, and Ma became chief executive of Yahoo's Chinese operations. In 2014, Alibaba made history when its $25 billion initial public offering on the New York Stock Exchange set a record for both the United States and the world. Ma is also preparing to launch 11 Main, a site specifically targeting American shoppers. Alibaba is making selective investments in innovative startups, including Lyft, the ride-sharing service that competes with Uber. Acknowledging that consumer awareness of Alibaba is low in the United States, executives are pursuing a "go-slow" approach to the U.S. market. As one insider said, "It would be a little naïve to think we can simply export our people and our business models into other markets, and specifically into markets as mature as the U.S."

**Sources:** David Barboza, "The Jack Ma Way," *The New York Times Sunday* Business (September 7, 2014), pp. 1, 4–5; David Gelles, Hiroko Tabuchi, and Michael J. de la Merced, "Alibaba's American Aspirations," *The New York Times* (May 24, 2014), pp. B1, B5; Jamil Anderlini, "The Billionaire Determined to Transform His Country," *Financial Times* (December 13, 2013), p. 9.

**Exhibit 15-4** Alibaba founder Jack Ma is a fan of Chinese kung fu novels. His company's initial public offering (IPO) in 2014 raised more than $20 billion.

**Source:** Ole Spata/dpa picture alliance/Alamy.

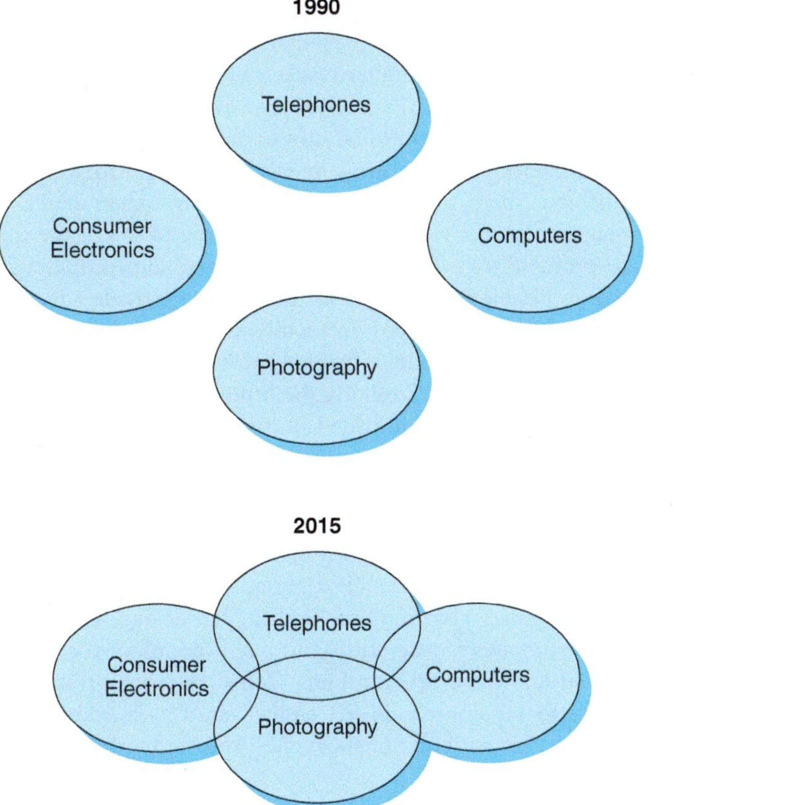


**FIGURE 15-1**
**Industry Convergence**

Today, however, Sony is in the "bits" business: Its core businesses incorporate digital technology and involve digitizing and distributing sound, images, and data. Now, Sony's competitors include Apple (music players, smartphones), Dell (computers), Canon (cameras), and Nokia (smartphones).

What kinds of challenges does convergence present? Consider the case of Kodak, the undisputed leader in photography-related products for more than a century. The company struggled to remake its business model as its sales of digital-related products grew from zero to $1 billion in five years. Because of convergence, Kodak's competitors came to include companies such as Dell and Hewlett-Packard. Moreover, Kodak's core businesses—film, photographic paper, and chemicals—were disrupted. Competition also came from the telecommunications industry. The cell phone camera was invented in 1997; a key benefit was the ability to download digital photos from the camera and post them on the Web or e-mail them to friends. Ironically, Motorola, a key player in the cell phone business, could have been one of the first companies to market a cell phone camera. However, management's attention was distracted by the ill-fated launch of the Iridium satellite phone. As a result, inventor Philippe Kahn took his idea to Japan, where the first cell phone cameras were introduced in 1999.[11] In 2010, annual sales of camera-equipped cell phones passed the 1-billion-unit mark.

> **"I think there will be an increasing convergence between content and commerce, that it will be about following consumers instead of making consumers come to you, and I am especially excited about the various platforms that will allow more and more access to customers."[12]**
>
> Natalie Massenet, founder, Net-a-Porter

## 15-3 Value Networks and Disruptive Technologies

As noted in the chapter introduction, the digital revolution has created both opportunities and threats.[13] Dell, IBM, Kodak, Motorola, Xerox, and Sony are just a few examples of global companies that have struggled to remake their businesses in the face of technological innovation.

[11]Kevin Maney, "Baby's Arrival Inspires Birth of Cell Phone Camera—and Societal Evolution," *USA Today* (January 24, 2007), p. 3B.
[12]Vanessa Friedman, "Ready for the Next Chapter in E-Tailing," *Financial Times* (April 5, 2010), p. 18.
[13]Much of the material in this section is adapted from Clayton Christensen, *The Innovator's Dilemma* (New York: HarperBusiness, 2003). See also Simon London, "Digital Discomfort: Companies Struggle to Deal with the 'Inevitable Surprise' of the Transition from Atoms to Bits," *Financial Times* (December 17, 2003), p. 17.

IBM missed out on the minicomputer market, in part because management believed minicomputers promised lower profit margins and represented a smaller market opportunity. DEC, Data General, and Prime created the minicomputer market, but these companies, in turn, missed the PC revolution. This time, however, IBM's executive team demonstrated that it had learned its lesson: It set up an independent organizational unit to create the company's first PC. However, IBM subsequently was slow to recognize growing market demand for laptops; new entrants included Apple, Dell, Toshiba, Sharp, and Zenith. Recently, IBM exited the PC market altogether.

How is it that managers at many companies fail to respond to change in a timely manner? According to Harvard professor Clayton Christensen, the problem is that executives become so committed to a current, profitable technology that they fail to provide adequate levels of investment in new, apparently riskier technologies. Ironically, companies fall into this trap by adhering to prevailing marketing orthodoxy, namely, listening to and responding to the needs of established customers. Christensen calls this situation the **innovator's dilemma**.

In every industry, companies are embedded in a **value network**. Each value network has a cost structure associated with it that dictates the margins needed to achieve profitability. The boundaries of the network are defined, in part, by the unique rank ordering of the importance of various product performance attributes. Parallel value networks, each built around a different definition of what makes a product valuable, may exist within the same broadly defined industry. Each network has its own "metrics of value." For example, for laptop computers, the metrics are small size, low weight and power consumption, and rugged design. During the 1980s, customers who bought portable computers were willing to pay a premium for smaller size; buyers of mainframe computers did not value this attribute. Conversely, mainframe buyers valued (i.e., were willing to pay more for) memory capacity as measured by megabytes; portable computer buyers placed less value on this attribute. In short, the value networks for mainframe computers and portable computers are different.

As firms gain experience within a given network, they are likely to develop capabilities, organizational structures, and cultures tailored to the distinctive requirements of their respective value networks. The industry's dominant firms—typically those with reputations as "well-managed" firms—lead in developing and/or adopting **sustaining technologies**, that is, incremental or radical innovations that improve product performance. According to Christensen, most new technologies developed by established companies are sustaining in nature; indeed, the vast majority of innovations are of this type. However, new entrants to an industry lead in developing **disruptive technologies** that redefine performance. The benefits associated with disruptive technologies go beyond enhancing product performance; disruptive technologies enable something to be done that was previously deemed impossible. Disruptive technologies typically enable new markets to emerge. As Christensen explains, "An innovation that is disrupting to one firm can be sustaining to another firm. The Internet was sustaining technology to Dell, which already sold PCs via direct marketing channels. But it was disruptive technology to Compaq, whose major distribution channel was retailers."[14]

To help managers recognize the innovator's dilemma and develop appropriate responses to environmental change, Christensen has developed five principles of disruptive innovations:

1. Companies depend on customers and investors for resources. As management guru Rosabeth Moss Kanter points out, the best innovations are user-driven; paradoxically, however, if management listens to established customers, opportunities for disruptive innovation may be missed.[15]
2. Small markets don't solve the growth needs of large companies. Small organizations can most easily respond to the opportunities for growth in a small market. This fact may require large organizations to create independent units to pursue new technologies, as IBM did in developing its PC.
3. Markets that don't exist can't be analyzed. Christensen recommends that companies embrace *agnostic marketing*. This is the explicit assumption that *no one*—not company personnel, not the company's customers—can know whether, how, or in what quantities a disruptive product can or will be used before they have experienced using it.

[14]Simon London, "Why Disruption Can Be Good for Business," *Financial Times* (October 3, 2003), p. 8.
[15]Rosabeth Moss Kanter, John Kao, and Fred Wiersema, *Innovation: Breakthrough Thinking at 3M, DuPont, GE, Pfizer, and Rubbermaid* (New York: HarperBusiness, 1997), p. 24.

4. An organization's capabilities define its disabilities. For example, Microsoft was once an industry trendsetter. Today, however, while it remains firmly committed to its Windows operating system, Microsoft lags behind new industry entrants in high-growth, consumer-oriented areas such as search and social networking.[16]
5. Technology supply may not equal market demand. Some products offer a greater degree of sophistication than the market requires. For example, developers of accounting software for small businesses overshot the functionality required by the market, thus creating an opportunity for a disruptive software technology that provided adequate, not superior, functionality and was simple and more convenient to use. This was the opportunity seized by Scott Cook, developer of Quicken and QuickBooks.

## 15-4 Global E-Commerce

The term **e-commerce** refers to the general exchange of goods and services using the Internet or a similar online network as a marketing channel. Global e-commerce sales surpassed $1.3 trillion in 2014. That figure includes hundreds of millions of Chinese consumers who are shopping online with greater frequency as smartphone penetration ramps up. According to Forrester Research, U.S. online retail sales revenues totaled $304 billion in 2014, a figure that represents about 7 percent of total U.S. retail sales. Internet penetration in some world regions is in the low single digits; this is especially true in Africa. For example, penetration is less than 10 percent in Eritrea, Burundi, Sierra Leone, Somalia, and other low-income countries. By contrast, in several countries, including South Korea, the Netherlands, Greenland, the UAE, Bahrain, and Qatar, more than 90 percent of the population is online. Consider the following:

- Every 48 hours, Yahoo! records more than 24 terabytes of data about its users' online activities. That is the equivalent of all the information contained in all the books in the Library of Congress.[17]
- Between 2003 and 2014, the number of Internet users in China increased from 68 million to 640 million. More than 460 million Chinese shop online, making China the world's largest e-commerce market. Local companies such as Alibaba are proving to be formidable competitors against global rivals such as Yahoo!, Google, and eBay.[18]
- According to Forrester Research, online retail and travel sales in Western Europe grew at a compound annual rate of 8 percent between 2008 and 2014. By 2018, it is expected that 75 percent of European Internet users will be shopping online, up from 65 percent in 2013.[19]

E-commerce activities can be divided into three broad categories: business-to-consumer (B2C or b-to-c), business-to-business (B2B or b-to-b), and consumer-to-consumer (peer-to-peer: P2P or p-to-p). People often associate e-commerce with well-known consumer-oriented sites such as Amazon.com, Apple's iTunes Store, and eBay. As noted in Chapter 14, Germany's Otto Group is the world's second-largest B2C e-commerce retailer. Overall, however, B2B commerce constitutes the biggest share of the Internet economy and will likely continue to do so for the foreseeable future. Industry forecasts call for global B2B revenues to reach $6.7 trillion by 2020, at which point B2C is expected to be $3.2 trillion (see Table 15-1).[20]

Problems can arise when a transaction site that is not designed to serve foreign customers nevertheless attracts them. Customer service can be a problem when customers are located in different time zones. For example, BlueTie is a small company based in Rochester, New York, that markets e-mail and office-software applications by subscription. The company's servers

[16] "Middle-Aged Blues," *The Economist* (June 11, 2011), p. 59.
[17] Kevin J. Delaney, "Lab Test: Hoping to Overtake Its Rivals, Yahoo Stocks Up on Academics," *The Wall Street Journal* (August 26, 2006), p. A8.
[18] Jason Dean, "China's Web Retailers Beat U.S. Rivals at Their Own Game," *The Wall Street Journal* (August 22, 2006), p. B1.
[19] Forrester Research, *Western European Online Retail and Travel Sales, 2008–2014* (March 16, 2009), p. 2. See also Michelle Beeson, *European Online Retail Forecast, 2013–2018*, Forrester Research (May 29, 2014), p. 4.
[20] Sarwant Singh, "B2B e-Commerce Market Worth $6.7 Trillion by 2020; Alibaba and China the Frontrunners," *Forbes* (November 6, 2014).

**TABLE 15-1 Forecast, Online Retail Sales, Select European Countries, 2013–2018 (millions)[a]**

| Country | 2013 | 2014(F) | 2015(F) | 2016(F) | 2017(F) | 2018(F) | CAGR |
|---|---|---|---|---|---|---|---|
| Germany | €31,509 | €35,555 | €39,924 | €44,573 | €49,501 | €54,688 | 11.7% |
| France | 25,492 | 29,797 | 33,975 | 38,267 | 42,856 | 47,465 | 13.2% |
| Spain | 4,898 | 5,877 | 7,000 | 8,306 | 9,794 | 11,506 | 18.6% |
| Western Europe[b] | 134,900 | 153,200 | 172,100 | 191,900 | 212,600 | 233,900 | 12.0% |

[a] Based on Michelle Beeson, *European Online Retail Forecast, 2013–2018,* Forrester Research (May 29, 2014), p. 5.
[b] Data is for EU-17: Austria, Belgium, Denmark, Finland, France, Germany, Greece, Ireland, Italy, Luxembourg, the Netherlands, Norway, Portugal, Spain, Sweden, Switzerland, and the United Kingdom.

continually update customer calendars and e-mail. When non-U.S. orders began to come in, BlueTie managers found it challenging to deliver correct times and dates. Fixing the problem required spending tens of thousands of dollars and tied up precious employee time.

Web sites can be classified by purpose: **Promotion sites** provide marketing communications about a company's goods or services, **content sites** provide news and entertainment and support a company's PR efforts, and **transaction sites** are online retail operations that allow customers to purchase goods and services. Typically, Web sites combine the three functions. Web sites can also be categorized in terms of content and audience focus.

For example, international students at your college or university may have learned about your school via the Internet, even though home-country prospective students constitute the primary target audience for the Web site. Similarly, Pandora, the online music service, only serves American listeners; Deezer, the French online music-streaming company, is operational in 160 countries. To date, Deezer has not launched in the United States. Why? For one thing, international copyright laws make it difficult to license performance rights for songs. As former Pandora CEO Joe Kennedy recently remarked, "The good news is that the Internet is global, but the bad news is that copyright law is country by country."[21] Apple's iTunes Music Store began as a U.S.-only retailer. During the next decade, the service was rolled out in dozens of countries. Netflix, the online movie distributor, has evolved from domestic to international in a similar way.

Companies such as FedEx and Gucci are global in scope, and the Internet constitutes a powerful, cost-effective communication tool. Similarly, the interactive marketing staff at Unilever PLC understands that the Web represents an important low-cost medium for promoting products. Unilever's vast archive of TV commercials has been digitized; Web surfers can download the videos for products such as Salon Selectives shampoo and watch them anytime. Recently, Unilever launched a 12-week series on Yahoo! Food titled *In Search of Real Food.* Hosted by Food Network TV star David Lieberman, the show was created around Hellman's mayonnaise. As Doug Scott, executive director of entertainment at the Ogilvy & Mather ad agency explained, "Content for broadband costs significantly less than TV productions and it allows you to distribute to a much larger audience."[22]

Companies can also seek e-commerce transactions with customers on a worldwide basis. Amazon.com is the most successful example of the transaction business model. Online book shoppers can choose from millions of book titles; many carry discounted prices. After assessing a number of potential products in terms of their suitability for online sales, company founder Jeffrey Bezos settled on books for two reasons. First, there are too many titles for any one "brick-and-mortar" store to carry. The second reason is related to industry structure: The publishing industry is highly fragmented, with thousands of publishers in the United States alone. That means that no single publisher has a high degree of supplier power. Bezos's instincts proved sound: Sales exploded after Amazon.com's Web site became operational in mid-1995. Within a year, orders were coming in from dozens of countries.

---

[21]Joe Mullin, "Pandora CEO: The Complexity of International Copyright Law Is a Big Problem," PaidContent.org (March 30, 2011). Accessed June 1, 2011.
[22]Susanne Vranica, "Hellmann's Targets Yahoo for Its Spread," *The Wall Street Journal* (June 27, 2007), p. B4.

Today, Amazon.com is the world's largest online retail site, with hundreds of millions of annual visitors. Amazon.com's twelve international sites generate between 40 percent and 50 percent of total sales. Germany, Japan, and the United Kingdom are Amazon's three biggest markets outside the United States.

Online retail in the United States passed the $300-billion mark in 2014. According to forecasts from Forrester Research, by 2017 U.S. online retail sales will total $370 billion. These figures include orders from abroad; Abercrombie & Fitch, Aéropostale, J. Crew, Macy's, Timberland, and Saks Fifth Avenue are just some of the U.S. retailers targeting foreign buyers by adding international shipping services to their Web sites. The dollar's strength, which translates into higher prices for shoppers paying in euros or other currencies, has prompted more U.S. consumers to order from abroad. Delivery giants FedEx, UPS, and DHL are making key acquisitions and partnering with other firms to help ensure seamless, frictionless ordering and delivery experiences for online shoppers.[23]

Some products are inherently not suitable candidates for sale via the Internet; for example, McDonald's doesn't sell hamburgers from its Web site. In some instances, global marketers make the strategic decision to establish a presence on the Web without offering transaction opportunities even though the product could be sold that way. Rather, such companies limit their Web activities to promotion and information in support of offline retail distribution channels. There are several reasons for this. First, companies may lack the infrastructure necessary to process orders from individual customers. Second, it can cost anywhere from $20 million to $30 million to establish a fully functioning e-commerce site. There may be other, product-specific reasons. The Web site for Godin Guitars, for example, provides a great deal of product information and a directory of the company's worldwide dealer network. However, company founder Robert Godin believes that the best way for a person to select a guitar is to play one, and that requires a visit to a music store.

For consumer products giant Procter & Gamble (P&G), the Internet represents a global promotion and information channel that is an integral part of its brand strategy. For example, Pampers is P&G's number 1 brand, with annual global sales of $10 billion. Pampers' online presence at www.pampers.com represents a new conceptualization of the brand. Previously, brand managers viewed Pampers disposable diapers as a way of keeping babies happy; the new view is that the Pampers brand is a child development aid. Visitors to the Pampers Village online community can read advice from the Pampers Parenting Institute as well as tips from mothers. Discount coupons are also available.

P&G launched www.thankyoumom.com to position P&G as "a proud sponsor of moms." In 2010, P&G used the site to award $100,000 in travel vouchers to help moms reunite with their families. P&G has also launched a retail Web site to sell Pantene shampoo, Pampers baby products, and other brands to consumers. This online strategy change brings P&G into direct competition with Walmart, Target, and other retailers that complement brick-and-mortar stores with Internet selling.[24]

Until recently, visitors to Web sites for most luxury goods purveyors were not given the opportunity to buy. The reason is simple: Top design houses strive to create an overall retail shopping experience that enhances the brand. This objective is basically at odds with e-commerce. As Forrester Research analyst Sucharita Mulpuru explained, "There was a belief that there was no way you could communicate your brand essence online."[25] This belief is changing, however. Some luxury goods marketers have developed smartphone and iPad apps to help consumers shop. Burberry, Chanel, Coach, Gucci, and other luxury brands are cultivating official online communities on Facebook. According to Reggie Bradord, CEO of a social media management company, they are doing the right thing. He says, "Luxury brands should be thinking about 'how can we create a dialogue and get consumers connecting with our brand?'"[26]

---

[23]Laura Stevens, "Borders Matter Less and Less in E-Commerce," *The Wall Street Journal* (June 24, 2015), p. B8. See also Stephanie Clifford, "U.S. Stores Learn How to Ship to Foreign Shoppers," *The New York Times* (March 21, 2012), pp. B1, B7.

[24]Ellen Byron, "P&G Goes on the Defensive for Pampers," *The Wall Street Journal* (June 15, 2010), p. B5.

[25]David Gelles, "Innovation Brings a Touch of Class to Online Shopping," *Financial Times Special Report: Business of Luxury* (June 14, 2010), p. 7.

[26]David Gelles, "Social Media: Tarnish the Brand or Build an Aspirational Following?" *Financial Times* (June 14, 2010); see also Gary Silverman, "How May I Help You?" *Financial Times* (February 4–5, 2006), p. W2.

As the Internet has developed into a crucial global communication tool, decision makers in virtually all organizations are realizing that they must include this new medium in their communications planning. Many companies purchase banner ads on popular Web sites; the ads are linked to the company's home page or product- or brand-related sites. Advertisers pay when users click the link. Although creative possibilities are limited with banner ads and **click-through rates**—the percentage of users who click on an advertisement that has been presented—are typically low, the number of companies that use the Web as a medium for global advertising is expected to increase dramatically over the next few years.

An important trend is **paid search advertising**, whereby companies pay to have their ads appear when users type certain search terms. Yahoo! paid $1.6 billion to acquire Overture, a company specializing in paid search advertising. As a Yahoo! spokesperson noted, "Paid search is just starting to take off globally. So this acquisition wasn't just part of our strategy for search, it was important for our international strategy as well."[27]

One of the most interesting aspects of the digital revolution has been noted by Chris Anderson, the editor of *Wired* magazine and author of *The Long Tail.* The book's title refers to the use of the efficient economics of online retail to aggregate a large number of relatively slow-selling products. *The Long Tail* helps explain the success of eBay, Amazon.com, Netflix, and iTunes, all of which offer far more variety and choice than traditional retailers can. As Anderson explains, "The story of the Long Tail is really about the economics of abundance—what happens when the bottlenecks that stand between supply and demand in our culture start to disappear and everything becomes available to everyone." Anderson notes that "below-the-radar" products—for example, obscure books, movies, and music—are driving revenues at e-commerce merchants such as Amazon.com, Netflix, and iTunes. He says, "These millions of fringe sales are an efficient, cost-effective business. . . . For the first time in history, hits and niches are on equal economic footing."[28]

## 15-5 Web Site Design and Implementation

To fully exploit the Internet's potential, company executives must be willing to integrate interactive media into their marketing mixes.[29] Web sites can be developed in-house, or an outside firm can be contracted to do the job. During the past few years, a new breed of interactive advertising agency has emerged to help companies globalize their Internet offerings (see Table 15-2). Some of these agencies are independent; others are affiliated with other advertising agency brands and holding companies (see Chapter 13). Whether Web development is handled in-house or by an outside agency, several issues must be addressed when setting up for global e-commerce. These include choosing domain names, arranging payment, localizing sites, addressing privacy issues, and setting up a distribution system.

**TABLE 15-2 Top Five Digital Agency Networks by 2014 Interactive Marketing Revenue**

| Agency (Parent Company) | Headquarters | Clients |
|---|---|---|
| IBM Interactive Experience (IBM) | New York | Jaguar Land Rover; U.S. Open |
| Deloitte Digital (Deloitte) | New York | TOMS; Intel; Activision |
| Accenture Interactive (Accenture) | New York/ London | AGL; Casual Male Retail Group |
| Epsilon (Alliance Data Systems) | Texas | Dell; American Express |
| Wunderman (WPP) | New York | Land Rover; Microsoft; Coca-Cola |

**Source:** Adapted from "World's 15 Largest Digital Agency Networks," *Advertising Age* (April 25, 2015), p. 32.

[27]Bob Tedeschi, "E-Commerce Report," *The New York Times* (January 12, 2004), p. C6.
[28]Chris Anderson, *The Long Tail: Why the Future of Business Is Selling Less of More* (New York: Hyperion, 2006), p. 13.
[29]Much of the discussion in this section is adapted from Alexis D. Gutzman, *The E-Commerce Arsenal* (New York: Amacom, 2001).

**TABLE 15-3 Select Amazon.com Domain Names**

| Domain Name | Country |
|---|---|
| amazon.com.br | Brazil |
| amazon.ca | Canada |
| amazon.cn | China |
| amazon.fr | France |
| amazon.de | Germany |
| amazon.it | Italy |
| amazon.co.jp | Japan |
| amazon.es | Spain |
| amazon.co.uk | United Kingdom |

A critical first step is registering a country-specific domain name. Thus, Amazon.com has a family of different domain names, one for each country in which it operates (see Table 15-3). Although it is certainly possible for European consumers to browse Amazon.com's U.S. site, they may prefer a direct link to a site with a local domain name. From both a marketing and a consumer perspective, this makes sense: The Web site of choice will be one that quotes prices in euros rather than dollars, offers a product selection tailored to local tastes, and ships from local distribution points. However, as noted earlier, the weak dollar may make it less expensive for shoppers in, say, Europe, to order from U.S. online retailers.

Moreover, research suggests that visitors spend more time at sites that are in their own language; they also tend to view more pages and make more purchases. Many people will seek information about sites on local versions of well-known search engines. For example, in France, Yahoo!'s local site is http://fr.Yahoo.com. The same principle applies to non-U.S. companies targeting the American online consumer market. Waterford Wedgwood PLC, Harrods, Johnnie Boden, and other well-known companies have acquired U.S. domain names and created sites with prices listed in dollars.[30]

While registering a ".com" domain name is a relatively straightforward procedure in the United States, requirements can vary elsewhere. In some countries, for example, a company must establish a legal entity before it can register a site with a local domain-name extension. **Cybersquatting**—the practice of registering a particular domain name for the express purpose of reselling it to the company that should rightfully use it—is also a problem. Avon, Panasonic, and Starbucks are some of the companies that have been victims of cybersquatting.

Payment can be another problem; in some countries, including China, credit card use is low. In such situations, e-commerce operators must arrange payment by bank check or postal money order; cash on delivery is also an option. Another issue is credit card fraud; Indonesia, Russia, Croatia, and Bosnia are among the countries where fraud is rampant. Extra identity measures may have to be taken, such as requiring buyers to fax the actual credit card they are using as well as photo IDs.[31] In Japan, consumers pay for online purchases at convenience stores (*konbini*). After selecting an item online, the buyer goes to a nearby convenience store (e.g., a 7-Eleven) and pays cash for the item; the clerk transfers the money to the online seller's account. However, foreign companies can't participate in the *konbini* system; this means that a foreign online retailer must establish an alliance with a local company.

Ideally, each country-specific site should reflect local culture, language usage, customs, and aesthetic preferences. Logos and other elements of brand identity should be included on the site, with adjustments for color preferences and meaning differences when necessary. For

[30]Jessica Vascellaro, "Foreign Shopping Sites Cater to U.S. Customers," *The Wall Street Journal* (October 12, 2005), pp. D1, D14.

[31]Peter Loftus, "Internet Turns Firms into Overseas Businesses," *The Wall Street Journal* (December 16, 2003), p. B4. See also Matt Richtel, "Credit Card Theft Is Thriving Online as Global Market," *The New York Times* (May 13, 2002), p. A1.

example, the shopping cart icon is familiar to online shoppers in the United States and many European countries. However, online companies must determine whether that icon is appropriate in all country markets. Subtle but important language differences can also occur even in English-speaking countries. For example, www.figleaves.com and www.figleaves.com/uk are, respectively, the American and British Web addresses for a UK-based lingerie marketer. However, the U.S. site refers to "panties," whereas the UK site has a listing for "briefs." When two or more different languages are involved, translators should be used to ensure that copy reflects current language usage. It is also important not to "reinvent the wheel" by translating the same terms over and over again. Local translators should have access to an in-house dictionary that contains preferred translations of company-specific terms. The database system should be capable of identifying content that has already been translated and then reusing that content.

After Yao Ming joined the Houston Rockets in 2002, the NBA's Chinese Web site was launched in conjunction with www.SOHU.com, China's leading Internet portal. Written entirely in Chinese characters, the site is designed to capitalize on basketball's increasing popularity in the world's largest market. The NBA has also launched country-specific English-language sites in Africa, Australia, Canada, India, New Zealand, the Philippines, and the United Kingdom. In addition, there are sites in several other languages, including German, Greek, Hebrew, Italian, Portuguese, and Spanish.

As the NBA's Chinese site illustrates, it is not enough to simply translate a Web site from the home-country language into other languages. Thus, another basic step is localizing a Web site in the native language and business nomenclature of the target country. From a technical point of view, Web sites designed to support English, French, German, and other languages that use the Latin alphabet store only a maximum of 256 characters in the American Standard Code for Information Interchange (ASCII) format. Even so, there are language-specific needs; for example, a German-language Web site requires more than double the capacity of an English-language site because German copy takes more space.[32] However, languages such as Japanese and Chinese require a database that supports double-ASCII. For this reason, it is wise to start with a double-ACSII platform when designing a Web site's architecture. The site's architecture should also be flexible enough to allow different date, currency, and money formatting. For example, to someone living in the United Kingdom, "7/10/16" means October 7, 2016. To an American, it means July 10, 2016.

Another critical global e-commerce issue is privacy. The EU's regulations are among the world's strictest; companies are limited in terms of how much personal information—a customer's age, marital status, and buying patterns, for example—can be gathered and how long the information can be retained. In 2012, EU Justice Commissioner Viviane Reding announced an overhaul of the EU's data collection rules (see Exhibit 15-5). The rules will apply to companies based outside the EU—Apple, Google, and Facebook, for example—if they offer services to EU citizens. Customers living in the EU have the "right to be forgotten"—that is, they can request to have their personal data deleted. Moreover, EU citizens must give explicit consent before companies can share their data.[33] By contrast, Washington's reluctance to protect privacy is due in part to First Amendment issues as well as to national security concerns stemming from the terrorist attacks of 2001. To help ensure compliance with privacy laws, American companies have created a new executive-level job position: chief privacy officer.[34]

A number of issues are related to physical distribution decisions. As online sales increase in a particular country or region, it may be necessary to establish local warehouse facilities to speed delivery and reduce shipping costs. In the United States, such a step has tax implications, meaning that the marketer may have to collect sales tax. To allay consumer concerns about ordering merchandise online, companies may opt to waive shipping fees and offer free returns and money-back guarantees.

---

[32]Patricia Riedman, "Think Globally, Act Globally," *Advertising Age* (June 19, 2000), p. 48.
[33]Frances Robinson, "EU Unveils Web-Privacy Rules," *The Wall Street Journal* (January 26, 2012), p. B9.
[34]David Scheer, "For Your Eyes Only: Europe's New High-Tech Role: Playing Privacy Cop to the World," *The Wall Street Journal* (October 10, 2003), p. A1.

**Exhibit 15-5** Viviane Reding is the European Commissioner for Justice, Fundamental Rights, and Citizenship. In her official capacity, Reding has spoken out about data privacy issues. One concern in the EU is the widespread corporate practice of gathering and using consumer data without permission. One key issue is the "right to be forgotten," which would require companies such as Google to delete user data if requested to do so.

**Source:** © epa european pressphoto agency b.v./Alamy.

## 15-6 New Products and Services

The digital revolution has spurred innovations in many different industries. Companies in all parts of the world are developing a new generation of products, services, and technologies. These include broadband networks, mobile commerce, wireless connectivity, and smartphones (see Exhibit 15-6).

"Increased broadband penetration is opening up possibilities that didn't exist even 2 years ago. . . . We need to realize that online is now an important part of the overall communications mix. . . . We are not an online business. We're a beverage business. But we have to develop compelling marketing platforms that are relevant to the lives of young people."[35]

Tim Kopp, vice president of global interactive marketing, Coca-Cola

### Broadband

A **broadband** communication system is one that has sufficient capacity to carry multiple voice, data, or video channels simultaneously. *Bandwidth* determines the range of frequencies that can pass over a given transmission channel. For example, traditional telephone networks offered quite limited bandwidth compared with state-of-the-art digital telephone networks. As a result, a traditional telephone call sounds "lo-fi." Bandwidth is measured in bits-per-second (Bps); a full page of English text is about 16,000 bits. For example, a 56 Kpbs modem connected to a conventional telephone line can move 16,000 bits per second; by comparison, a broadband Internet connection that utilizes coaxial cable can move up to 10 gigabits per second.

South Korea currently boasts the world's fastest average Internet speeds. However, technology upgrades currently underway will mean even higher speeds: The government intends to ensure that every Korean household has a 1-gigabit Internet connection. As Choi Gwang-gi, the engineer overseeing the project, explains, "A lot of Koreans are early adopters, and we thought we needed to be prepared for things like 3D TV, Internet Protocol TV, high-definition multimedia, gaming and videoconferencing, ultra-high definition TV, and cloud computing."[36] Consumers won't be the only beneficiaries of the upgrade; corporations will also be able to harness gigabit Internet connections for high-definition global videoconferencing and other applications.

As South Korea and other countries forge ahead with massive investment in broadband infrastructure upgrades, politicians and union leaders in laggard countries are taking a keen interest in the issue. A recent study declared that South Korea and several other countries are "ready for tomorrow" in terms of Internet speed. A second tier of countries falls into the category "below today's applications threshold." The United States, Germany, and Hong Kong all fall into this category.[37] U.S. President Barack Obama responded to this situation in 2011 by promising $18.7 billion to improve America's broadband network.

[35] Andrew Ward, "Coke Taps into Brand New Internet Craze," *Financial Times* (August 8, 2006), p. 15.
[36] Mark McDonald, "Home Internet May Get Even Faster in South Korea," *The New York Times* (February 22, 2011), p. B3.
[37] Alan Cane, "Leaders Look to Future in Broadband Race," *Financial Times* (October 23, 2009).

**Exhibit 15-6** The Linux open source operating system was created by Linus Torvalds, shown here with the software's iconic penguin mascot. Although Linux is distributed for free, annual sales of Linux-related software grew from about $12 billion in 2008 to more than $35 billion in 2013. The Linux Foundation was created to deal with competitive issues pertaining to Microsoft and its Windows operating system. It also deals with technical, legal, and standards issues.
Source: Paul Sakuma/AP Images.

Why are policymakers following the broadband race so closely? Broadband offers multiple marketing opportunities to companies in a variety of industries. Broadband also allows Internet users to access **streaming media** such as **streaming audio** and **streaming video**. Personalized radio services such as Apple Radio, Pandora, Spotify, and iHeartRadio allow users to list their favorite artists and songs. Pandora uses a proprietary technology called the Music Genome Project to make recommendations for new music that are similar to a listener's current favorites. Streaming media is having a profound impact on the television industry, with Amazon.com, iTunes, Netflix, YouTube, and other services offering movie and TV show downloads and streaming as viewing options.

Streaming media represents a major market opportunity for the video game industry, which includes electronics companies (e.g., Microsoft and Sony), game publishers (e.g., Electronic Arts), and Internet portals (e.g., Google). Gamers in different locations, even different countries, can compete against each other using PCs or Xbox or PlayStation consoles. These are sometimes called *massively multiplayer online games* (MMOG); the most popular MMOG is *World of Warcraft.* Microsoft's Xbox Live service has more than 48 million subscribers worldwide. Consumer interest in online gaming has been fueled by powerful next-generation game consoles such as Microsoft's Xbox One and Sony's PlayStation 4.

## Cloud Computing

In the preceding section, *cloud computing* was referenced as one driver of higher broadband speeds. The term refers to next-generation computing that is performed "in the cloud." Rather than installing software such as iTunes or Microsoft Office on a computer hard drive, such applications will be delivered through a Web browser. Cloud computing means that archives—including music and movie files, photos, and documents—are stored on massive remote servers and data centers rather than on individual users' computers. Computer files can be accessed remotely, via the Internet, from any location and from any computer.

Google's Chrome operating system, which has been described as "a new computing paradigm," is designed to exploit the opportunities of cloud computing. Another industry trendsetter, Amazon.com, has set up Amazon Web Services (AWS) to offer cloud-computing resources to businesses. AWS is a variation on the outsourcing trend that was discussed in Chapter 8; Netflix, Foursquare, and thousands of other companies use the service instead of running their own data centers. However, cloud computing is still in its infancy; a recent service interruption of AWS caused widespread disruptions among its clients. Despite such setbacks, cloud computing is expected to grow at an annual torrid pace of 25 percent over the next several years.[38]

[38]Steve Lohr, "Amazon's Trouble Raises Cloud Computing Doubts," *The New York Times* (April 23, 2011), p. B1.

## INNOVATION, ENTREPRENEURSHIP, AND THE GLOBAL STARTUP

### Reed Hastings, Netflix

SYNC • THINK • LEARN

MyMarketingLab

Reed Hastings is an entrepreneur. He developed an innovative service, created a brand, and started a company to market it. By applying the basic tools and principles of modern marketing, Hastings has achieved remarkable success. As is true with many entrepreneurs, Hastings's idea was based on his recognition of a problem that needed to be solved and his own experience as a consumer. Like many people, he had forgotten to return some videocassettes that he had rented. When he finally did take them back to the video store, he had to pay some hefty late fees. He said to himself, "There has to be a better way." A business model that seemed to make more sense was the one used by many health clubs: In return for a monthly fee, members can use the club any time they want. With this in mind, in 1997 Hastings started Netflix, a mail-order DVD rental service (see Exhibit 15-7).

Within a few years, red-and-white Netflix envelopes were appearing in mailboxes throughout the United States. The company enjoyed robust subscriber growth, and by mid-2011 its stock had soared to nearly $300 per share. Netflix's popularity was due in part to its "star ratings" recommendation feature that helped subscribers find new shows and movies based on prior viewing habits and the ratings they gave to the programming that they watched. Netflix's success came at the expense of competitors in the brick-and-mortar video rental business; in 2010, for example, Blockbuster filed for bankruptcy.

Hastings was at the forefront in a video industry that was undergoing rapid transformation. However, more change was to come: As the user base of household broadband and lightning-fast 4G mobile networks reached critical mass, streaming video was supplanting physical DVDs as the viewing medium of choice. Hastings responded by offering streaming-content subscriptions for $7.99 per month in addition to DVD rentals. However, Netflix faced competition from Redbox, an upstart DVD rental company with very low prices, as well as from streaming services such as Hulu and Amazon Prime.

By mid-2011, Hastings was searching for new sources of growth. As one analyst said, "The only option for Netflix is to go international." That is exactly what Hastings had in mind. Canada was Netflix's first international market entry, with operations commencing in 2010. In 2011, Latin America was added, and in 2012 the United Kingdom, Ireland, Denmark, Finland, Norway, and Sweden came online as well. However, global expansion is expensive. Copyright laws require licensing content on a country-by-country basis, and marketing costs are significant as well. One of Hastings's goals is to negotiate worldwide licensing deals that will provide better terms than the country-by-country approach.

Netflix predicts it will have operations in 200 countries by the end of 2016. Irrespective of location, streaming subscribers pay roughly the equivalent of the U.S. subscription rate—about $8.00 per month. Netflix content can also be accessed on more than 1,000 different devices, including smartphones, tablets, and, of course, televisions.

Meanwhile, Hastings is moving ahead with plans to create original content. The first season of political thriller *House of Cards* met with popular and critical acclaim and was renewed. Subscribers returned, the company's fortunes turned around, and the stock has more than quadrupled from its 2011 lows. Says Hastings, "We think of the technology as a vehicle for creating a better, more modern experience for the content we have. What we're really competing for quite broadly is people's time."

**Sources:** Emily Steel, "Netflix Accelerates Ambitious Global Expansion as U.S. Growth Slows," *The New York Times* (January 21, 2015), p. B3; Sam Schechner, "Netflix Tries to Woo a Wary Europe," *The Wall Street Journal* (September 8, 2014), p. B1; Ashlee Vance, "The Man Who Ate the Internet (Cover Story)," *BloombergBusinessweek* (May 13, 2013), pp. 56–60; Amol Sharma and Nathalie Tadena, "Viewers Stream to Netflix," *The Wall Street Journal* (April 23, 2013), pp. B1, B4; Greg Bensinger, "Netflix Transition Rattles Investors," *The Wall Street Journal* (July 26, 2012), p. B3.

**Exhibit 15-7** Netflix shares slumped in mid-2011 after company founder Reed Hastings announced plans to separate the streaming video business from the DVD rental business. Less than two years later, however, the stock rebounded sharply as original Netflix programs such as *House of Cards, Orange Is the New Black,* and *Daredevil* became well received by viewers and critics alike.

**Source:** © ZUMA Press, Inc./Alamy.

## Smartphones

Cell phones have been one of the biggest new-product success stories of the digital revolution. Worldwide, 1.3 billion smartphones were shipped in 2014. Soaring demand has boosted the fortunes of manufacturers such as Apple, HTC, Motorola, RIM, and Samsung, as well as AT&T, Deutsche Telekom, U.S. Cellular, Verizon, and other service providers. New features and functionality give consumers a reason to upgrade their handsets on a regular basis. Conventional cell phones (sometimes called feature phones) allow text messaging via **short message service (SMS)**, a globally accepted wireless standard for sending alphanumeric messages of up to 160 characters. SMS is the technology platform that is the basis for Twitter's microblogging service. Industry experts expect marketers to integrate SMS with communication via other digital channels, such as interactive digital TV, the Internet, and e-mail.

**Smartphones** have much greater functionality than feature phones, incorporating many of the capabilities of computers. Worldwide, smartphones represent about one-fourth of all cell phone sales. Case in point: Apple's wildly successful iPhone comes equipped with a full-blown version of the company's iOS and Web browser. The popularity of smartphones is due, in part, to the availability of apps such as Action Movie FX, Angry Birds, Pinterest, and Uber. In 2013, Apple's iTunes store sold its 50 billionth iPhone app. Apple commemorated the milestone with a "50 Billion Apps Download Promotion": the lucky person who downloaded the 50 billionth app won a $10,000 gift card—to be redeemed on iTunes, of course! Many of Apple's rivals use Android, a mobile operating system developed by Google.

| | |
|---|---|
| $1 billion | The amount Facebook paid to acquire Instagram in 2012 |
| 300 million | The number of Instagram users as of December 2014 |
| 65 percent | Instagram users outside the United States |

## Mobile Advertising and Mobile Commerce

**Mobile advertising** and **mobile commerce (m-commerce)** are terms that describe the use of cell phones as channels for delivering advertising messages and conducting product and service transactions. Most smartphone and tablet users can access the Internet via **Wi-Fi**; in addition, cell phone service providers typically offer data plans that allow Internet connections via 3G or 4G networks. This allows Apple, AOL, Crisp Media, Google, Medialets, Mobext, and other companies to offer clients mobile ad services. For example, Unilever, Nissan, and other companies use Apple's iAd service to place interactive ads inside iPhone and iPod apps.[39]

Total worldwide spending for mobile ads was only about $1 billion in 2007; according to eMarketer, at the end of 2014, the figure was nearly $43 billion. The United States leads all other nations, with eMarketer reporting that 2014 mobile advertising totaled $18.9 billion.[40] Mobile search and mobile display advertising are growing in importance as consumers migrate away from their desktops and spend more time on mobile devices. In fact, in 2015, Google announced that it was tweaking its vaunted search algorithms to favor "mobile-friendly sites" with text that can be read on small screens and content that fits the screen. Web sites that are not optimized for mobile will be demoted in the search process.

A smartphones that is equipped with a **global positioning system (GPS)** can determine the user's exact geographic position. This capability has created new opportunities for location-based mobile platforms, such as Foursquare and Uber. The popularity of GPS-equipped mobile devices is driving interest in *location-based advertising*. For example, Alcatel-Lucent, the French telecommunications equipment manufacturer, has launched a service that sends tailored text messages when smartphone users are near a specific location, such as a store, hotel, or restaurant. The service, which is managed by San Francisco–based 1020 Placecast, provides addresses and telephone numbers of the businesses and can also provide links to coupons or other types of sales promotions. Users "opt in" by signing up to receive ads.

[39]Yukari Iwatani Kane and Emily Steel, "Apple's iAd Helping Rivals," *The Wall Street Journal* (November 11, 2010), p. B4.
[40]Felicia Greiff, "Global Mobile Ad Spending Will Rise to $100 Billion in 2016," *Advertising Age* (April 2, 2015).

NAVTEQ Media Solutions™
Case Study
McDonald's is lovin' the results of their location-aware ad campaign with NAVTEQ
McDonald's achieves a 7% click-thru rate with 39% clicking to route them to the nearest McDonald's restaurant
McDonald's Finland wanted to test the impact of a location-targeted mobile ad campaign on driving foot traffic into their locations. The goal of the campaign was to entice mobile-connected consumers to come to a nearby McDonald's restaurant.
The plan called for targeting consumers within a certain distance of a McDonald's restaurant with a location-aware ad heralding a special offer, which would in turn trigger a mobile map and directions to the nearest restaurant. Together with NAVTEQ, the leading provider of map, traffic, and location data, McDonald's demonstrated that location-based advertising is a powerful means of converting a mere passer-by to a paying in-store customer.
"We are thrilled with the results from this campaign. NAVTEQ LocationPoint proved that location targeted mobile advertising does indeed drive foot traffic into our restaurants. Targeting consumers when they are near our locations and then navigating them right into our stores is powerful marketing for McDonald's."
— Tomi Wirtanen Head of marketing, McDonald's Finland
MCDONALD'S
Helsinki, Finland
McDonald's
JUUSTO
Menu
Back
www
OK
Enabled by NAVTEQ LocationPoint™ Advertising, McDonald's delivered location-relevant mobile ads to users of Nokia Ovi Maps when they were within five miles of any of McDonald's 82 restaurants in Finland. The ad campaign promoted a McDonald's cheese burger for 1 euro, resulting in a solid, measureable ROI, a 7% click-thru rate. Consumers clicked on the ads to see promotion details and receive directions to the nearest store location. Of users who clicked through, 39% selected the click-to-navigate option which offered "drive to" or "walk to" navigation to the nearest McDonald's location.
One of the most important objectives for a retail marketer is getting people to walk in the door. Location targeting combined with click-to-navigate functionality in a mobile campaign like this one is transforming mobile into a direct response channel for brick and mortar advertisers like McDonalds.
Good advertising moves people.
Great advertising moves with them.
©2010 NAVTEQ. All Rights Reserved.
NAVTEQ
Media Solutions™
www.navteqmedia.com


**Exhibit 15-8** NAVTEQ provides digital map data for location-based devices such as smartphones. NAVTEQ data is also used in vehicle navigation devices from Garmin.
Source: NAVTEQ Media Solutions.

NAVTEQ Media Solutions is a digital map data company owned by Nokia. NAVTEQ provides location-based advertising services using the company's proprietary technology, LocationPoint Advertising (Exhibit 15-8). NAVTEQ's global clients include Best Western Germany, Domino's Pizza India, and McDonald's Finland. Recent campaigns for a variety of clients have demonstrated that mobile campaigns can provide marketers with important metrics that can be used to calculate return on investment (ROI).

In one campaign, mobile users who were within a five-mile radius of any McDonald's location in Finland received an offer to buy a cheeseburger for 1 euro. The result was a 7 percent click-through rate. Of those users, 39 percent used the ad's click-to-navigate option to request walking or driving directions to the nearest McDonald's. In India, a campaign to reach existing and prospective Domino's customers was also successful. Ads were delivered to smartphone users; banner ads were also placed on Nokia's Ovi Services portal. The results were impressive:

22.6 percent of users clicked for the map, 10.8 percent clicked to call for home-delivery options, and 8 percent used the ad to access Domino's Web site.[41]

Cell phone usage is exploding in India. As Manoj Dawane, CEO of Mumbai software company People Infocom, explains, "In India, mobile phone penetration is high compared to other forms of media like television or the Internet. You can't have a better place than India for mobile advertising." One factor driving mobile ads in India is the low rates that subscribers pay—as little as 2 cents per minute. Demographics play an important role, too. About two-thirds of the Indian population lives in rural areas where television ownership and newspaper readership are low. Cellular operators such as BPL Mobile have built networks that reach tens of thousands of Indian villages. Arif Ali, head of brand communications at BPL, has ideas that will keep subscriber costs low. "We are thinking of providing 30- to 60-second commercials over the phone where we will pass on some kind of benefit," he said.[42]

**Bluetooth** mobile communication technology has the advantage of consuming less power than Wi-Fi.[43] This makes Bluetooth well suited for use with cell phones. However, Bluetooth works over shorter distances than Wi-Fi. Both Bluetooth and Wi-Fi technology are being incorporated into automobiles and home appliances such as refrigerators, lighting systems, and microwave ovens. In short, the "Internet of things" is rapidly coming into being.

Likewise, the Internet-connected car is becoming a reality as automakers rush to incorporate technology into their vehicles. Indeed, many drivers view their cars as an extension of their digital selves, and a variety of apps permit various kinds of interactions. cale nameplates such as Porsche and BMW have developed Apple Watch apps that enable drivers to remotely check, say, whether the doors are locked and the windows are up. Electric car owners can also check to see whether their cars' batteries are fully charged. Mainstream manufacturers such as Ford and Hyundai are also launching their own apps. Most global automakers and suppliers have established research laboratories in California's Silicon Valley tech hub (see Exhibit 15-9).

## Mobile Music

Because of rampant illegal sharing of music files, the music companies are searching for new sources of revenue. Thanks to technology convergence, the new generation of smartphones is driving change in the mobile music industry. **Mobile music** is music that is purchased and played on a smartphone or other mobile device.

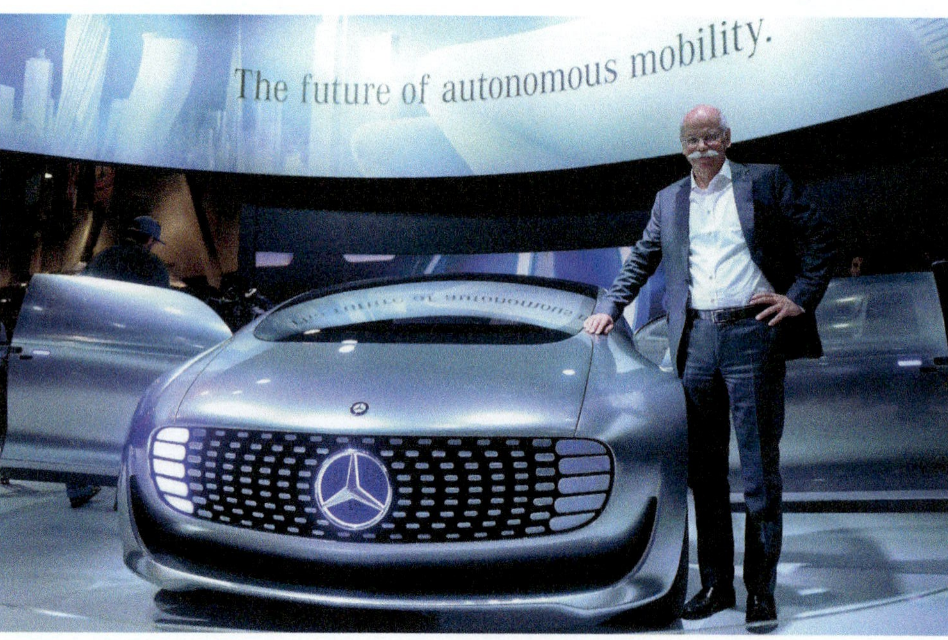
The future of autonomous mobility.

**Exhibit 15-9** Dr. Dieter Zetsche, Chairman of Daimler AG and head of Mercedes-Benz, delivered the keynote address at the 2015 International Consumer Electronics Show in Las Vegas. In his remarks, Dr. Zetsche discussed the future of autonomous vehicle technology and other innovations.

**Source:** Britta Pedersen/epa european pressphoto agency b.v./Alamy.

---

[41]Sara Silver and Emily Steel, "Alcatel Gets into Mobile Ads," *The Wall Street Journal* (May 21, 2009), p. B9; NAVTEQ, "Domino's," http://navteqmedia.com/mobile/case-studies/dominos (accessed May 24, 2011); NAVTEQ, "McDonald's," http://navteqmedia.com/mobile/case-studies/mcdonalds (accessed May 24, 2011).

[42]Eric Bellman and Tariq Engineer, "India Appears Ripe for Cell Phone Ads," *The Wall Street Journal* (March 10, 2008), p. B3.

[43]*Bluetooth* is the Anglicized version of a Scandinavian epithet for Harald Blatand, a Danish Viking and king who lived in the tenth century.

For more than a decade, the market for paid, legal, full-track music downloads was dominated by Apple's iTunes Store. Music purchased from iTunes can be played back on computers and mobile devices such as Apple's iPod, iPhone, and iPad. In 2006, iTunes reached a milestone of 1 billion downloads; today, Apple is the world's number 1 music seller, with a cumulative total of 25 billion downloads. (The 25-billionth song was downloaded in Germany in 2013, and the lucky iTunes customer won a €10,000 Apple Gift Card.) Apple's competitors tried, without much success, to develop music players and download services to rival the iPod/iTunes combination.

The market for paid downloads has matured rapidly as consumers opt for streaming services. According to figures compiled by the International Federation for the Phonographic Industry (IFPI), annual global download revenues peaked in 2012 at about $4 billion. Also in 2012, streaming revenues totaled about $1 billion. However, streaming revenues are exhibiting strong growth, while download revenues are in decline. In response, Apple launched Apple Music in 2015. Some streaming sites—Spotify, for example—offer a free tier as well as a paid, "premium" level of service. The difference is that the paid tier is ad-free while the free tier requires users to listen to mobile ads. Apple's new service is subscription-only. Apple Music executives believe their service will offer better personalization features and superior artist recommendations compared to other services.[44]

Cloud computing, which was discussed earlier in the chapter, is expected to have a major impact on the mobile music business. Cloud-based music services represent a hybrid of the subscription and online store business models; the new approach addresses some of the shortcomings of the existing methods. For example, iPod owners had to sync their iPods to their computers or other devices. Also, the pricing schemes for the various subscription services can be confusing. By contrast, cloud-based music services, including iTunes Match, Google Play, and Amazon Cloud Player, offer users a music locker; the locker is "in the cloud," and music files that have been purchased or uploaded can be accessed from a variety of mobile devices.

## Mobile and Online Gaming

Mobile gaming is gaining in popularity; revenues were expected to reach $17.6 billion in 2015, up from $3.77 billion in 2010. Worldwide, Apple's iPhone, iPod, and iPad are the dominant mobile-gaming platforms. Game of War: Fire Age, and Clash of Clans are two of the most popular mobile games. Other popular games include Zynga Poker, solitaire, blackjack, and other card and casino games; Sudoku; and board games such as Monopoly.

Some games are available on a free-to-play basis; others sell for the equivalent of a few dollars. How can a marketer monetize a free game? For a small fee, free games can be upgraded to premium versions. In addition, many games offer users the opportunity to make in-game purchases of virtual goods. Game of War is a case in point: It generates $1 million in revenue every day for parent company Machine Zone. Indeed, the word "free" can be misleading, as network operators typically charge fees for downloading the games.[45]

In the past few years, online gaming has also morphed into a spectator sport. In fact, the term **e-sport** has been coined to describe video game competitions in which professional gamers compete for cash prizes that can reach $1 million. Examples include the StarCraft II 2014 World Championship Global Finals and the League of Legends World Championship that was held in South Korea. Fans in the United States can watch the matches from locations such as the Ignite lounge in Chicago or the Staples Center in Los Angeles (see Exhibit 15-10).

## Mobile Payments

Mobile payments—payments using smartphones—received a major boost when Apple launched Apple Pay in conjunction with the iPhone 6 in 2014. Users link their smartphones to their bank accounts; a technology called **near-field communication (NFC)** allows users to "swipe" their phones near a payment terminal to complete a purchase. Previous payment systems, including Google Wallet and Square, had not been particularly popular. However, a series of well-publicized credit card data cyber-thefts at Target, Home Depot, and other retailers raised consumer interest in a payment system that would offer increased speed and security.

---

[44] Tim Bradshaw and Matthew Garrahan, "Apple Streaming Service Leaves iTunes Behind," *Financial Times* (June 6/7, 2015), p. 10.

[45] Daisuke Wakabayashi and Spencer E. Ante, "Mobile Game Fight Goes Global," *The Wall Street Journal* (June 14, 2012), p. B1.

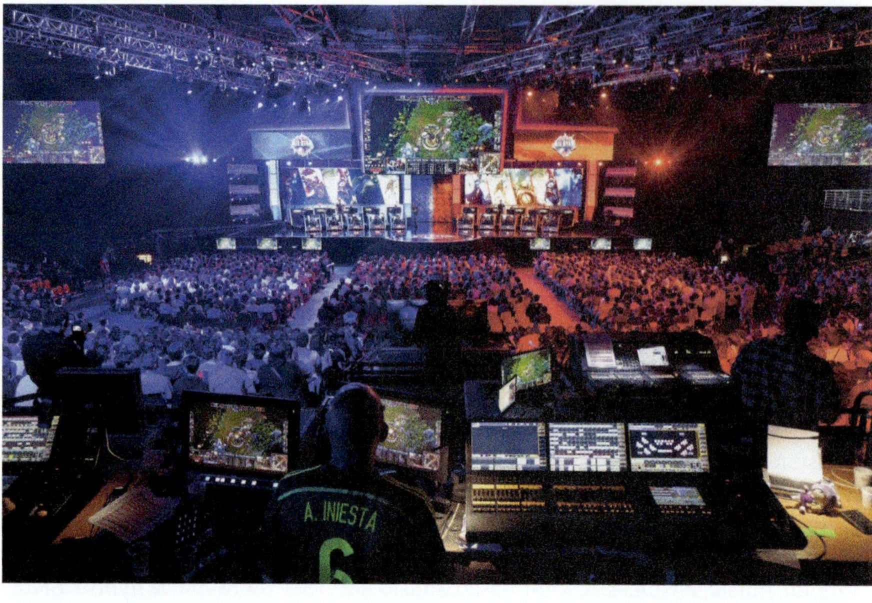


**Exhibit 15-10** E-sports are exploding in popularity as thousands of fans pack arenas to watch competitive video gaming.
Source: Lionel Bonaventure/AFP/Getty Images.

## Streaming Video

Global penetration of broadband Internet service has fueled the growing popularity of global digital video services such as YouTube. Other players operating in the space include Facebook, Instagram, Twitter, and, as discussed in the "Global Startup" sidebar, Netflix. One recent innovation is Meerkat, a streaming app that allows users to stream live video using their Twitter accounts. Some industry observers predict that Meerkat and similar apps will lead to major changes in the way people consume news and live events such as sports.

| | |
|---|---|
| 1 billion | Number of people who tune into YouTube each day |
| 300 million | Number of hours of video viewed on YouTube each day |
| 300 | Number of hours of new content uploaded to YouTube every minute |

## Internet Phone Service

For the telecommunications industry, Internet telephone service is the "next big thing." **Voice over Internet Protocol (VoIP)** technology allows the human voice to be digitized and broken into data packets that can be transmitted over the Internet and converted back into normal speech. If a call is placed to a conventional phone, it must be switched from the Internet to a traditional phone network; local telephone companies generally own the lines into residences and businesses. However, if the call is made between two subscribers to the same VoIP provider, it bypasses the traditional network altogether. The implications are clear: VoIP has the potential to render the current telecommunications infrastructure—consisting primarily of twisted copper and fiber optic cable—obsolete.

Currently, VoIP accounts for only a small percentage of global calls. However, it has the potential to be a disruptive innovation that will upset the balance of power in the telecommunications industry. The promise of a global growth market has resulted in soaring stock values for startups. In Europe, Niklas Zennström, cofounder of the Kazaa music file-sharing service, started Skype Ltd. to offer Internet telephone service. As hundreds of thousands of new users—many in China, India, and Sweden—joined each day, Skype became a global phenomenon. In 2005, eBay acquired Skype for $2.6 billion. However, eBay struggled to create synergies between the communication system and the company's core auction business. In 2009, eBay spun off Skype as a separate company. In 2011, Microsoft bought Skype for $8.6 billion.

## Digital Books and Electronic Reading Devices

The digital revolution has had a dramatic impact on traditional print media such as newspapers and magazines. Publishers are experiencing dramatic downturns in readership as people spend more time online. At the same time, the global recession forced many companies to cut back on print advertising. Caught in a squeeze, magazines are folding and newspapers are declaring bankruptcy. However, electronic readers (e-readers) such as Amazon.com's Kindle, Barnes & Noble's Nook, and Apple's iPad may help lure subscribers back.

**Exhibit 15-11** Amazon.com founder and CEO Jeff Bezos unveils the Kindle Fire, the latest version of his company's wireless reading device. Amazon.com's e-book sales recently overtook sales of titles in traditional paperback and hardback formats. Bezos is hoping that the Kindle will gain acceptance among college students.
**Source:** © ZUMA Press, Inc./Alamy.

Amazon.com sold the first Kindle for $359; prices for the latest generation Kindle Fire HD start at $99 (see Exhibit 15-11). Amazon.com has taken the Kindle global with the launch of a smaller, less expensive version that can be used in more than 100 countries. Apple launched the iPad in March 2010; by the end of the year, 15 million units had been sold. By mid-2014, Apple had sold more than 200 million of the devices.

Industry observers think that colleges and universities will be instrumental in building awareness and encouraging adoption of e-readers and e-books. The reason is simple: Electronic versions of textbooks represent a huge market opportunity. For example, the textbook you are reading is available directly from the publisher in the form of an electronic "subscription" at www.coursesmart.com. The online version requires users to be connected to the Internet; the text can be accessed from an unlimited number of computers. Buyers can use the e-book for 180 days before the subscription expires. The price is approximately half of what bookstores charge for a new copy of the physical textbook. Usually, students can print as many as 10 pages at a time; it is also possible to cut and paste, highlight, and take notes directly on the computer.

As is the case with music and movies, digital piracy is a growing problem with e-books. A number of Web sites and file-sharing services distribute unauthorized copies of popular copyrighted material. What do authors themselves think of the problem? Some view digital piracy as a way to gain new readers. Others say that they simply want fair compensation for their work. A third camp includes authors who don't think pursuing the pirates is worth the effort. As best-selling author Stephen King said recently, "The question is, how much time and energy do I want to spend chasing these guys? And to what end? My sense is that most of them live in basements floored with carpeting remnants, living on Funions and discount beer."[46]

## Wearables

Wearable technology—including fitness bands, Google Glass, Apple Watch, and other products—are reaching a tipping point in terms of sales growth. Technology research firm IDC predicts that annual sales will reach 113 million units by 2018, up from 6 million units in 2013. Glass at Work, a new program from Google, is designed to encourage adoption of Google Glass in hospitals, construction, and other workplaces where employees work with their hands.

## Summary

The *digital revolution* has created a global electronic marketplace. The revolution has gained momentum over the course of 75-plus years, during which time technological breakthroughs included the digital mainframe computer; the *transistor*; the *integrated circuit (IC)*; the *personal computer*

[46]Motoko Rich, "New Target for Digital Pirates: The Printed Word," *The New York Times* (May 12, 2009), p. A1

*(PC)*; the *spreadsheet*; the PC *operating system*; and the *Internet*, which originated as an initiative of the *Defense Advanced Research Projects Agency (DARPA)*. Three key innovations by Tim Berners-Lee—*URLs*, HTTP, and HTML—led to the creation in the early 1990s of the *World Wide Web*.

The digital revolution has resulted in a process known as *convergence*, meaning that previously separate industries and markets are coming together. In this environment, the *innovator's dilemma* means that company management must decide whether to invest in current technologies or try to develop new technologies. Although leading firms in an industry often develop *sustaining technologies* that result in improved product performance, the revolution has also unleashed a wave of *disruptive technologies* that are creating new markets and reshaping industries and *value networks*.

*E-commerce* is growing in importance for both consumer and industrial goods marketers. Generally, commercial Web sites can have a domestic or a global focus; in addition, they can be classified as *promotion sites, content sites*, or *transaction sites*. Global marketers must take care when designing Web sites. Country-specific domain names must be registered and local-language sites developed. In addition to addressing issues of technology and functionality, content must reflect local culture, customs, and aesthetic preferences. *Cybersquatting* can hinder a company's effort to register its corporate name as an Internet destination.

The Internet is a powerful tool for advertisers; *click-through rates* are one measure of effectiveness. Another trend is *paid search advertising*. New products and services spawned by the digital revolution include *broadband*, which permits transmission of *streaming media* over the Internet; *mobile commerce (m-commerce)*, which is made possible by *Wi-Fi, Bluetooth*, and other forms of wireless connectivity; *global positioning systems (GPS)*; and *short message service (SMS)*. *Smartphones* are creating new markets for *mobile music* downloads and streaming; smartphones can also be used for mobile gaming and Internet phone service using *VoIP*.

---

MyMarketingLab

To complete the problems with the ✪, go to EOC Discussion Questions in the MyLab.

## Discussion Questions

**15-1.** Briefly review the key innovations that culminated in the digital revolution. What is the basic technological process that made the revolution possible?

✪**15-2.** What is convergence? How is convergence affecting Sony? Kodak? Nokia?

**15-3.** What is the innovator's dilemma? What is the difference between a sustaining technology and a disruptive technology? Briefly review Christensen's five principles of disruptive innovation.

**15-4.** What is the Long Tail? What implications does this have for market segmentation?

✪**15-5.** Review the key products and services that have emerged during the digital revolution. What are some new products and services that are not mentioned in the chapter?

**15-6.** You have the option of purchasing electronic editions of many of your college textbooks. Is this something that you are interested in doing?

✪**15-7.** Which pricing model do you think is better for music downloads, the iTunes Store's "pay-per-track" or Rhapsody's subscription service? Do you think cloud-based music services will be successful?

**CASE 15-1** **CONTINUED (REFER TO PAGE 468)**

## Africa 3.0

Investment in telecommunications and other sectors in Africa is being driven by a variety of factors. Several demographic trends are clear. For example, nearly half the population is under the age of 15. The World Bank reports that half the population lives on $1.25 per day. However, according to a study by the African Development Bank, Africa's middle class now comprises 34 percent of the population, some 313 million people in all. The report defines "middle class" as those who spend between $2 and $20 per day. A narrower definition would include the 120 million people (21 percent) who spend between $4 and $20 per day.

Demand from this emerging middle class has been a boon to telecommunications companies. Between 2006 and 2010, compound revenue growth in the sector averaged 40 percent. In Africa, a cell phone is often a person's most valuable possession; more than 450 million people are cell phone subscribers. Kenya, for example, is home to more than 21 million active phone numbers for a population of 40 million people. In most parts of Africa, mobile networks suffer service interruptions. As a result, many people use more than one cell phone and have multiple providers.

Key industry players include Safaricom, Kenya's leading mobile phone service provider and the largest, most profitable company in East Africa. South Africa's MTN Group is the continent's leading mobile provider in terms of subscribers. MTN gained prominence in 2010 when it became the first African company to have a sponsorship for World Cup soccer. Globacon is in Nigeria.

One of the biggest African success stories involves Celtel International, a telecom created by Sudanese businessman Mo Ibrahim. In 2005, Ibraham sold the company to Zain, based in Kuwait, for $3.4 billion. In 2010, India's Bharti Airtel paid $10.7 billion for Zain's African assets. Zain has operations in 15 African countries, including Malawi, Chad, and Zambia. The acquisition makes Bharti the world's largest mobile provider—165 million subscribers in all—with operations only in emerging markets.

Not surprisingly, the market opportunity is also attracting investment from other global telecom operators. For example, France Telecom has tens of millions of users in 22 countries in Africa and the Middle East. Executives are extending the company's African reach to span the entire continent; the goal is to become the "champion of rural Africa" by rolling out a range of new, low-cost mobile services under the Orange brand. For example, the company's E-Recharge service lets users exchange credits via text messaging. Price discounts of up to 99 percent for off-peak calls are also very popular.

Kenya has become a key battleground, as service providers cut prices to attract customers. Airtel Kenya has squared off against Safaricom, Orange Kenya, and other rivals; Airtel recently cut rates by 50 percent, to $0.03 per minute for voice calls and $0.01 for text messages. Parent company Bharti Airtel had previously used this tactic in India, where customers are making longer calls because airtime is less expensive. For his part, Safaricom CEO Robert Collymore says his company will focus on data and mobile banking services.

Arguably the biggest mobile innovation in Africa is M-Pesa (M for "mobile"; *pesa* is Swahili for "money"). M-Pesa is a mobile phone–based money transfer service developed by Safaricom Kenya and Vodaphone, with backing from Britain's Department for International Development. In 2014, Safaricom partnered with KCB, Kenya's biggest bank.

Today, M-Pesa is the dominant mobile money platform and a case study of the way telecommunication companies are transforming the banking industry in Africa. About one-third of Kenya's population uses M-Pesa regularly, with daily transactions adding up to about $44 million. For example, Kenyans use M-Pesa to get cash and make payments for bills, school fees, and airline tickets. Safaricom's service boasts a network of more than 100,000 agents. As competitors across the continent enter the mobile payments space, interoperability between service providers will increase in importance.

Just a decade ago, many mainstream banks would not have found it feasible to do business with low-income customers; the meager returns did not justify opening branch networks or setting up ATMs. As a result, a person with a city job would have to give money to a friend or a bus driver to deliver to relatives at home. Needless to say, highway robbery was a constant threat.

Today, however, banks can work with shopkeepers and bar owners who dispense or collect cash and then credit or debit a customer's mobile phone account. The target market is the "unbanked"; that is, people who do not have bank accounts. In Kenya alone, the majority of adults have access to financial services today, compared with only 5 percent in 2006. In Nigeria, a country of 150 million people, only 20 percent of the population has a bank account. Nigeria's Central Bank (CBN) is taking the lead, creating a system in which telecommunications companies will provide the infrastructure for offering financial services. This approach is necessary because there are several dominant cell phone service providers in Nigeria.

Price wars are just one of the challenges of doing business on the continent. Africa is at the bottom of the World Bank's "Ease of Doing Business" rankings. Widespread corruption is part of the problem; as Sudanese telecom magnate Ibrahim puts it, "There is a crisis of leadership and governance in Africa and we must face it." Moreover, he notes, "These guys know that millions of children are going to bed without dinner. The blood of those children is on the hands of those who spend the money on arms and private jets."

Data compiled by Global Financial Integrity, a nongovernmental organization, support Ibrahim's assessment of the business environment. According to a recent report, more than $350 billion flowed out of Africa as a result of corruption and illicit deals.

## Discussion Questions

**15-8.** The United States and Latin America have been far slower than countries in Africa and Europe in adopting mobile payments technology. Why is this the case?

**15-9.** Further economic liberalization in Africa depends, in part, on government leaders overcoming suspicions that foreign companies want to exploit Africa. How quickly is this likely to happen?

**15-10.** If marketers "think local and act local," what are some of the new products and services that are likely to emerge from Africa in the next few years?

**Sources:** Katrina Manson and Jude Webber, "Simple Phone Technology Promises to Revolutionise Access to Finance," *Financial Times* (January 30, 2015), p. 14; Nichole Sobecki, "Making Change: Mobile Pay in Africa," *The Wall Street Journal* (January 2, 2015), p. B6; Chad Bray and Reuben Kyama, "Tap to Pay (Not So Much in the U.S.)," *The New York Times* (April 2, 2014), pp. F1, F8; Kevin J. O'Brien, "Microsoft and Huawei of China to Unite to Sell Low-Cost Windows Smartphones in Africa," *The New York Times* (February 5, 2013), p. B2; Peter Wonacott, "A New Class of Consumers Grows in Africa," *The Wall Street Journal* (May 2, 2011), p. A8; Sarah Childress, "Telecom Giants Battle for Kenya," *The Wall Street Journal* (January 14, 2011), pp. B1, B7; Ben Hall, "France Telecom Targets Rural Africa for Growth," *Financial Times* (November 10, 2010), p. 16; Parselelo Kantai, "Telecoms: Mobile May Be the Future of Banking," *Financial Times* (September 29, 2010); Gordon Brown, "To Combat Poverty, Get Africa's Children to School," *Financial Times* (September 20, 2010), p. 9; William Wallis and Tom Burgis, "Attitudes Change to Business in Region," *Financial Times* (June 4, 2010), p. 6; Wallis, "Outlook Brightens for Frontier Market," *Financial Times* (June 2, 2010), p. 7; Robb M. Stewart and Will Connors, "For Bharti, Africa Potential Outweighs Hurdles," *The Wall Street Journal* (February 17, 2010), pp. B1, B2; Jamie Anderson, Martin Kupp, and Ronan Moaligou, "Lessons from the Developing World," *The Wall Street Journal* (August 17, 2009), p. R6; Tom Burgis, "Case Study: Text Messages Give Shopkeepers the Power to Bulk Buy," *Financial Times Special Report: Digital Business* (May 29, 2009), p. 8; Cassell Bryan-Low, "New Frontiers for Cellphone Service," *The Wall Street Journal* (February 13, 2007), pp. B1, B5.

## MyMarketingLab

Go to the Assignments section of your MyLab to complete these writing exercises.

**15-11.** What key issues must be addressed by global companies that engage in e-commerce?

**15-12.** Briefly outline Web design issues as they pertain to global marketing.

# 16 Strategic Elements of Competitive Advantage

## LEARNING OBJECTIVES

**16-1** Identify the forces that shape competition in an industry and illustrate each force with a specific company or industry example.

**16-2** Define *competitive advantage* and identify the key conceptual frameworks that guide decision makers in the strategic planning process.

**16-3** Explain how a nation can achieve competitive advantage, and list the forces that may be present in a national "diamond."

**16-4** Define *hypercompetitive industry* and list the key arenas in which dynamic strategic interactions take place.

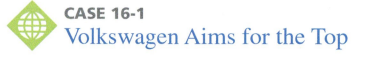

## CASE 16-1
## Volkswagen Aims for the Top

In May 2011, production began at Volkswagen's new $1 billion assembly plant in Chattanooga, Tennessee. The Passat sedans coming off the line are a striking symbol of the German automaker's ambitious strategic goal: Volkswagen CEO Martin Winterkorn intends to overtake Toyota and become the world's number 1 automaker by 2018. Winterkorn has vowed that VW will sell 1 million cars in the United States by 2018.

Volkswagen's sole previous U.S. plant, in Westmoreland, Pennsylvania, was closed in 1988. Several factors explain Winterkorn's decision to once again establish a manufacturing operation in the United States. For one thing, the strength of the euro—1 euro was equal to $1.40 when the plant opened—makes it difficult to export cars from Germany to the United States and sell them profitably (Exhibit 16-1). A "German-engineered, American-made" value proposition should also strengthen VW's place in the U.S. auto industry. And, by locating the new plant in the South, VW is taking advantage of much lower wage rates than at older plants operated by GM, Ford, and Chrysler in Detroit.

Winterkorn's declaration caused quite a stir in the auto industry. Volkswagen Auto Group of America markets both the VW and Audi nameplates in the United States; in 2014, unit sales for the group totaled nearly 550,000 vehicles. However, the VW brand has been hampered by perceptions of hit-and-miss quality; in a recent J.D. Power Initial Quality Study, VW ranked 31st out of 33 brands. In addition to a new model produced in Chattanooga, VW is also launching a revamped version of its iconic Bug as well as a new Jetta. To find out more about VW's global marketing strategy, turn to the continuation of Case 16-1 at the end of the chapter.

**Exhibit 16-1** VW's 20-story "Autostadt storage tower" in Wolfsburg.
**Source:** John MacDougall/AFP/Getty Images/Newscom.

The essence of marketing strategy is successfully relating the strengths of an organization to its environment. As the horizons of marketers have expanded from domestic to regional and global, so, too, have the horizons of competitors. Global competition is the reality in almost every industry today, including auto manufacturing. This fact of life puts an organization under increasing pressure to master techniques for conducting industry analysis and competitor analysis and understanding competitive advantage at both the industry and the national levels. This chapter covers these topics in detail.

## 16-1 Industry Analysis: Forces Influencing Competition

A useful way of gaining insight into competitors is through industry analysis. As a working definition, an *industry* can be defined as a group of firms that produce products that are close substitutes for each other. In any industry, competition works to drive down the rate of return on invested capital toward the rate that would be earned in the economist's "perfectly competitive" industry. Rates of return that are greater than this so-called "competitive" rate will stimulate an inflow of capital either from new entrants or from existing competitors making additional investments. The global smartphone industry is a case in point: Apple's success with the iPhone prompted Samsung and others to enter the market. Rates of return below this competitive rate will result in withdrawal from the industry and a decline in the levels of activity and competition.

Harvard University's Michael E. Porter, a leading authority on competitive strategy, developed a **five forces model** that explains competition in an industry: the threat of new entrants, the threat of substitute products or services, the bargaining power of buyers, the bargaining power of suppliers, and the competitive rivalry among current members of the industry. In industries such as soft drinks, pharmaceuticals, and cosmetics, the favorable nature of the five forces has resulted in attractive returns for competitors. However, pressure from any of the forces can limit profitability, as evidenced by the recent fortunes of some competitors in the PC and semiconductor industries. A discussion of each of the five forces follows.

## Threat of New Entrants

New entrants to an industry bring new capacity; a desire to gain market share and position; and, quite often, new approaches to serving customer needs. The decision to become a new entrant in an industry is often accompanied by a major commitment of resources. New players mean prices will be pushed downward and margins squeezed, resulting in reduced industry profitability in the long run. Porter describes eight major sources of barriers to entry, the presence or absence of which determines the extent of threat by new industry entrants.[1]

The first barrier, **economies of scale**, refers to the decline in per-unit product costs as the absolute volume of production per period increases. Although the concept of scale economies is frequently associated with manufacturing, it is also applicable to research and development (R&D), general administration, marketing, and other business functions. Honda's efficiency at engine R&D, for example, results from the wide range of products it produces that feature gasoline-powered engines. When existing firms in an industry achieve significant economies of scale, it becomes difficult for potential new entrants to be competitive.

*Product differentiation*, the second major entry barrier, is the extent of a product's perceived uniqueness—in other words, whether it is a commodity. Differentiation can be achieved as a result of unique product attributes or effective marketing communications, or both. Product differentiation and brand loyalty "raise the bar" for would-be industry entrants who are required to make substantial investments in R&D or advertising. For example, Intel achieved differentiation and erected a barrier in the microprocessor industry with its "Intel Inside" advertising campaign and logo that appears on many brands of PCs.

A third entry barrier relates to *capital requirements*. Capital is required not only for manufacturing facilities (fixed capital) but also for financing R&D, advertising, field sales and service, customer credit, and inventories (working capital). The enormous capital requirements in such industries as pharmaceuticals, mainframe computers, chemicals, and mineral extraction present formidable entry barriers.

A fourth barrier to entry is the one-time *switching costs* resulting from the need to change suppliers and products. These might include retraining costs, ancillary equipment costs, the cost of evaluating a new source, and so on. The perceived cost to customers of switching to a new competitor's product may present an insurmountable obstacle, preventing industry newcomers from achieving success. For example, Microsoft's huge installed base of Windows operating systems and applications presented a formidable entry barrier for many years.

A fifth barrier to entry is access to *distribution channels*. If channels are full, or unavailable, the cost of entry is substantially increased because a new entrant must invest time and money to gain access to existing channels or to establish new channels. Some Western companies have encountered this barrier in Japan.

*Government policy,* the sixth barrier, is frequently a major entry barrier. In some cases, the government will restrict competitive entry. This is true in a number of industries, especially those outside the United States, that have been designated as "national" industries by their respective governments. Japan's postwar industrialization strategy was based on a policy of preserving and protecting national industries in their development and growth phases. The result was a market that proved difficult for non-Japanese competitors to enter, an issue that was targeted by the Bill Clinton administration. American business executives in a wide range of industries urged adoption of a government policy that would reduce some of these barriers and open the Japanese market to more U.S. companies.

---

[1] Michael E. Porter, *Competitive Strategy* (New York: Free Press, 1980), pp. 7–33.

Established firms may also enjoy *cost advantages independent of scale economies* that present a seventh barrier to entry. Access to raw materials, a large pool of low-cost labor, favorable locations, and government subsidies are several examples.

Finally, expected *competitor response,* the eighth barrier, can be a major entry barrier. If new entrants expect existing competitors to strongly oppose the entry, the entrants' expectations about the rewards of entry will certainly be affected. A potential competitor's belief that entry into an industry or market will be an unpleasant experience may serve as a strong deterrent. Bruce Henderson, former president of the Boston Consulting Group, used the term "brinkmanship" to describe a recommended approach for deterring competitive entry. Brinkmanship occurs when industry leaders convince potential competitors that any market-entry effort will be countered with vigorous and unpleasant responses. This is an approach that Microsoft has used many times to maintain its dominance in software operating systems and applications.

In the three decades since Porter first described the five forces model, the digital revolution appears to have altered the entry barriers in many industries. First and foremost, technology has lowered the cost for new entrants. For example, Barnes & Noble watched an entrepreneurial upstart, Amazon.com, storm the barriers protecting traditional brick-and-mortar booksellers. Amazon.com founder Jeff Bezos identified and exploited a glaring inefficiency in book distribution: Bookstores ship unsold copies of books back to publishers to be shredded and turned into pulp. Amazon.com's centralized operations and increasingly personalized online service enable customers to select from millions of different titles at discount prices and have them delivered to their homes within days. For a growing number of book-buying consumers, Amazon.com eclipses the value proposition of local bookstores that offer "only" a few thousand titles and gourmet coffee bars. Since Bezos founded Amazon.com in 1995, sales have grown to $61 billion and the company has expanded into new product lines, including CDs, DVDs, streaming movies and music, and e-books. The company serves tens of millions of customers in more than 160 countries. Barnes & Noble responded by entering the online book market itself even as it continues to be profitable in its traditional bricks-and-mortar business. In the meantime, Bezos has repositioned Amazon.com as an Internet superstore selling electronics and general merchandise.

## Threat of Substitute Products

A second force influencing competition in an industry is the threat of substitute products. The availability of substitute products places limits on the prices market leaders can charge in an industry; high prices may induce buyers to switch to the substitute. Once again, the digital revolution is dramatically altering industry structures. In addition to lowering entry barriers, the digital era means that certain types of products can be converted to bits and distributed in pure digital form. For example, the development of the MP3 file format for music was accompanied by the increased popularity of peer-to-peer (p-to-p or P2P) file swapping among music fans. Napster and other online music services offered a substitute to consumers who were tired of paying $15 or more for a CD. Although a U.S. court severely curtailed Napster's activities, other services—including several outside the United States—sprang up in its place. The top players in the music industry were taken by surprise, and today, Sony BMG, Warner Music, and Universal Music Group are still struggling to develop new strategies in response to the changing business environment.

**"Walmart is the 800-pound gorilla. You're going to want to do more things for a customer who is growing as fast as Walmart is."[2]**

Ted Taft, Meridian Consulting Group

## Bargaining Power of Buyers

In Porter's model, "buyers" refers to manufacturers (e.g., General Motors [GM]) and retailers (e.g., Walmart) rather than consumers. The ultimate aim of such buyers is to pay the lowest possible price to obtain the products or services that they require. Usually, therefore, if they can, buyers drive down profitability in the supplier industry. To accomplish this, the buyers have to gain leverage over their vendors. One way they can do this is to purchase in such large quantities that supplier firms are highly dependent on the buyers' business. Second, when the suppliers' products are viewed as commodities—that is, as standard or undifferentiated—buyers are likely to bargain hard for low prices because many firms can meet their needs. Buyers will also bargain hard when the supplier industry's products or services represent a significant portion of the buying firm's costs. A fourth source of buyer power is the willingness and ability to achieve backward integration.

[2]Melanie Warner, "Its Wish, Their Command," *The New York Times* (March 3, 2006), p. C1.

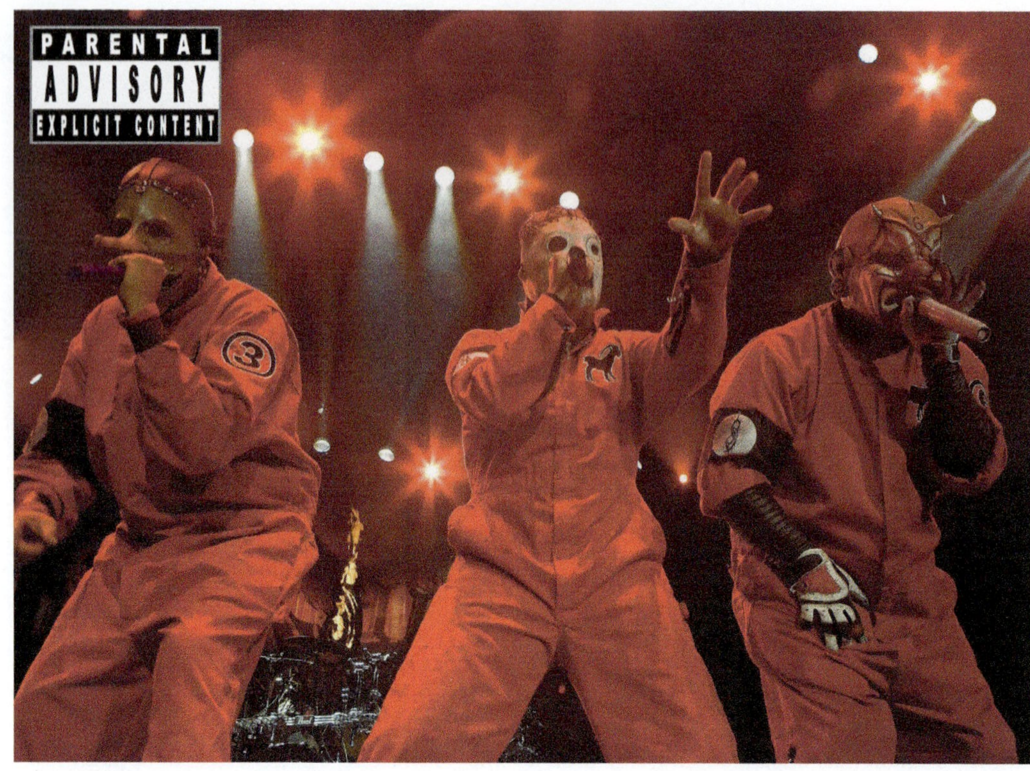


**Exhibit 16-2** Walmart exercises its buying power by refusing to stock CDs bearing "Parental Advisory" stickers warning of controversial or potentially offensive lyrics; Slipknot's debut CD is one example.

In response to the "corporatization" of record retailing, independent shop owners have launched an annual international promotion called Record Store Day. On the third Saturday in April, discerning music fans are urged to patronize their local indie shop.

Slipknot vocalist/lyricist Corey Taylor acknowledges that many of the band's fans have little choice but to shop at their local Walmart. To prove that he could do it, Taylor intentionally wrote lyrics that avoided profanity on *Vol. 3: (The Subliminal Verses)*.

For example, because it purchases massive quantities of goods for resale, Walmart is in a position to dictate terms to any vendor wishing to distribute its products through the retail giant's stores. Walmart's influence also extends to the recorded music industry; Walmart refuses to stock CDs bearing parental advisory stickers for explicit lyrics or violent imagery. Recording artists who want their recordings available at Walmart have the option of altering lyrics and song titles or deleting offending tracks. Likewise, artists are sometimes asked to change album cover art if Walmart deems it offensive (see Exhibit 16-2). In addition, Walmart has launched Soundcheck, which consists of performances by up-and-coming recording artists that are broadcast every Friday night on the in-house television network found in each store. Exclusive tracks featuring special versions of songs by the Soundcheck sessions' artists are also available.[3]

## Bargaining Power of Suppliers

Supplier power in an industry is the converse of buyer power. If suppliers have enough leverage over industry firms, they can raise prices high enough to significantly influence the profitability of their organizational customers. Several factors determine suppliers' ability to gain leverage over industry firms. Suppliers will have the advantage if they are large and relatively few in number. Second, when the suppliers' products or services are important inputs to user firms, are highly differentiated, or carry switching costs, the suppliers will have considerable leverage over buyers. Suppliers will also enjoy bargaining power if alternative products do not threaten their business. A fourth source of supplier power is their willingness and ability to develop their own products and brand names if they are unable to get satisfactory terms from industry buyers.

[3]Jonathan Birchall, "Walmart, the Record Label," *Financial Times* (January 31, 2006), p. 17.

## EMERGING MARKETS BRIEFING BOOK

### Cemex

MyMarketingLab SYNC • THINK • LEARN

Mexico's S.A.B. de C.V. Cemex is a global building solutions company with operations in more than 50 countries. Chief executive Lorenzo Zambrano, the grandson of the company's founder, holds an MBA from Stanford University. To help drive sales in Mexico, where Cemex commands more than 50 percent of the market, the company devised an innovative payment method. Migrant workers in the United States can pay for cement that their friends and relatives in Mexico can pick up at a local store.

Zambrano introduced sophisticated technology to the company's operations. For example, satellites and computer software allow company engineers in Mexico to monitor temperatures in kilns across the ocean in Spain. As Zambrano explained, "A cement company is not supposed to be high-tech, but we showed it can be. It is supposed to be boring, but we showed it is not." Under Zambrano's leadership, Cemex had 2010 revenues of $14 billion.

Starting in the early 1990s, Zambrano began extending Cemex's global reach by acquiring Spain's two largest cement companies for $1 billion. Other acquisitions followed in Indonesia, Panama, the Philippines, the United States, Venezuela, and elsewhere. Unfortunately, after a string of successes, one acquisition turned out to be disastrous. In 2007, Zambrano paid more than $15 billion to acquire Australia's Rinker Materials Corp. Rinker was a major supplier to the U.S. housing market; as the economic crisis worsened, sales to the United States declined.

There was more bad news; the global credit crunch made it very difficult for Zambrano to refinance some of the debt burden that Cemex had taken on. Moreover, as investors sought security by holding dollars, the greenback's value rose while other currencies weakened. The weaker peso meant that Cemex's dollar-denominated debt was even more of a burden. Rossana Fuentes Berain, author of a biography of the Cemex chief, summed up Zambrano's predicament this way: "For 20 years, he managed Cemex flawlessly. Now people are obviously asking why such brilliant people like Lorenzo could not see this coming. Why weren't they more cautious? Why didn't they ask the right questions?"

**Sources:** Amy Kamzin and James Fontanella-Khan, "Mexico's Cemex Eyes Indian Cement Group," *Financial Times* (November 23, 2010); Joel Millman, "Hard Times for Cement Man," *The Wall Street Journal* (December 11, 2008), pp. A1, A14.

In the tech world, Microsoft and Intel are two companies with substantial supplier power. Because about 90 percent of the world's 1-billion-plus PCs run on Microsoft's operating systems and 80 percent use Intel's microprocessors, the two companies enjoy a great deal of leverage relative to Dell, Hewlett-Packard, and other computer manufacturers. Microsoft's industry dominance prompted both the U.S. government and the European Union (EU) to launch separate antitrust investigations. Today, the shift is to new electronic devices such as smartphones, netbooks, and tablets. Many of these new products use the Apple, Android, or Linux operating systems instead of Windows; the chips are from competitors such as Qualcomm and Texas Instruments. As these trends take hold, Microsoft and Intel will find their supplier power diminishing.[4]

## Rivalry Among Competitors

Rivalry among firms refers to all the actions taken by firms in an industry to improve their positions and gain advantage over each other. Rivalry manifests itself in price competition, advertising battles, product positioning, and attempts at differentiation. To the extent that rivalry among firms forces companies to rationalize costs, it is a positive force. To the extent that it drives down prices (and therefore profitability) and creates instability in the industry, it is a negative factor.

Several factors can create intense rivalry. Once an industry becomes mature, firms focus on market share and how it can be gained at the expense of other firms. Second, industries characterized by high fixed costs are always under pressure to keep production at full capacity to cover the fixed costs. Once the industry accumulates excess capacity, the drive to fill capacity will push prices—and profitability—down. A third factor affecting rivalry is lack of differentiation or an absence of switching costs, which encourages buyers to treat the products or services as commodities and shop for the best prices. Again, there is downward pressure on prices and profitability. Fourth, firms with high strategic stakes in achieving success in an industry generally are destabilizing because they may be willing to accept below-average profit margins to establish themselves, hold position, or expand.

[4]Olga Kharif, Peter Burrows, and Cliff Edwards, "Windows and Intel's Digital Divide," *BusinessWeek* (February 23, 2009), p. 58.

## 16-2 Competitive Advantage

> **"The only way to gain lasting competitive advantage is to leverage your capabilities around the world so that the company as a whole is greater than the sum of its parts. Being an international company—selling globally, having global brands or operations in different countries—isn't enough."[5]**
>
> David Whitwam, former CEO, Whirlpool

**Competitive advantage** exists when there is a match between a firm's distinctive competencies and the factors critical for success within its industry. Any superior match between company competencies and customers' needs permits the firm to outperform competitors. Competitive advantage can be achieved in two ways. First, a firm can pursue a low-cost strategy that enables it to offer products at lower prices than competitors' prices. Competitive advantage may also be gained by a strategy of differentiating products so that customers perceive unique benefits, often accompanied by a premium price. Note that both strategies have the same effect: They both contribute to the firm's overall value proposition. Porter explored these issues in two landmark books, *Competitive Strategy* (1985) and *Competitive Advantage* (1990); the latter is widely considered to be one of the most influential management books in recent years.

Ultimately, customer perception decides the quality of a firm's strategy. Operating results such as sales and profits are measures that depend on the level of psychological value created for customers: The greater the perceived consumer value, the better the strategy. A firm may market a better mousetrap, but the ultimate success of the product depends on customers deciding for themselves whether to buy it. Value is like beauty; it's in the eye of the beholder. In sum, creating more value than the competition achieves competitive advantage, and customer perception defines value.

Two different models of competitive advantage have received considerable attention. The first offers "generic strategies," four routes or paths that organizations choose to offer superior value and achieve competitive advantage. According to the second model, generic strategies alone did not account for the astonishing success of many Japanese companies in the 1980s and 1990s. The more recent model, based on the concept of "strategic intent," proposes four different sources of competitive advantage. Both models are discussed in the following paragraphs.

### Generic Strategies for Creating Competitive Advantage

In addition to the "five forces" model of industry competition, Porter has developed a framework of so-called generic business strategies based on the two types or sources of competitive advantage mentioned previously: *low cost* and *differentiation*. The relationship of these two sources with the scope of the target market served (narrow or broad) or product mix width (narrow or wide) yields four **generic strategies**: *cost leadership, product differentiation, cost focus*, and *focused differentiation*.

Generic strategies aiming at the achievement of competitive advantage or superior marketing strategy demand that a firm make choices. The choices concern the *type of competitive advantage* it seeks to attain (based on cost or differentiation) and the *market scope* or *product mix width* within which competitive advantage will be attained.[6] The nature of the choice between types of advantage and market scope is a gamble, and it is the nature of every gamble that it entails *risk*: By choosing a given generic strategy, a firm always risks making the wrong choice.

**BROAD MARKET STRATEGIES: COST LEADERSHIP AND DIFFERENTIATION Cost leadership** is competitive advantage based on a firm's position as the industry's low-cost producer, in broadly defined markets or across a wide mix of products. This strategy has gained widespread appeal in recent years as a result of the popularization of the experience curve concept. In general, a firm that bases its competitive strategy on overall cost leadership must construct the most efficient facilities (in terms of scale or technology) and obtain the largest share of market so that its cost per unit is the lowest in the industry. These advantages, in turn, give the producer a substantial lead in terms of experience with building the product. Experience then leads to more refinements of the entire process of production, delivery, and service, which lead to further cost reductions.

Whatever its source, cost leadership advantage can be the basis for offering lower prices (and more value) to customers in the late, more-competitive stages of the product life cycle. In Japan, companies in a range of industries—photography and imaging, consumer electronics and entertainment equipment, motorcycles, and automobiles—have achieved cost leadership on a worldwide basis.

[5]Regina Fazio Maruca, "The Right Way to Go Global: An Interview with Whirlpool CEO David Whitwam," *Harvard Business Review* 72, no. 2 (March–April 1994), p. 135.

[6]Michael E. Porter, *Competitive Advantage: Creating and Sustaining Superior Performance* (New York: Free Press, 1985), p. 12.

Cost leadership, however, is a sustainable source of competitive advantage only if barriers exist that prevent competitors from achieving the same low costs. In an era of increasing technological improvements in manufacturing, manufacturers constantly leapfrog over one another in pursuit of lower costs. At one time, for example, IBM enjoyed the low-cost advantage in the production of computer printers. Then the Japanese took the same technology and, after reducing production costs and improving product reliability, gained the low-cost advantage. IBM fought back with a highly automated printer plant in North Carolina, where the number of component parts was slashed by more than 50 percent and robots were used to snap many components into place. Despite these changes, IBM ultimately chose to exit the business.

When a firm's product has an actual or perceived uniqueness in a broad market, it is said to have achieved competitive advantage by **differentiation**. This can be an extremely effective strategy for defending market position and obtaining superior financial returns; unique products often command premium prices (see Exhibit 16-3). Examples of successful differentiation include Maytag in large home appliances, Caterpillar in construction equipment, and almost any

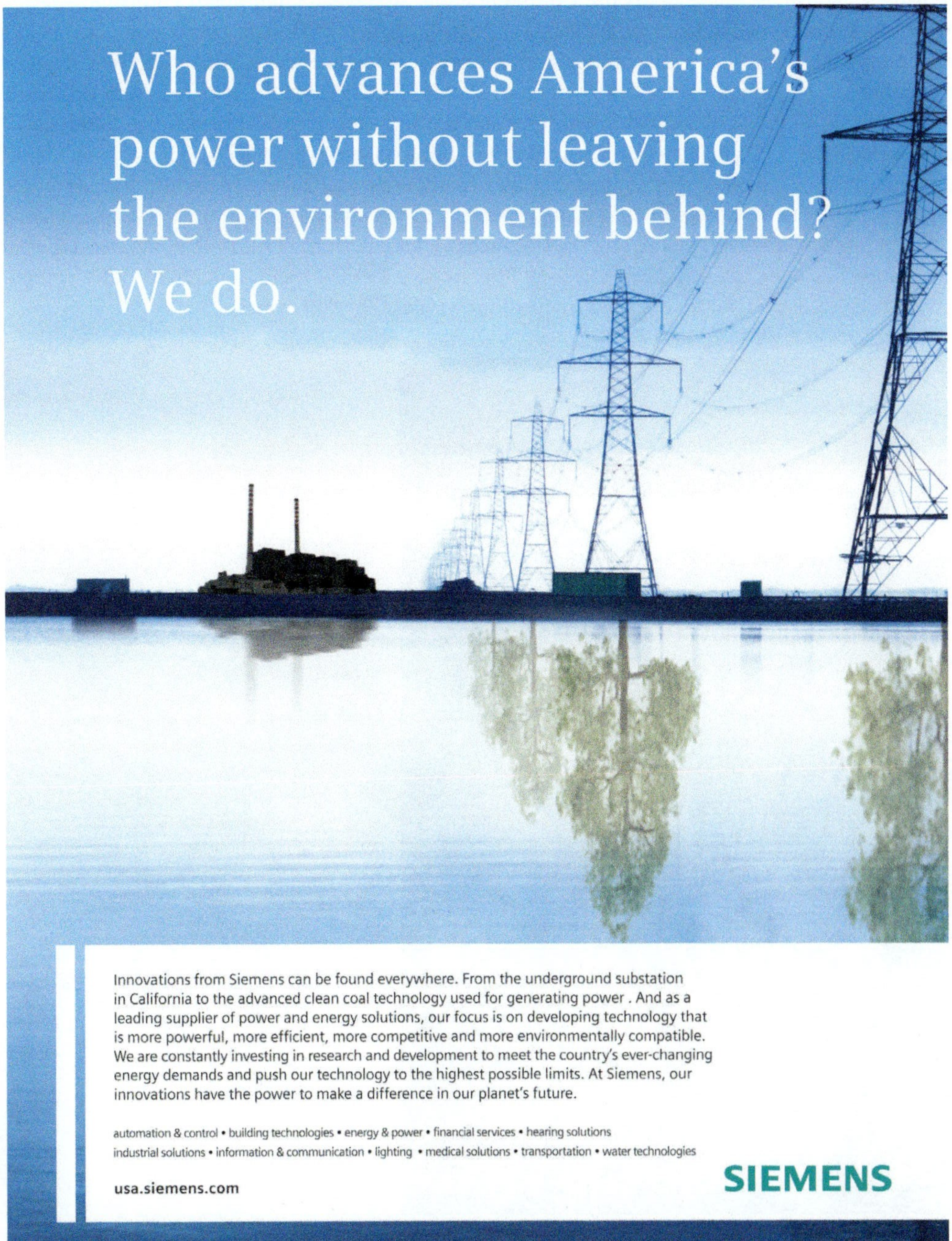

**Exhibit 16-3** Munich-based Siemens AG is a key global player in a variety of engineering sectors. Worldwide, public interest in energy-related issues has increased significantly. This advertisement for Siemens' U.S. unit underscores the company's commitment to innovation in power generation, transmission, and distribution to ensure that the nation's energy needs are met.
**Source:** Courtesy of Siemens Corporation.

"We're living in a very polarized world now. You're either an absolute price leader—you're a Ryanair, a Southwest Airlines, a Walmart and you're just hugely efficient and you will not be touched on price or cost. Or you're over on the quality end of the market with the Guccis and the Pradas and you're a quality leader."[7]

Steve Ridgway, CEO of Virgin Atlantic Airways

successful branded consumer product. IBM traditionally has differentiated itself with a strong sales/service organization and the security of the IBM standard in a world of rapid obsolescence. Among athletic shoe manufacturers, Nike has positioned itself as the technological leader thanks to unique product features found in a wide array of shoes.

**NARROW TARGET STRATEGIES: COST FOCUS AND FOCUSED DIFFERENTIATION** The preceding discussion of cost leadership and differentiation considered only the impact on broad markets. By contrast, strategies to achieve a narrow-focus advantage target a narrowly defined market or customer. This advantage is based on an ability to create more customer value for a narrowly targeted segment and results from a better understanding of customer needs and wants. A narrow-focus strategy can be combined with either cost- or differentiation-advantage strategies. In other words, whereas a *cost focus* means offering low prices to a narrow target market, a firm pursuing *focused differentiation* will offer a narrow target market the perception of product uniqueness at a premium price.

Germany's *Mittelstand* companies have been extremely successful in pursuing **focused differentiation** strategies backed by a strong export effort. The world of "high-end" audio equipment offers another example of focused differentiation. A few hundred small companies design speakers, amplifiers, and related hi-fi gear that cost thousands of dollars per component. While audio components represent a $21 billion market worldwide, annual sales in the high-end segment are only about $1.1 billion. American companies such as Audio Research, Conrad-Johnson, Krell, Mark Levinson, Martin-Logan, and Thiel dominate the segment, which also includes hundreds of smaller enterprises with annual sales of less than $10 million (see Exhibit 16-4). The state-of-the-art equipment these companies offer is distinguished by superior craftsmanship and performance and is highly sought after by audiophiles in Asia (especially Japan and Hong Kong) and Europe. Market growth has slowed in recent years, however, as technological advances mean that inexpensive gear offers improved sound quality. Also, many audiophiles are turning their attention to other components such as flat-screen televisions and multi-room wireless speaker systems.

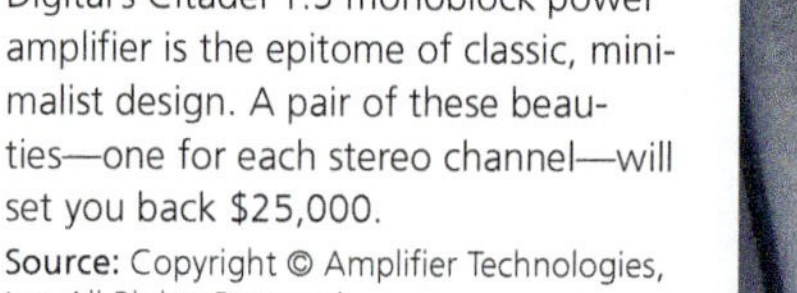

**Exhibit 16-4** In keeping with the aesthetics of high-end audio gear, Theta Digital's Citadel 1.5 monoblock power amplifier is the epitome of classic, minimalist design. A pair of these beauties—one for each stereo channel—will set you back $25,000.

**Source:** Copyright © Amplifier Technologies, Inc. All Rights Reserved.

[7]Daniel Michaels, "No, the CEO Isn't Sir Richard Branson," *The Wall Street Journal* (July 30, 2007), pp. B1, B3.

**Exhibit 16-5** For more than 100 years, Germany's Aldi has offered shoppers a tightly focused assortment of unbranded merchandise at very low prices in a no-frills setting. Now, taking a cue from its Trader Joe unit in the United States, Aldi is making major improvements in its home-country market. German shoppers want more than low prices; they also want a nice ambience and a more appealing atmosphere.

**Source:** © Lannis Waters/The Palm Beach Post/ZUMAPRESS.com/Alamy.

The final strategy is **cost focus**, which is when a firm's lower-cost position enables it to focus on a narrow target market and offer lower prices than the competition (see Exhibit 16-5). In the shipbuilding industry, for example, Polish and Chinese shipyards offer simple, standard vessel types at low prices that reflect low production costs.[8] Germany's Aldi, a no-frills "hard discounter" with operations in numerous countries, offers a very limited selection of household goods at extremely low prices. In 1976, Aldi opened its first U.S. stores in southeastern Iowa. It expanded slowly, opening a handful of stores each year. Private-label products help keep costs and prices down, allowing Aldi to expand in the key U.S. markets despite the recent poor economic climate. Recently, Aldi opened its first store in New York City.[9]

IKEA, the Swedish furniture company, has grown into a successful global company by using the cost-focus strategy (see Case 16-2). As George Bradley, president of Levitz Furniture in Boca Raton, Florida, noted two decades ago, "[IKEA] has really made a splash. They're going to capture their niche in every city they go into." Such a strategy can be risky. As Bradley explained, "Their market is finite because it is so narrow. If you don't want contemporary, knock-down furniture, it's not for you. So it takes a certain customer to buy it. And remember, fashions change."[10]

The issue of sustainability is central to this strategy concept. As noted, cost leadership is a sustainable source of competitive advantage only if barriers exist that prevent competitors from achieving the same low costs. Sustained differentiation depends on continued perceived value and the absence of imitation by competitors.[11] Several factors determine whether focus can be sustained as a source of competitive advantage. First, a cost focus is sustainable if a firm's competitors are defining their target markets more broadly. A focuser doesn't try to be all things to all people: Competitors may diminish their advantage by trying to satisfy the needs of a broader market segment—a strategy that, by definition, means a blunter focus. Second, a firm's differentiation focus advantage is sustainable only if competitors cannot define the segment even more narrowly. Also, focus can be sustained if competitors cannot overcome barriers that prevent imitation of the focus strategy, and if consumers in the target segment do not migrate to other segments that the focuser doesn't serve.

---

[8]Michael E. Porter, *The Competitive Advantage of Nations* (New York: Free Press, 1990), p. 39.

[9]Cecilie Rohwedder and David Kesmodel, "Aldi Looks to U.S. for Growth," *The Wall Street Journal* (January 13, 2009), p. B1. For an excellent discussion of Aldi's corporate history, see Michael J. Silverstein, *Treasure Hunt: Inside the Mind of the New Consumer* (New York: Portfolio, 2006), Chapter 3, pp. 66–75.

[10]Jeffrey A. Trachtenberg, "Home Economics: IKEA Furniture Chain Pleases with Its Prices, Not with Its Service," *The Wall Street Journal* (September 17, 1991), pp. A1, A5.

[11]Michael E. Porter, *Competitive Advantage: Creating and Sustaining Superior Performance* (New York: Free Press, 1985), p. 158.

## Creating Competitive Advantage via Strategic Intent

An alternative framework for understanding competitive advantage focuses on competitiveness as a function of the pace at which a company implants new advantages deep within its organization. This framework identifies **strategic intent**, growing out of ambition and obsession with winning, as the means for achieving competitive advantage. Writing in the *Harvard Business Review*, Gary Hamel and C. K. Prahalad note:

> Few competitive advantages are long lasting. Keeping score of existing advantages is not the same as building new advantages. The essence of strategy lies in creating tomorrow's competitive advantages faster than competitors mimic the ones you possess today. An organization's capacity to improve existing skills and learn new ones is the most defensible competitive advantage of all.[12]

This approach is founded on the principles of W. E. Deming, who stressed that a company must commit itself to continuing improvement in order to be a winner in a competitive struggle. For years, Deming's message fell on deaf ears in the United States, while the Japanese heeded his message and benefited tremendously. Japan's most prestigious business award is named after him. Eventually, however, U.S. manufacturers responded, and Detroit's current resurgence is evidence that they have made much progress.

The significance of Hamel and Prahalad's framework becomes evident when comparing Caterpillar and Komatsu. As noted earlier, Caterpillar is a classic example of differentiation: The company became the largest manufacturer of earthmoving equipment in the world because it was fanatical about quality and service. Caterpillar's success as a global marketer has enabled it to achieve a 40 percent share of the worldwide market for earthmoving equipment, more than half of which represents sales to developing countries. The differentiation advantage was achieved with product durability, global spare parts service (including guaranteed parts delivery anywhere in the world within 48 hours), and a strong network of loyal dealers.

However, Caterpillar has faced a very challenging set of environmental pressures over the last several decades. Many of Caterpillar's plants were closed by a lengthy strike in the early 1980s; a worldwide recession at the same time caused a downturn in the construction industry. This hurt companies that were Caterpillar customers. In addition, the strong dollar gave a cost advantage to foreign rivals.

Compounding Caterpillar's problems was a new competitive threat from Japan. Komatsu was the world's number 2 construction equipment company and had been competing with Caterpillar in the Japanese market for years. Komatsu's products were generally acknowledged to offer a lower level of quality. The rivalry took on a new dimension after Komatsu adopted the slogan "*Maru-c*," meaning "encircle Caterpillar." Emphasizing quality and taking advantage of low labor costs and the strong dollar, Komatsu surpassed Caterpillar as number 1 in earthmoving equipment in Japan and made serious inroads in the United States and other markets. However, the company continued to develop new sources of competitive advantage even after it achieved world-class quality. For example, new-product development cycles were shortened and manufacturing was rationalized. Caterpillar struggled to sustain its competitive advantage because many customers found that Komatsu's combination of quality, durability, and lower price created compelling value. Yet even as the recession and a strong yen put new pressure on Komatsu, the company sought new opportunities by diversifying into machine tools and robots.[13]

The Komatsu/Caterpillar saga illustrates the fact that global competitive battles can be shaped by factors other than the pursuit of generic strategies. Many firms have gained competitive advantage by *disadvantaging* rivals through "competitive innovation." Hamel and Prahalad define *competitive innovation* as "the art of containing competitive risks within manageable proportions" and identify four successful approaches used by Japanese competitors. These are *building layers of advantage, searching for loose bricks, changing the rules of engagement*, and *collaborating*.

---

[12]Gary Hamel and C. K. Prahalad, "Strategic Intent," *Harvard Business Review* 67, no. 3 (May–June 1989), pp. 63–76. See also Hamel and Prahalad, "The Core Competence of the Corporation," *Harvard Business Review* 68, no. 3 (May–June 1990), pp. 79–93.

[13]Robert L. Rose and Masayoshi Kanabayashi, "Komatsu Throttles Back on Construction Equipment," *The Wall Street Journal* (May 13, 1992), p. B4.

**LAYERS OF ADVANTAGE** A company faces less risk in competitive encounters if it has a wide portfolio of advantages. Successful companies steadily build such portfolios by establishing layers of advantage on top of one another. Komatsu is an excellent example of this approach. Another is the TV industry in Japan. By 1970, Japan was not only the world's largest producer of black-and-white TV sets but was also well on its way to becoming the leader in producing color sets. The main competitive advantage for such companies as Matsushita at that time was low labor costs.

Because they realized that their cost advantage might be temporary, the Japanese also added an additional layer of *quality and reliability* advantages by building plants large enough to serve world markets. Much of this output did not carry the manufacturer's brand name. For example, Matsushita Electric sold products to other companies such as RCA, which then marketed them under their own brand names. Matsushita was pursuing a simple idea: A product sold was a product sold, no matter whose label it carried.[14]

In order to build the next layer of advantage, the Japanese spent the 1970s investing heavily in marketing channels and Japanese brand names to gain recognition. This strategy added yet another layer of competitive advantage: the *global brand franchise*, that is, a global customer base. By the late 1970s, channels and brand awareness were established well enough to support the introduction of new products that could benefit from global marketing—VCRs and photocopy machines, for example. Finally, many companies have invested in *regional manufacturing* so their products can be differentiated and better adapted to customer needs in individual markets.

The process of building layers illustrates how a company can move along the value chain to strengthen competitive advantage. The Japanese began with manufacturing (an upstream value activity) and moved on to marketing (a downstream value activity) and then back upstream to basic R&D. All of these sources of competitive advantage represent mutually reinforcing layers that are accumulated over time.

**LOOSE BRICKS** A second approach takes advantage of the "loose bricks" left in the defensive walls of competitors whose attention is narrowly focused on a market segment or a geographic area to the exclusion of others. For example, Caterpillar's attention was focused elsewhere when Komatsu made its first entry into the Eastern Europe market. Similarly, Taiwan's Acer prospered by following founder Stan Shih's strategy of approaching the world computer market from the periphery. Shih's inspiration was the Asian board game *Go*, in which the winning player successfully surrounds opponents. Shih gained experience and built market share in countries overlooked by competitors such as IBM and Compaq. By the time Acer was ready to target the United States in earnest, it was already the number 1 PC brand in key countries in Latin America, Southeast Asia, and the Middle East.

Intel's loose brick was its narrow focus on complex microprocessors for PCs. The world's biggest chip maker in terms of sales, it currently commands about 80 percent of the global market for PC processors. However, even as it built its core business, demand for non-PC consumer electronics products began to explode. The new non-PC products, such as set-top boxes for televisions, digital cameras, smartphones, and tablets, require chips that are cheaper and use less power than those produced by Intel. Competitors such as LSI Logic and Arm Holdings recognized the opportunity and beat Intel into an important new market. Intel has responded by developing new chips incorporating 3D technology that use half as much power as current designs.[15]

**CHANGING THE RULES** A third approach involves **changing the rules of engagement** and refusing to play by the rules set by industry leaders. For example, in the copier market, IBM and Kodak imitated the marketing strategies used by market leader Xerox. Meanwhile, Canon, a Japanese challenger, wrote a new rulebook.

While Xerox built a wide range of copiers, Canon built standardized machines and components, reducing manufacturing costs. While Xerox employed a huge direct-sales force, Canon chose to distribute through office-product dealers. Canon also designed serviceability, as well as reliability, into its products so that it could rely on dealers for service rather than incurring the

[14] James Lardner, *Fast Forward: Hollywood, the Japanese, and the VCR Wars* (New York: New American Library, 1987), p. 135.
[15] Chris Nuttal, Robin Kwong, and Maija Palmer, "Intel Wants to Get a Grip on Mobile Market," *Financial Times* (May 6, 2011), p. 17.

expense required to create a national service network. Canon further decided to sell rather than lease its machines, freeing the company from the burden of financing the lease base. In another major departure, Canon targeted its copiers at secretaries and department managers rather than at the heads of corporate duplicating operations.[16]

Canon introduced the first full-color copiers and the first copiers with "connectivity"—the ability to print images from such sources as video camcorders and computers. The Canon example shows how an innovative marketing strategy—with fresh approaches to the product, pricing, distribution, and selling—can lead to overall competitive advantage in the marketplace. Canon is not invulnerable, however; in 1991 Tektronix, a U.S. company, leapfrogged past Canon in the color copier market by introducing a plain-paper color copier that offered sharper copies at a much lower price.[17]

**COLLABORATING** A final source of competitive advantage is using know-how developed by other companies. Such *collaboration* may take the form of licensing agreements, joint ventures, or partnerships. History has shown that the Japanese have excelled at using the collaborating strategy to achieve industry leadership. One of the legendary licensing agreements of modern business history is Sony's licensing of transistor technology from AT&T's Bell Labs subsidiary in the 1950s for $25,000. This agreement gave Sony access to the transistor and allowed the company to become a world leader. Building on its initial successes in the manufacturing and marketing of portable radios, Sony has grown into a superb global marketer whose name is synonymous with a wide assortment of high-quality consumer electronics products.

More recent examples of Japanese collaboration are found in the aircraft industry. Today, Mitsubishi Heavy Industries Ltd. and other Japanese companies manufacture airplanes under license to U.S. firms and also work as subcontractors for aircraft parts and systems. Many observers fear that the future of the American aircraft industry may be jeopardized as the Japanese gain technological expertise. The next section discusses various examples of "collaborative advantage."[18]

## Global Competition and National Competitive Advantage

An inevitable consequence of the expansion of global marketing activities is the growth of competition on a global basis.[19] In industry after industry, global competition is a critical factor affecting success. As Yoshino and Rangan have explained, **global competition** occurs when a firm takes a global view of competition and sets about maximizing profits worldwide, rather than on a country-by-country basis. If, when expanding abroad, a company encounters the same rival in market after market, then it is engaged in global competition.[20] In some industries, global companies have virtually excluded all other companies from their markets. An example is the detergent industry, in which three companies—Colgate, Unilever, and Procter & Gamble—dominate an increasing number of detergent markets in Latin America and the Pacific Rim. Many companies can make a quality detergent, but brand-name muscle and the skills required for quality packaging overwhelm local competition in market after market.[21]

---

[16]Gary Hamel and C. K. Prahalad, "Strategic Intent," *Harvard Business Review* 67, no. 3 (May–June 1989), p. 69.

[17]G. Pascal Zachary, "Color Printer Gives Tektronix Jump on Canon," *The Wall Street Journal* (June 14, 1991), p. B1.

[18]Hamel and Prahalad have continued to refine and develop the concept of strategic intent since it was first introduced in their groundbreaking 1989 article. During the 1990s, the authors outlined five broad categories of resource leverage that managers can use to achieve their aspirations: concentrating resources on strategic goals via convergence and focus; accumulating resources more efficiently via extracting and borrowing; complementing one resource with another by blending and balancing; conserving resources by recycling, co-opting, and shielding; and rapid recovery of resources in the marketplace. Gary Hamel and C. K. Prahalad, "Strategy as Stretch and Leverage," *Harvard Business Review* 71, no. 2 (March–April 1993), pp. 75–84.

[19]This section draws heavily on Chapter 3, "Determinants of National Competitive Advantage," and Chapter 4, "The Dynamics of National Advantage," in Porter, *The Competitive Advantage of Nations*, 1990. For an extended country analysis based on Porter's framework, see Michael Enright, Antonio Francés, and Edith Scott Assavedra, *Venezuela: The Challenge of Competitiveness* (New York: St. Martin's Press, 1996).

[20]Michael Y. Yoshino and U. Srinivasa Rangan, *Strategic Alliances: An Entrepreneurial Approach to Globalization* (Boston: Harvard Business School Press, 1995), p. 56.

[21]See Joseph Kahn, "Cleaning Up: P&G Viewed China as a National Market and Is Conquering It," *The Wall Street Journal* (September 12, 1995), pp. A1, A6.

The automobile industry has also become fiercely competitive on a global basis. Part of the reason for the initial success of foreign automakers in the United States was the reluctance—or inability—of U.S. manufacturers to design and manufacture high-quality, inexpensive small cars. The resistance of U.S. manufacturers was based on the economics of car production: Bigger cars equaled bigger profits. Under this formula, small cars meant smaller unit profits. Sadly, U.S. car manufacturers mostly ignored the increasing preference of U.S. drivers for smaller cars, a classic case of ethnocentrism and management myopia. European and Japanese manufacturers always offered cars smaller than those made in the United States, in part because market conditions were much different: less space, higher taxes on engine displacement and fuel, and greater market interest in functional design and engineering innovations.

First Volkswagen, and then Japanese automakers such as Nissan and Toyota, discovered a growing demand for their cars in the U.S. market. For most of the past twenty years, the Toyota Camry has been the best-selling passenger car in North America. Ironically, the Camry plants are located in Kentucky and Indiana, and Cars.com rates the Camry as "the most American car" in its American-Made Index! But the competitive environment continues to evolve. Today, South Korea's Hyundai and Kia have joined the ranks of world-class automakers. Meanwhile, Korea's Automobile Journalist Association named Camry the "Korea Car of the Year" for 2013; however, those Korea-bound Camrys come from U.S. plants. Doubly ironic! And, as noted in Case 16-1, for Volkswagen to achieve its strategic goal of becoming the world's top automaker, it must significantly boost U.S. sales.

The effect of global competition has been highly beneficial to consumers around the world. In the two examples cited, detergents and automobiles, consumers have benefited. In Central America, detergent prices have fallen as a result of global competition. Global automakers provide consumers with the models, performance, and price characteristics they want. If smaller, lower-priced imported cars had not been available, it is unlikely that Detroit's manufacturers would have responded as quickly to the changing market conditions. What is true for automobiles in the United States is true for every product category around the world: Global competition expands the range of products available and increases the likelihood that consumers will get what they want.

The downside of global competition is its impact on the producers of goods and services. Global competition creates value for consumers, but it also has the potential to destroy jobs and profits. When a company—Toyota, for example—offers consumers in other countries a better product at a lower price, it takes customers away from domestic firms such as GM. Unless the domestic firm can create new values and find new customers, the jobs and livelihoods of the domestic supplier's employees are threatened.

This section addresses the following issue: Why is a particular nation a good home base for specific industries? Why, for example, is the United States the home base for the leading competitors in tablets and smartphones, software, credit cards, and filmed entertainment? Why is Germany home to so many world leaders in printing presses, chemicals, and luxury cars? Why are so many leading pharmaceutical, chocolate/confectionery, and trading companies located in Switzerland? How does one account for Italy's success in wool textiles, knitwear, and apparel?

Harvard professor Michael E. Porter explored these issues in his groundbreaking 1990 book *The Competitive Advantage of Nations.* The book was hailed as a valuable guide for shaping national policies on competitiveness. According to Porter, the presence or absence of particular attributes in individual countries influences industry development, not just the ability of individual firms to create core competencies and competitive advantage.[22] Porter describes these attributes in terms of a national "diamond." You can visualize these attributes relative to a baseball diamond: Demand conditions are on "first base"; firm strategy, structure, and rivalry occupy "second base"; factor conditions are on "third base"; and related and supporting industries are at "home plate." The diamond shapes the environment in which firms compete. Activity in any one of the four points of the diamond impacts all the other points, and vice versa.

## Factor Conditions

**Factor conditions** refers to a country's endowment with resources. Factor resources may have been created or inherited. *Basic factors* may be inherited or created without much difficulty; because they can be replicated in other nations, they are not sustainable sources of **national**

[22]Michael E. Porter, *The Competitive Advantage of Nations* (New York: Free Press, 1990).

**Exhibit 16-6** As Michael Porter discusses in his book *The Competitive Advantage of Nations*, Italy's strength as an exporter is due in part to clusters of successful industries including textiles and apparel; glass, ceramics, and stone products; and many others. A case in point is the town of Impruneta in the Italian province of Florence. Impruneta is a source of high-quality terracotta; the high iron content of the area's clay means that the finished pieces can withstand temperatures as low as –20 degrees F. Many artisan pieces are rolled by hand, including those imported in the United States by Seibert & Rice.

**Source:** © Kristoffer Tripplaar/Alamy.

**advantage**. Specialized factors, by contrast, are more advanced and provide a more sustainable source for advantage. Porter describes five categories of factor conditions: human, physical, knowledge, capital, and infrastructure.

**HUMAN RESOURCES** The quantity of workers available, the skills possessed by these workers, the wage levels, and the overall work ethic of the workforce together constitute a nation's human resource factor. Countries with a plentiful supply of low-wage workers have an obvious advantage in the production of labor-intensive products. However, such countries may be at a *disadvantage* when it comes to the production of sophisticated products requiring highly skilled workers capable of working without extensive supervision.

**PHYSICAL RESOURCES** The availability, quantity, quality, and cost of land, water, minerals, and other natural resources determine a country's physical resources (see Exhibit 16-6). A country's size and location are also included in this category, because proximity to markets and sources of supply, as well as transportation costs, are strategic considerations. These factors are important advantages—or disadvantages—to industries dependent on natural resources. Brazil is a case in point. With a large landmass, temperate climate, and abundant water supply, Brazil is a leading producer of agricultural commodities, including coffee, soybeans, and sugar.

**KNOWLEDGE RESOURCES** The availability within a nation of a significant portion of the population having scientific, technical, and market-related knowledge means that the nation is endowed with knowledge resources. The presence of this factor is usually a function of the number of research facilities and universities—both government and private—operating in the country. This factor is important to success in sophisticated products and services, and to doing business in sophisticated markets. This factor relates directly to Germany's leadership in chemicals; for nearly 200 years, Germany has been home to top university chemistry programs, advanced scientific journals, and apprenticeship programs.

**CAPITAL RESOURCES** Countries vary in the availability, amount, cost, and types of capital available to the country's industries. The nation's savings rate, interest rates, tax laws, and government deficit all affect the availability of this factor. The advantage enjoyed by industries in countries with low capital costs versus those located in nations with relatively high capital costs is sometimes decisive. Firms paying high capital costs are frequently unable to stay in a market where the competition comes from a nation with low capital costs. The firms with the low cost of capital can keep their prices low and force the firms paying high costs to either accept low returns on investment or leave the industry.

**INFRASTRUCTURE RESOURCES** Infrastructure includes a nation's banking system, health care system, transportation system, and communications system, as well as the availability and cost

**INNOVATION, ENTREPRENEURSHIP, AND THE GLOBAL STARTUP**

## Italian Entrepreneurs Combine Fashion and Function



As Michael Porter notes in *The Competitive Advantage of Nations*:

> Entrepreneurship thrives in Italy, feeding rivalry in existing industries and the formation of clusters. Italians are risk takers. Many are individualistic and desire independence. They aspire to have their own company. They like to work with people they know well, as in the family, and not as part of a hierarchy.... Recently, the entrepreneur has become celebrated in Italy, and a number of business magazines are full of nothing but profiles of successful entrepreneurs. (p. 447)

So, what is an entrepreneur? Management guru Peter Drucker used the term to describe someone who introduces innovations. Entrepreneurs, by definition, are always pioneers in introducing new products. Drucker writes:

> They are people with exceptional abilities who seize opportunities that others are oblivious to or who create opportunities through their own daring and imagination.... Innovation is the specific instrument of entrepreneurship. Innovation is the act that endows resources with a new capacity to create wealth.... Through innovation, entrepreneurs create new satisfactions or new consumer demand.

Leonardo del Vecchio is an entrepreneur. He developed an innovative approach to an existing product and, in 1961, founded a company that manufactures and markets it. By applying the basic tools and principles of modern marketing, del Vecchio has achieved remarkable success. He grew up in an orphanage, but today he is one of Europe's richest men. His insight: Although eyeglasses are critical for vision, they also reflect the wearer's personality. As a product, then, eyeglass frames serve two purposes; one is functional, the other is aesthetic. This insight fueled the growth of del Vecchio's company, Luxottica, into the world's top producer of eyeglass frames.

In the 1960s, del Vecchio approached Milan-based designer Giorgio Armani and asked, "Have you ever thought about glasses and your brand name and your style?" Armani's response? "Great idea! Let's go!" he said. The rest, as they say, is history. Today, Luxottica has 60,000 employees worldwide, and is vertically integrated. It designs and manufactures frames in its own factories, and also is involved in distribution through fully owned chains such as Sunglass Hut, LensCrafters, and Pearle Vision. It owns top eyewear brands including Oakley, Ray-Ban, and Vogue. The company also produces frames under license for a veritable who's who of luxury brands: Burberry, Dolce & Gabbana, Donna Karan, Prada, Ralph Lauren, Versace, and many others. Ray-Ban is Luxottica's biggest-selling brand, with more than €2 billion ($2.2 billion) in sales each year. Del Vecchio's business principles include the following (see Exhibit 16-7):

- "Made in Italy" is important!
- Must cut costs to keep production at home.
- Invest in automation: Robots, not workers, weld on hinges, set rhinestones, affix brand logos.

Diego Della Valle is another Italian entrepreneur. He developed an innovative approach to an existing product and then leveraged his family's business to manufacture and market it. By applying the basic tools and principles of modern marketing, Della Valle and his family have achieved remarkable success. As is true with many entrepreneurs, Della Valle's idea was based on his recognition that "there had to be a better way." While visiting the United States as a young man, he spotted "these strange, very badly made shoes from Portugal." They were marketed as a driving accessory. He brought a pair back to Italy and showed his father, Dorino. The elder Della Valle thought they were "horrible" and told his son to throw them away. Dorino Della Valle then reconsidered. His son says, "He changed the way we think about shoes. In the past, expensive shoes were rigid, heavy. So he had the idea of making them soft, to fit like a glove, using the best quality leather."

Today, Tod's S.p.A., the family business that was started in the 1920s, is closely identified with its iconic driving shoe. The company's strategic focus is on shoes and handbags; annual sales are $1 billion. CEO Diego Della Valle says, "We want to guarantee our customers we're giving them the best." The CEO continues, "Pure Italian style is identifiable anywhere in the world. When I am walking in Central Park, I recognize the Italians because an Italian, even when he jogs, he's dressed perfect." The need to maintain a quality image is one reason that all Tod's production—including six sewing factories—takes place in Italy. Analyst Davide Vimercati notes, "Tod's is proof that if you manage your brand consistently and you build brand equity over the years, you reach a stage where demand remains strong, even in tough times."

**Sources:** Bill Emmott, *Good Italy, Bad Italy: Why Italy Must Conquer Its Demons to Face the Future* (New Haven, CT: Yale University Press, 2012), Chapter 7; Liz Alderman, "A Shoemaker That Walks but Never Runs," *The New York Times* (October 10, 2010), p. B1; Vincent Boland, "Italy's Entrepreneur with Sole," *Financial Times* (April 22, 2009); "Employment, Italian Style," *The Wall Street Journal* (June 26, 2012), p. A14; Christina Passariello, "Fitting Shades for Chinese," *The Wall Street Journal* (April 21, 2011), p. B5; Rachel Sanderson, "The Real Value of Being 'Made in Italy,'" *Financial Times* (January 19, 2011); Emanuela Scarpellini, *Material Nation: A Consumer's History of Modern Italy* (New York: Oxford University Press, 2011); David Segal, "Is Italy Too Italian?" *The New York Times* (August 1, 2010), p. B1; Michael E. Porter, *The Competitive Advantage of Nations* (New York: The Free Press, 1990), Chapter 8.

of using these systems. More sophisticated industries are more dependent on advanced infrastructures for success.

Competitive advantage accrues to a nation's industry if the mix of factors available to the industry is such that it facilitates pursuit of a generic strategy (i.e., low-cost production or the production of a highly differentiated product or service). Nations that have selective factor *disadvantages* may also indirectly create competitive advantage. For example, the absence of

**Exhibit 16-7** Luxottica, the world's leading eyewear manufacturer, also owns and operates retail chains in key global markets. Generally speaking, customers in the United States tend to emphasize function (e.g., brands such as Ray-Ban and Oakley) and are somewhat more conservative and traditional in their tastes. By contrast, European and Asian customers share the desire for an emotional connection with the things they buy—including eyeglass frames. The company is ramping up efforts to expand in Brazil, India, Turkey, and China.
**Source:** Kris Tripplaar/SIPA/Newscom.

suitable labor may force firms to develop forms of mechanization or automation that give the nation an advantage. High transportation costs may motivate firms to develop new materials that are less expensive to transport.

## Demand Conditions

The nature of home demand conditions for the firm's or industry's products and services is important because it determines the rate and nature of improvement and innovation by the firms in the nation. **Demand conditions** are the factors that either train firms for world-class competition or that fail to adequately prepare them to compete in the global marketplace. Four characteristics of home demand are particularly important to the creation of competitive advantage: the composition of home demand, the size and pattern of the growth of home demand, the rapid home-market growth, and the means by which a nation's home demand pushes or pulls the nation's products and services into foreign markets.

**COMPOSITION OF HOME DEMAND** This demand element determines how firms perceive, interpret, and respond to buyer needs. Competitive advantage can be achieved when the home demand sets the quality standard and gives local firms a better picture of buyer needs, at an earlier time, than what is available to foreign rivals. This advantage is enhanced when home buyers pressure the nation's firms to innovate quickly and frequently. The basis for advantage is the fact that the nation's firms can stay ahead of the market when the firms are more sensitive and more responsive to home demand and when that demand, in turn, reflects or anticipates world demand.

**SIZE AND PATTERN OF GROWTH OF HOME DEMAND** These are important only if the composition of the home demand is sophisticated and anticipates foreign demand. Large home markets offer opportunities to achieve economies of scale and learning while dealing with familiar, comfortable markets. There is less apprehension about investing in large-scale production facilities and expensive R&D programs when the home market is sufficient to absorb the increased capacity. If the home demand accurately reflects or anticipates foreign demand, and if the firms do not become content with serving the home market, the existence of large-scale facilities and programs will be an advantage in global competition.

**RAPID HOME-MARKET GROWTH** This is yet another incentive to invest in and adopt new technologies faster and to build large, efficient facilities. The best example of this is in Japan, where rapid home-market growth provided the incentive for Japanese firms to invest heavily in modern, automated facilities. *Early home demand*, especially if it anticipates international demand, gives local firms the advantage of getting established in an industry sooner than foreign rivals. Equally important is *early market saturation*, which puts pressure on a company to expand into international markets and innovate. Market saturation is especially important if it coincides with rapid growth in foreign markets.

**MEANS BY WHICH A NATION'S PRODUCTS AND SERVICES ARE PUSHED OR PULLED INTO FOREIGN COUNTRIES** The issue here is whether a nation's people and businesses go abroad and then demand the home nation's products and services in those second countries. For example, when the U.S. auto companies set up operations in foreign countries, the auto parts industry followed. The same is true for the Japanese auto industry. Similarly, when overseas demand for the services of U.S. engineering firms skyrocketed after World War II, those firms, in turn, established demand for U.S. heavy construction equipment. This provided an impetus for Caterpillar to establish foreign operations.

A related issue is that of a nation's people going abroad for training, pleasure, business, or research. After returning home, they are likely to demand the products and services with which they became familiar while abroad. Similar effects can result from professional, scientific, and political relationships between nations. Those involved in the relationships begin to demand the products and services of the recognized leaders.

It is the interplay of demand conditions that produces competitive advantage. Of special importance are those conditions that lead to initial and continuing incentives to invest and innovate and to continuing competition in increasingly sophisticated markets.

## Related and Supporting Industries

A nation has an advantage when it is home to globally competitive companies in business sectors that comprise **related and supporting industries**. Globally competitive supplier industries provide inputs to downstream industries. The latter, in turn, are likely to be globally competitive in terms of price and quality and thus gain competitive advantage from this situation. Downstream industries will have easier access to these inputs and the technology that produced them, and to the managerial and organizational structures that made them competitive. Access is a function of proximity both in terms of physical distance and cultural similarity. It is not the inputs themselves that give advantage. It is the *contact* and *coordination* with the suppliers, the opportunity to structure the value chain so that linkages with suppliers are optimized. These opportunities may not be available to foreign firms.

Similar advantages are present when there are globally competitive, related industries in a nation. Opportunities are available for coordinating and sharing value chain activities. Consider, for example, the opportunities for sharing between computer hardware manufacturers and software developers. Related industries also create "pull through" opportunities, as described previously. For example, non-U.S. sales of PCs from Hewlett-Packard, Lenovo, Dell, Acer, and others have bolstered demand for software from Microsoft and other U.S. companies. Porter notes that the development of the Swiss pharmaceuticals industry can be attributed, in part, to Switzerland's large synthetic dye industry; the discovery of the therapeutic effects of dyes, in turn, led to the development of pharmaceutical companies.[23]

## Firm Strategy, Structure, and Rivalry

The **nature of firm strategy, structure, and rivalry** is the final determinant of a nation's diamond. Domestic rivalry in a single national market is a powerful influence on competitive advantage. The PC industry in the United States is a good example of how a strong domestic rivalry keeps an industry dynamic and creates continual pressure to improve and innovate. The rivalry between Dell, Hewlett-Packard, and Apple forces all the players to develop new products, improve existing ones, lower costs and prices, develop new technologies, and continually improve quality and service to keep customers happy. Rivalry with foreign firms may lack this intensity. Domestic rivals have to fight each other not just for market share, but also for employee talent, R&D breakthroughs, and prestige in the home market. Eventually, strong domestic rivalry will push firms to seek international markets to support expansions in scale and R&D investments, as Japan amply demonstrates. In contrast, the absence of significant domestic rivalry can lead to complacency in the home firms and eventually cause them to become noncompetitive in the world markets.

[23]Michael E. Porter, *The Competitive Advantage of Nations* (New York: Free Press, 1990), p. 324.

**Exhibit 16-8** Well-known and highly esteemed in its own country, India's Tata Group participates in a variety of industries, including heavy vehicles, cars, department stores, and tea. Now the group's management team is hoping to maintain that brand image as an international strategy is implemented. Historically, Tata's Group's competitive advantage was based on scouring the globe to find the lowest-cost, highest-quality production inputs—be they raw materials or skilled labor—and then selling them in the global marketplace at a substantial profit. In 2006, the Group's Taj Hotels Resorts and Palaces subsidiary announced plans to buy the Ritz-Carlton Hotel in Boston.
Source: Kuni/AP Images.

It is not the number of domestic rivals that is important; rather, it is the intensity of the competition and the quality of the competitors that make the difference. It is also important that there be a fairly high rate of new business formation to create new competitors and prevent the older companies from becoming comfortable with their market positions and products and services. As noted earlier in the discussion of the five forces model, new industry entrants bring new perspectives and new methods. They frequently define and serve new market segments that established companies have failed to recognize.

Differences in management styles, organizational skills, and strategic perspectives also create advantages and disadvantages for firms competing in different types of industries, as do differences in the intensity of domestic rivalry (see Exhibit 16-8). In Germany, for example, company structure and management style tend to be hierarchical. Managers tend to come from technical backgrounds and to be most successful when dealing with industries that demand highly disciplined structures, like chemicals and precision machinery. Italian firms, in contrast, tend to look like, and be run like, small family businesses that stress customized over standardized products, niche markets, and substantial flexibility in meeting market demands.

There are two final external variables to consider in the evaluation of national competitive advantage—chance and government.

## Chance

Chance events play a role in shaping the competitive environment. Chance events are occurrences that are beyond the control of firms, industries, and usually governments. Included in this category are such things as wars and their aftermaths; major technological breakthroughs; sudden, dramatic shifts in a factor or an input cost, like an oil crisis; dramatic swings in exchange rates; and so on.

Chance events are important because they create major discontinuities in technologies that allow nations and firms that were not competitive to leapfrog over former competitors and become competitive, even leaders, in the changed industry. For example, the development of microelectronics allowed many Japanese firms to overtake U.S. and German firms in industries that had been based on electromechanical technologies—areas traditionally dominated by the Americans and Germans.

From a systemic perspective, the importance of chance events lies in the fact that they alter conditions in the diamond. The nation with the most favorable "diamond," however, will be the one most likely to take advantage of these chance events and convert them into competitive advantage. For example, Canadian researchers were the first to isolate insulin, but they could not convert this breakthrough into a globally competitive product. However, firms in the United States and Denmark were able to make that conversion because of their respective national "diamonds."

### Government

Although it is often argued that government is a major determinant of national competitive advantage, in actuality, government is not a determinant but rather an influence on determinants. Government influences determinants by virtue of its roles as a buyer of products and services and a maker of policies on labor, education, capital formation, natural resources, and product standards. It also influences determinants by its role as a regulator of commerce—for example, by telling banks and telephone companies what they can and cannot do.

By reinforcing determinants in industries where a nation has competitive advantage, government improves the competitive position of the nation's firms. Governments devise legal systems that influence competitive advantage by means of tariffs and nontariff barriers and laws requiring local content and labor. In the United States, for example, the dollar's decline over the past decade has been due, in part, to a deliberate policy to enhance U.S. export flows and stem imports. In other words, government can improve or lessen competitive advantage, but it cannot create it.

## 16-4 Current Issues in Competitive Advantage

Porter's work on national competitive advantage has stimulated a great deal of further research. The Geneva-based World Economic Forum issues an annual report ranking countries in terms of their competitiveness. A decade and a half ago, Morgan Stanley used the Porter framework to identify 238 companies with a sustainable competitive advantage worldwide. "National advantage" was then assessed by analyzing how many of these companies were headquartered in a particular country. The United States ranked first, with 125 companies identified as world leaders (see Table 16-1). Among the world's automakers, Morgan Stanley's analysts considered only BMW, Toyota, and Honda to have worldwide competitive advantage.[24]

### Hypercompetitive Industries

In a book published in the mid-1990s, Dartmouth College professor Richard D'Aveni suggested that the Porter strategy frameworks fail to adequately address the dynamics of competition in the 1990s and the new millennium.[25] D'Aveni took a different approach. He noted that the business environment at the time was characterized by short product life cycles, short product design cycles, new technologies, and globalization. All of these factors and forces interacted to undermine market stability. The result? An escalation and acceleration of competitive forces.

In light of these changes, D'Aveni believed the goal of strategy was shifting from sustaining to disrupting advantages. The limitation of the Porter models, D'Aveni argued, is that they are

**TABLE 16-1 Location of Companies with Global Competitive Advantage**

| Country | Number of Companies |
|---|---|
| 1. United States | 125 |
| 2. United Kingdom | 21 |
| 3. Japan | 19 |
| 4. France | 12 |
| 5. Germany | 10 |
| 6. Netherlands | 7 |
| 7. Canada | 6 |
| 8. Switzerland | 6 |
| 9. Sweden | 3 |
| 10. Finland | 3 |

[24] Tony Jackson, "Global Competitiveness Observed from an Unfamiliar Angle," *Financial Times* (November 21, 1996), p. 18.
[25] Richard D'Aveni, *Hypercompetition: Managing the Dynamics of Strategic Maneuvering* (New York: Free Press, 1994).

static; that is, they provide a snapshot of competition at a given point in time. Acknowledging that Hamel and Prahalad broke new ground in recognizing that few advantages are sustainable, D'Aveni aimed to build upon their work in order to shape "a truly dynamic approach to the creation and destruction of traditional advantages." D'Aveni used the term **hypercompetition** to describe a dynamic competitive world in which no action or advantage can be sustained for long. In such a world, D'Aveni argued, "everything changes" because of the dynamic maneuvering and strategic interactions by hypercompetitive firms such as Microsoft and Gillette.

According to D'Aveni's model, competition unfolds in a series of dynamic strategic interactions in four areas: cost/quality, timing and know-how, entry barriers, and deep pockets. Each of these arenas is "continuously destroyed and recreated by the dynamic maneuvering of hypercompetitive firms." Also, according to D'Aveni, the only source of a truly sustainable competitive advantage is a company's ability to manage its dynamic strategic interactions with competitors by means of frequent movements and countermovements that maintain a relative position of strength in each of the four arenas (see Table 16-2).

**TABLE 16-2 Dynamic Strategic Interactions in Hypercompetitive Industries**

| Arena | Dynamic Strategic Interaction |
|---|---|
| 1. Cost/Quality | **1.** Price wars |
| | **2.** Quality and price positioning |
| | **3.** "The middle path" |
| | **4.** "Cover all niches" |
| | **5.** Outflanking and niching |
| | **6.** The move toward an ultimate value marketplace |
| | **7.** Escaping from the ultimate value marketplace by restarting the cycle |
| 2. Timing and know-how | **1.** Capturing first-mover advantages |
| | **2.** Imitation and improvement by followers |
| | **3.** Creating impediments to imitation |
| | **4.** Overcoming the impediments |
| | **5.** Transformation or leapfrogging |
| | **6.** Downstream vertical integration |
| 3. Entry barriers | **1.** Building a geographic stronghold by creating and reinforcing entry barriers |
| | **2.** Targeting the product market strongholds of competitors in other countries |
| | **3.** Incumbents make short-term counter-responses to guerrilla attacks |
| | **4.** Incumbents realize they must respond fully to the invaders by making strategic responses to create new hurdles |
| | **5.** Competitors react to new hurdles |
| | **6.** Long-run counter-responses via defensive or offensive moves |
| | **7.** Competition between the incumbent and entrant is exported to entrant's home turf |
| | **8.** An unstable standoff between the competitors is established |
| 4. Deep pockets | **1.** "Drive'em out" |
| | **2.** Smaller competitors use courts or Congress to derail deep-pocketed firm |
| | **3.** Large firm thwarts antitrust suit |
| | **4.** Small firms neutralize the advantage of the deep pocket |
| | **5.** The rise of a countervailing power |

**Exhibit 16-9** Swatch Group was an Official Partner of the 2015 Venice Biennale International Art Exposition. Swatch often commissions new styles from well-known artists. Nick Hayek, the son of Swatch founder Nicolas Hayek, is the company's current CEO. Nayla Hayek, Nick's sister, is the group's chairwoman. Swatch recently introduced a new mechanical watch, the Sistem51, that is produced by automated machines in less than 30 seconds.
**Source:** Fabrice Coffrini/AFP/Getty Images.

**COST/QUALITY** Competition in the first arena, cost/quality, occurs via seven dynamic strategic interactions: price wars, quality and price positioning, "the middle path," "cover all niches," outflanking and niching, the move toward an ultimate value marketplace, and escaping from the ultimate value marketplace by restarting the cycle. D'Aveni cites the global watch industry as an example of hypercompetitive behavior in the cost/quality arena. In the 1970s, the center of the watch industry shifted from Switzerland to Japan as the Japanese created high-quality quartz watches that could be sold cheaply.

In the early 1980s, the merger of two Swiss companies into Société Suisse Microélectronique et d'Horlogerie SA (SMH) was followed by a highly automated manufacturing innovation that allowed a quartz movement to be integrated into a stylish plastic case. As a result of this innovation and a strong marketing effort in support of the Swatch brand, the center of the watch industry shifted back to Switzerland. In 2013, for the company's 30th anniversary, Swatch announced the Sistem51, the world's first watch built entirely by automation. The Sistem51 line currently produces 4,000 watches per day.[26]

Today, the Swatch Group is the world's largest watchmaker. The watch industry continues to be highly segmented, with prestige brands competing on reputation and exclusivity; as with many other luxury goods, higher prices are associated with higher perceived quality. In the low-cost segment, brands compete on price and value (see Exhibit 16-9).

**TIMING AND KNOW-HOW** The second arena for hypercompetition is based on organizational advantages derived from timing and know-how. As described by D'Aveni, a firm that has the skills to be a "first mover" and arrive first in a market has achieved a *timing advantage*. A *know-how advantage* is the technological knowledge—or other knowledge of a new method of doing business—that allows a firm to create an entirely new product or market.[27]

D'Aveni identifies six dynamic strategic interactions that drive competition in this arena: capturing first-mover advantages, imitation and improvement by followers, creating impediments to imitation, overcoming the impediments, transformation or leapfrogging, and downstream vertical integration. As the consumer electronics industry has globalized, Sony and

[26]Robin Swithinbank, "Manufactured, Assembled and Decorated—in 28.5 Seconds," *Financial Times Special Report—Watches and Jewellery* (June 5, 2015), p. 8.
[27]Richard D'Aveni, *Hypercompetition: Managing the Dynamics of Strategic Maneuvering* (New York: Free Press, 1994), p. 71.

its competitors have exhibited hypercompetitive behavior in this second arena. Sony has an enviable history of first-mover achievements based on its know-how in audio technology: first pocket-sized transistor radio, first consumer VCR, first portable personal stereo, and first compact disc player.

Although each of these innovations literally created an entirely new market, Sony has fallen victim to the risks associated with being a first mover. The second dynamic strategic interaction—imitation and improvement by followers—can be seen in the successful efforts of JVC and Matsushita to enter the home VCR market a few months after Sony's Betamax launch. VHS technology offered longer recording times and was the dominant consumer format worldwide until the advent of the DVD era.

After years of moves and countermoves among Sony and its imitators, Sony progressed to downstream vertical integration with the 1988 purchase of CBS Records for $2 billion and then, later, the purchase of Columbia Pictures. The acquisitions, which represent the sixth dynamic strategic interaction, were intended to complement Sony's core "hardware" businesses (e.g., TVs, VCRs, and hi-fi equipment) with "software" (e.g., videocassettes and CDs). However, Matsushita quickly imitated Sony by paying $6 billion for MCA Inc. Initially, neither Sony nor Matsushita proved successful at managing their acquisitions. More recently, however, Sony Pictures Entertainment has enjoyed huge successes with the *Spider-Man* movies and *Spectre*, the latest James Bond film.

Sony is also facing serious challenges to its core electronics businesses. The digital revolution rendered Sony's core competencies in analog audio technology obsolete. The company must develop new know-how resources if it is to continue to lead in the Information Age. Sony has found technological leaps harder to achieve, as evidenced by the fact that Apple's iPod is now the world's best-selling portable music player. Sony was also slow to grasp the speed with which consumers would embrace flat-panel TV technology; its home entertainment and sound businesses have been losing money for years. In fact, a hedge fund manager has called for top management to spin off a portion of the entertainment business to boost profitability.[28]

Hypercompetition is showing up in other ways, too. For example, after 20 years, sales of Sony's Handycam camcorders started to decline. Meanwhile, an inexpensive device called the Flip from startup Pure Digital Technologies quickly became a best seller after its launch in 2006. Belatedly, Sony rolled out the Webbie Internet-ready camcorder. During the product's development, the U.S.-based marketing director for the design team asked Tokyo for permission to make the camcorder available in orange and purple.[29] Today, of course, many consumers are using their smartphones to capture and share video images, rendering stand-alone camcorder devices unnecessary.

**ENTRY BARRIERS** Industries in which barriers to entry have been built up comprise the third arena in which hypercompetitive behavior is exhibited. As described earlier in the chapter, these barriers include economies of scale, product differentiation, capital investments, switching costs, access to distribution channels, cost advantages other than scale, and government policies. D'Aveni describes how aggressive competitors erode these traditional entry barriers via eight strategic interactions. For example, a cornerstone of Dell's global success in the PC industry is a direct-sales approach that bypasses dealers and other distribution channels.

The first dynamic strategic interaction comes as a company builds a geographic "stronghold" by creating and reinforcing barriers. After securing a market—especially the home-country market—competitors begin to seek markets outside the stronghold. Thus, the second dynamic strategic interaction takes place when companies target the product market strongholds of competitors in other countries. Honda's geographic expansion outside Japan with motorcycles and automobiles—a series of forays utilizing guerrilla tactics—is a case in point. The third dynamic strategic interaction comes when incumbents make short-term counter-responses to the guerrilla attacks. Strong incumbents may try to turn back the invader with price

---

[28]Hiroko Tabuchi, "Investor's Next Target Is Sony," *The New York Times* (May 15, 2013), p. B1.
[29]Daisuke Wakabayashi and Christopher Lawton, "At Sony, Culture Shift Yields a Low-Cost Video Camera," *The Wall Street Journal* (April 16, 2009), p. B1.

wars, factory investment, or product introductions; or they may adopt a wait-and-see attitude before responding. In the case of both Harley-Davidson and the Detroit-based U.S. auto industry, management originally underestimated and rationalized away the full potential of the threat from Honda and other Japanese companies. Realizing that its company was a weak incumbent, Harley-Davidson management then had little choice but to appeal for government protection. The resulting "breathing room" allowed Harley to put its house in order. Similarly, the U.S. government heeded Detroit's pleas for relief and imposed tariffs and quotas on Japanese auto imports. This gave the Big Three time to develop higher-quality, fuel-efficient models to offer U.S. consumers.

The fourth dynamic strategic interaction occurs when the incumbent realizes it must respond fully to the invader by making strategic responses to create new hurdles. U.S. automakers, for example, waged a PR campaign urging U.S. citizens to "Buy American." The fifth dynamic strategic interaction takes place when competitors react to these new hurdles. In an effort to circumvent import quotas as well as co-opt the "Buy American" campaign, the Japanese automakers built plants in the United States. The sixth dynamic strategic interaction consists of long-run counter-responses to the attack via defensive or offensive moves. GM's 1990 introduction of Saturn is a good illustration of a well-formulated and executed defensive move. As the second decade of the twenty-first century continues, GM is launching another defensive move; in an effort to defend its Cadillac nameplate from Lexus, Acura, and Infiniti, GM is developing a global strategy for Cadillac.

Competition in the third arena continues to escalate; in the seventh dynamic strategic interaction, competition between the incumbent and the entrant is exported to the entrant's home turf. President Clinton's threat of trade sanctions against Japanese automakers in 1995 was intended to send a message that Japan needed to open its auto market. In 1997, GM intensified its assault on Japan by exporting right-hand-drive Saturns to the Japanese market. The eighth and final dynamic strategic interaction in this arena consists of an unstable standoff between the competitors. Over time, the stronghold erodes as entry barriers are overcome, leading competitors to the fourth arena.

As the preceding discussion shows, the irony and paradox of the hypercompetition framework is that in order to achieve a sustainable advantage, companies must seek a series of *unsustainable* advantages! D'Aveni is thus in agreement with the late Peter Drucker, who long counseled that the roles of marketing are innovation and the creation of new markets. Innovation begins with abandonment of the old and obsolete. Sumantra Ghoshal and Christopher Bartlett make a similar point in *The Individualized Corporation*:

> Managers are forced to refocus their attention from a preoccupation with defining defensible product-market positions to a newly awakened interest in how to develop the organizational capability to sense and respond rapidly and flexibly to change. . . . Managers worldwide have begun to focus less on the task of forecasting and planning for the future and more on the challenge of being highly sensitive to emerging changes. Their broad objective is to create an organization that is constantly experimenting with appropriate responses, then is able to quickly diffuse the information and knowledge gained so it can be leveraged by the entire organization. The age of strategic planning is fast evolving into the era of organizational learning.[30]

Likewise, D'Aveni urges managers to reconsider and reevaluate the use of what he believes are old strategic tools and maxims. He warns of the dangers of commitment to a given strategy or course of action. The flexible, unpredictable player may have an advantage over the inflexible, committed opponent. D'Aveni notes that, in hypercompetition, pursuit of generic strategies results in short-term advantage, at best. The winning companies are the ones that successfully move up the ladder of escalating competition, not the ones that lock into a fixed position. D'Aveni is also critical of the five forces model. The best entry barrier, he argues, is one that maintains the initiative, not mounts a defensive attempt to exclude new entrants.

[30]Sumantra Ghoshal and Christopher Bartlett, *The Individualized Corporation* (New York: HarperBusiness, 1997), p. 71.

**Exhibit 16-10** Luciano Benetton is one of four siblings who founded the Italian fashion company that bears the family's name. Luciano recently stepped down as chairman of the Benetton Group and turned over control of the company to son Alessandro. The change comes as Benetton faces increased competition from fleet-footed global rivals such as Sweden's Hennes & Mauritz (H&M) and Spain's Zara. Some industry observers note that Benetton's business model, which involves partnerships with regional sales agents, will need to be adjusted to reflect the business environments in key emerging markets such as China and India.
**Source:** Marcelo del Pozo/Reuters/Corbis Images.

## The Flagship Firm: The Business Network with Five Partners

According to Professors Alan Rugman and Joseph D'Cruz, Porter's model is too simplistic given the complexity of today's global environment.[31] Rugman and D'Cruz have thus developed an alternative framework based on business networks that they call the **flagship model**. Japanese vertical *keiretsu* and Korean *chaebol* have succeeded, Rugman and D'Cruz argue, by adopting strategies that are mutually reinforcing within a business system and by fostering a collective long-term outlook among partners in the system. Moreover, the authors note, "long-term competitiveness in global industries is less a matter of rivalry between firms and more a question of competition between business systems."

A major difference between the flagship model and Porter's is that Porter's is based on the notion of corporate individualism and individual business transactions. For example, as discussed previously, Microsoft's tremendous supplier power allows it to dictate to, and even prosper at the expense of, the computer manufacturers it supplies with operating systems and applications. The flagship model, by contrast, is evident in the strategies of Ford, Volkswagen, and other global automakers; Sweden's IKEA and Italy's Benetton are additional examples (see Exhibit 16-10).

The flagship firm is at the center of a collection of five partners; together, they form a business system that consists of two types of relationships. The flagship firm provides the leadership, vision, and resources to "lead the network in a successful global strategy." *Key suppliers* are those that perform some value-creating activities, such as manufacturing of critical components, better than the flagship. This is a network relationship, with a sharing of strategies, resources, and responsibility for the success of the network. Other suppliers are kept at "arm's length." Likewise, the flagship has network relationships with *key customers* and more traditional, arm's-length commercial relationships with *key consumers*.

In the case of Volkswagen, for example, dealers are its key customers while individual car buyers are its key consumers; in other words, strictly speaking, Volkswagen sells to dealers, and dealers sell to consumers. Similarly, Benetton's key customers are its retail outlets while the individual clothes shopper is the key consumer. *Selected competitors* are companies with which

[31]The following discussion is adapted from Alan M. Rugman and Joseph R. D'Cruz, *Multinationals as Flagship Firms* (Oxford, England: Oxford University Press, 2000).

the flagship develops alliances, such as those described at the end of Chapter 9. The fifth partner is the *non-business infrastructure* (NBI), composed of universities, governments, trade unions, and other entities that can supply the network with intangible inputs such as intellectual property and technology. In the flagship model, flagship firms often play a role in the development of a country's industrial policy.

Benetton's success in the global fashion industry illustrates the flagship model. Benetton is the world's largest purchaser of wool, and its centralized buying enables the company to reap scale economies. The core activities of cutting and dyeing are retained in-house, and Benetton has made substantial investments in computer-assisted design and manufacturing. However, Benetton is linked to approximately 400 subcontractors that produce finished garments in exclusive supply relationships with the company. In turn, a network of 80 agents who find investors, train managers, and assist with merchandising link the subcontractors to the 6,000 Benetton retail shops. As Rugman and D'Cruz note, "Benetton is organized to reward cooperation and relationship building and the company's structure has been created to capitalize on the benefits of long-term relationships."

## Blue Ocean Strategy

One of the most important recent strategy frameworks was proposed by Professors Renée Mauborgne and Kim Chan. In books and articles devoted to "Blue Ocean Strategy," the authors define two categories of competitive spaces: red oceans and blue oceans. Red oceans are, in essence, existing markets or industries with well-defined boundaries where the "rules" are understood by all the players. By contrast, blue oceans are markets or industries that do not currently exist.[32]

The researchers advise company executives to avoid getting bloodied in a "red ocean" of cost cutting and imitation. Far better, they assert, is for a company to create a new space, a blue ocean of "uncontested market space," where hypercompetitive forces don't operate. The authors cite eBay as one example; in this instance, founder Pierre Omidyar created a completely new industry. Cirque du Soleil is another example; in this instance, however, founder Guy Laliberté innovated within the boundaries of an existing industry—the circus. Likewise, while Sony and Microsoft were ramping up speed and power with their PlayStation and Xbox gaming systems, Nintendo created a blue ocean with the low-tech, lower-priced Wii console and family-oriented games. Launched in 2006, Wii emphasized "fun, magic, and joy" rather than processing power.[33]

## Additional Research on Competitive Advantage

Other researchers have challenged Porter's thesis that a firm's home-base country is the main source of core competencies and innovation. For example, Indiana University Professor Alan Rugman has argued that the success of companies based in small economies such as Canada and New Zealand stems from the "diamonds" found in a particular set or combination of home and related countries. For example, a company based in an EU nation may rely on the national "diamond" of one of the 28 other EU members. Similarly, one impact of NAFTA on Canadian firms is to make the U.S. "diamond" relevant to competency creation. Rugman argues that, in such cases, the distinction between the home nation and the host nation becomes blurred. He proposes that Canadian managers must look to a "double-diamond" and assess the attributes of both Canada and the United States when formulating corporate strategy.[34] In other words, he argues that, for smaller countries, the nation is not the relevant unit of analysis in formulating strategy. Rather, corporate strategists must look beyond the nation to the region or to sets of closely linked countries.

[32]Renée Mauborgne and Kim Chan, "Blue Ocean Strategy," *Harvard Business Review* 82, no. 10 (October 2004), pp. 76–84.

[33]John Gapper, "Nintendo's Wizards Put the Magic Into Video Games," *Financial Times* (July 16, 2015), p. 9.

[34]Alan M. Rugman and Lain Verbeke, "Foreign Subsidiaries and Multinational Strategic Management: An Extension and Correction of Porter's Single Diamond Framework," *Management International Review* 3, no. 2 (1993), pp. 71–84.

Other critics have argued that Porter generalized inappropriately from the American experience, while confusing industry-level competition with trade at the national level. In the *Journal of Management Studies*, Howard Davies and Paul Ellis assert that nations can, in fact, achieve sustained prosperity without becoming innovation driven; the authors also note the absence of strong diamonds in the home bases of many global industries.[35]

As for Michael Porter, his views on corporate strategy and competitive advantage have evolved during the last three decades. In a 1997 interview with the *Financial Times*, he emphasized the difference between operational efficiency and corporate strategy. The former, in Porter's view, concerns improvement via time-based competition or total quality management; the latter entails "making choices." Porter explains, "'Choice' arises from doing things differently from the rival. And strategy is about trade-offs, where you decide to do this and not that. Strategy is the deliberate choice not to respond to some customers, or choosing which customer needs you are going to respond to." Porter is not convinced of the validity of competitive advantage models based on core competency or hypercompetitive industries. He feels that a nation has an advantage when it is home to globally competitive companies in business sectors that are related and supporting industries.

In 2008, Porter revisited his five forces model in an article in the *Harvard Business Review*. Despite all the changes and challenges brought about by the global financial crisis, Porter believes his model is as relevant and robust as ever. As he told the *Financial Times* in 2011, the five forces are

> more and more and more fundamentally important and visible, because a lot of the barriers and the distortions that would blunt or mitigate these distortions and the need for strategy and competitive advantage . . . have been swept away.

The factors contributing to this, Porter says, are globalization, increased transparency of information, and the reduction in trade barriers.[36]

## Summary

In this chapter, we focused on the factors that help industries and countries achieve *competitive advantage*. According to Porter's *five forces model*, industry competition is a function of the threat of new entrants, the threat of substitutes, the bargaining power of suppliers and buyers, and the rivalry among existing competitors. Managers can use Porter's *generic strategies* model to conceptualize possible sources of competitive advantage. A company can pursue broad market strategies of *cost leadership* and *differentiation* or the more targeted approaches of *cost focus* and *focused differentiation*. Rugman and D'Cruz have developed a framework known as the *flagship model* to explain how networked business systems have achieved success in global industries. For pursuing competitive advantage, Hamel and Prahalad have proposed an alternative framework that grows out of a firm's *strategic intent* and use of competitive innovation. A firm can build *layers of advantage*, search for *loose bricks* in a competitor's defensive walls, *change the rules of engagement*, or *collaborate with competitors* and utilize their technology and know-how.

Today, *global competition* is a reality in many industry sectors. Thus, competitive analysis must be carried out on a global scale. Global marketers, however, must also have an understanding of national sources of competitive advantage. Porter has described four determinants of *national advantage*. *Factor conditions* include human, physical, knowledge, capital, and infrastructure resources. *Demand conditions* include the composition, size, and growth pattern of home demand. The rate of home-market growth and the means by which a nation's products are pulled into foreign markets also affect demand conditions. The final two determinants are the presence of *related and supporting industries* and the *nature of firm strategy, structure,*

---

[35]Howard Davies and Paul Ellis, "Porter's Competitive Advantage of Nations: Time for the Final Judgment?" *Journal of Management Studies* 37, no. 8 (December 2000), pp. 1189–1213.
[36]Andrew Hill, "An Academic Who Shares His Values," *Financial Times* (September 25, 2011), p. 14.

*and rivalry*. Porter notes that chance and government also influence a nation's competitive advantage. Porter's work has been the catalyst for promising new research into strategy issues, including D'Aveni's work on *hypercompetition*, Rugman's *double-diamond framework* for national competitive advantage and Mauborgne and Chan's *blue-ocean* framework.

---

**MyMarketingLab**

To complete the problems with the ✪, go to EOC Discussion Questions in the MyLab.

## Discussion Questions

**16-1.** Outline Porter's five forces model of industry competition. How are the various barriers to entry relevant to global marketing?

✪ **16-2.** How does the five partners (flagship) model developed by Rugman and D'Aveni differ from Porter's five forces model?

**16-3.** Briefly describe Hamel and Prahalad's framework for competitive advantage.

✪ **16-4.** How can a nation achieve competitive advantage?

**16-5.** According to current research on competitive advantage, what are some of the shortcomings of Porter's model?

✪ **16-6.** What is the connection, if any, between *national* competitive advantage and *company* competitive advantage? Explain.

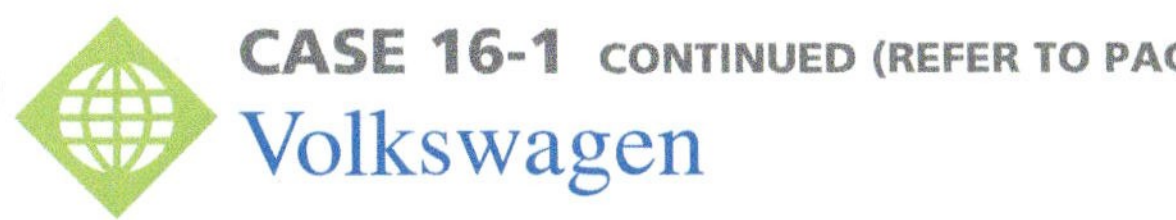

## CASE 16-1 CONTINUED (REFER TO PAGE 494)

# Volkswagen

Volkswagen executives acknowledge that if they are to triple the number of vehicles sold in the United States, they must make cars that appeal to American drivers. Although VW's portfolio of brands includes upscale nameplates such as Audi, Bentley, Bugatti, Lamborghini, and Porsche, the Volkswagen brand itself accounts for about 50 percent of annual revenues.

### Company Background

Historically, one of VW's sources of competitive advantage has been its core competence in the design and manufacture of small, fuel-efficient gasoline engines. Diesel engines are another strength; both types of engines offer the kind of money-saving performance that drivers seek when gasoline prices are high. Several VW models also rank high for crash safety. Given these strengths, why does VW currently rank only second among global automakers? And why has it captured only 3 percent of the U.S. car market? Christian Klinger, Volkswagen Group board member and the executive in charge of sales and marketing for the Volkswagen brand, offers this explanation: "We need the right products and local production," he says. "In the past maybe we had the right product but not the right price. Or the right price and not the right product."

Volkswagen enjoys the distinction of being the number 1 car maker in Europe and the second-largest in the world. Worldwide, the company sold 10 million vehicles in 2014. The compact Golf is the best-selling car in Europe. Volkswagen's market share in Western Europe is 24.4 percent; in Central and Eastern Europe, its share is 15.4 percent. When the new midsize Passat was introduced, initial European demand for it was so strong that there was an eight-month waiting list. The company can boast that its giant Wolfsburg plant is home to the most automated production line in the world, capable of completing 80 percent of a car's assembly by machine. Outside Europe, Volkswagen has also achieved considerable success. In Mexico, for example, the company's share of the passenger car market is 16.7 percent. Volkswagen is also the number 1 Western auto manufacturer in China, where it commands nearly 21 percent of the market.

A deeper understanding of Volkswagen's place in the auto industry requires an overview of then chairman Carl Hahn's attempts to implement his vision of VW as Europe's first global automaker. Indeed, management guru Peter Drucker credited Volkswagen for developing the first truly global strategy more than 40 years ago. By 1970, the Beetle was a mature product in Europe; sales were still moderately strong in the United States and were booming in Brazil. Drucker described what happened next:

> The chief executive officer of Volkswagen proposed switching the German plants entirely to the new model, the successor to the Beetle, which the German plants would also supply to the United States market. But the continuing demand for Beetles in the United States would be satisfied out of Brazil, which would then give Volkswagen do Brasil the needed capability to enlarge its plants and to maintain for another ten years the Beetle's leadership in the growing Brazilian market. To assure the American customers of the "German quality" that was one of the Beetle's main attractions, the critical parts such as engines and transmissions for all cars sold in North America would, however, still be made in Germany. The finished car for the North American market would be assembled in the United States.

Unfortunately, this visionary strategy failed. One problem was resistance on the part of German unions. A second problem was confusion among American dealers about a car that was equally "made in Germany," "made in Brazil," and "made in the USA."

Two decades later, as described in an interview with the *Harvard Business Review*, Hahn's strategic plan for the 1990s and beyond called for a decentralized structure of four autonomous divisions. In pursuit of this vision, Hahn invested tens of billions of dollars in Czechoslovakia's Skoda autoworks and SEAT in Spain. The Volkswagen, Audi, Skoda, and SEAT units each would have its own chief executive. As a whole, the company would be capable of turning out more than 4 million cars annually in low-cost plants located close to buyers. The company's R&D center, however, would continue to be in Germany. Highly automated plants in Germany would provide components such as transmissions, engines, and axles to assembly operations in other parts of the world.

In Spain, VW hoped to take advantage of labor rates 50 percent lower than those in West Germany and roughly on par with those paid by Japanese companies with factories in Britain. Because labor makes up a larger share of production costs for subcompacts than for larger models, and because annual demand in Spain amounted to 500,000 cars, Spain was an attractive location for small-car production. Besides serving the domestic market, VW intended to use Spain as a production source that would allow it to cut prices and boost margins in Europe. Today, cars produced by SEAT are positioned to appeal to budget-conscious car buyers.

Similar reasoning was behind VW's 1991 purchase of a 31 percent stake in Skoda from the Czechoslovak government. Located northeast of Prague in the city of Mlada Boleslav, the Skoda works enjoyed the distinction of being the most efficient plant in the former Soviet bloc. However, product quality was low, and the plant was a major source of pollution. With an eye to doubling production to 450,000 cars, VW pledged to invest $5 billion by the end of the decade. VW's presence also persuaded TRW, Rockwell International, and other parts suppliers interested in serving Skoda and other automakers in Central and Eastern Europe to establish operations in the Czech Republic.

However, to maintain their low-cost position and ensure quality control, VW and Skoda executives went a step beyond the Japanese-style "lean production" system that emphasizes just-in-time delivery from nearby suppliers: Several different suppliers manufactured components such as seats, instrument panels, and rear axles *inside* the plant itself. As Skoda CFO Volkhard Kohler explained in 1994, "We have to organize better than in the Western world and use supplier integration. Wages will increase, so we have to find other ways of being cost-effective. Supplier integration is part of the new thinking and what we do here can be a model for the West." Professor Daniel Jones of the Cardiff University Business School supported the effort: "It's physically integrated, but in terms of management and performance each runs his own show. It makes a lot of sense because you have the direct integration of [the] people making the parts and the people putting them in the car," he said in an interview.

Hahn also earmarked $3 billion for a project in which he took a keen personal interest: investment in the former East Germany, where he was born. On October 3, 1990, German reunification added 16 million people to Volkswagen's home-country market virtually overnight. Under communism, the citizens of East Germany had a choice of basically one car: the notoriously low-quality Trabant. Hahn's strategy for a reunited Germany included building a new, $1.9 billion factory that would employ 6,500 workers and produce a quarter of a million Golf and Polo models each year. The investment was justified in part by forecasts that East Germans would buy 750,000 cars each year; VW aimed to capture a third of that market, equal to its share in West Germany.

## The Piech Era

Ferdinand Piech, an autocratic leader with an engineering background who was "steely eyed and intense," succeeded Hahn as chairman in 1993. At the time, the company still had stakes in SEAT and Skoda. He immediately declared a state of crisis in the company and began taking drastic actions; cost cutting topped the list. Piech trimmed VW's worldwide employment, starting with 20,000 jobs in 1993. Piech also pledged to slash the number of auto platforms underlying VW's nameplates from 16 to 4 within a few years. During his tenure, a new car, the Passat, was launched, as were redesigned Jetta and Beetle models. He acquired three luxury automakers: Lamborghini, Bugatti, and Bentley. Piech also elevated the status of engineering in the company, and spending on R&D soared. Piech quickly gained a reputation for making key decisions himself.

With great fanfare, VW announced in March 1993 that it had succeeded in luring a new production chief away from General Motors. José Ignacio López de Arriortúa was expected to play a major role in cost cutting at VW, but he arrived amid accusations of industrial espionage. The controversy did not stop López from doing what he had been hired to do. He broke long-term contracts with many of VW's suppliers and put new contracts up for bid; as a result, a higher percentage of components were now sourced outside Germany. At VW's new General Pachecho plant in Buenos Aires, López subcontracted various aspects of production to a dozen outside companies. VW workers built a few crucial parts such as the chassis and power train; suppliers were responsible for various other tasks such as assembling instrument panels. In the end, however, the espionage controversy cost López his job, and Piech settled the civil case by agreeing to pay GM $100 million and buy $1 billion in GM parts.

Even though his tenure at VW was brief and stormy, the positive aspects of the López legacy endured. Maryann Kellar, author of a book about VW, calls the Czech experiment "something that has been talked about for years as the next great productivity and cost enhancement move by the industry." In 1996, Skoda rolled out the Octavia, the first new car developed by the Czech plant during the Volkswagen era and the first to use a VW chassis platform. Piech also won concessions from IG Metall, the German autoworkers union. The union agreed to 2.5 percent annual pay raises and a pledge of job security. In addition, the workday for many assembly-line workers was reduced to 5 hours and 46 minutes—in essence, a four-day week. CFO Bruno Adelt estimated that all the agreed-upon changes would boost productivity 4 to 5 percent.

Even as VW expanded production in emerging markets and introduced production efficiencies, it was devising a comeback strategy for the United States. Mexican production of a new version of the legendary Beetle began in 1997, with a U.S. launch in 1998. As board member Jens Neumann said, "The Beetle is the core of the VW soul. If we put it back in people's minds, they'll think of our products more." Like its predecessor, the new Beetle had curved body panels and running boards. However, it was a front-wheel-drive model with more headroom and legroom. Despite being priced at about $15,000, 10 percent higher than the company's entry-level Golf, the new Beetle was initially a huge success. Sales were strong through 2000; then, as the buzz surrounding the vehicle died down, sales began to slip. In 2003, hoping to recapture some "cool" and reenergize the Beetle brand, a convertible model was introduced.

## Volkswagen in the Twenty-First Century

After Bernd Pischetsrieder became chairman of Volkswagen AG in April 2002, he presided over the launch of several key new vehicles. The $35,000 Volkswagen Touareg was the company's first SUV. Named after a nomadic African tribe that makes an annual journey across the Sahara, the Touareg was introduced just as SUV sales were starting to decline in the United States. *Car and Driver* magazine named the Touareg the "best luxury SUV" of 2003. Another new vehicle was the Phaeton, the first super-luxury model to bear the VW nameplate. Developed at a cost of $700 million, the Phaeton boasted the world's finest automotive air conditioning system and carried a price tag of $85,000. Together, the Touareg and Phaeton were compelling evidence that Volkswagen intended to move upmarket.

For Pischetsrieder, 2006 was a turbulent year; he lost a boardroom battle with Chairman Piech over the ongoing efforts to cut costs and remain competitive in the face of increased competition from Toyota and other Asian automakers. At the beginning of 2007, another key executive resigned. Wolfgang Bernhard, chairman of the Volkswagen brand group, had initiated a series of cost-cutting measures; both Germany's powerful labor unions and Chairman Piech were opposed to some of his actions.

In 2007, Martin Winterkorn was named chief executive officer of Volkswagen AG; he was also CEO of the VW division. Winterkorn moved swiftly to reboot the cost-cutting efforts of his predecessors. Because cutting jobs at VW's six plants in Germany was not an option, productivity improvements would have to be achieved elsewhere. Winterkorn embraced a modular production technology pioneered by Scania, the Swedish truck manufacturer. Because it reduces both complexity and costs, modular architecture is being used in a variety of industrial settings. In addition to Volkswagen, Daimler, Siemens, and Electrolux are also using modular designs and production processes. As a Volkswagen spokesperson put it, "With the modular production toolbox we will in the future be able to build different models and different brands on the same production line."

In essence, the approach means that cars will be assembled from common building blocks that have standard interfaces; as much as 60 percent of core components can be shared. VW will use four core modular *baukasten* (toolboxes) as the basis for four vehicle types across eleven brands: small city cars, midsize cars, mid-engine sports cars, and large vehicles. Management insists that the high degree of component sharing will not result in a standardized, "one-size-fits-all" product design. Rather, it will allow VW to create vehicles such as the new Audi Q3 that respond to specific regional needs and preferences. It is the responsibility of Walter de Silva, VW's design chief, to make sure all the company's cars share a common design language without losing their distinctive identities. And, how does an Italian designer fit in with the corporate culture at a German car company? As de Silva notes, "There is obviously a very special chemistry between German engineering and Italian creativity—it's something you can't explain."

## Product Strategy: Jetta

Having conquered key emerging markets and modernized its production processes, VW must now shore up its U.S. business. To accomplish this, executives are determined to "Americanize" VW's cars; the first example of this effort was the 2011 Jetta. Developed at a cost of $1 billion, the new model was produced at VW's N80 assembly plant in Mexico City. The new Jetta arrived at dealers in fall 2010 backed by an advertising campaign that emphasized the $15,995 sticker price. The advertising tagline was "Great. For the price of good." The 2011 model was bigger than its 2010 predecessor, and cost-cutting changes were made to the rear brakes and suspension.

## Product Strategy: Beetle

VW had a lot riding on the launch of the third-generation Beetle. The original Beetle (also known as the Bug) featured an air-cooled engine (no radiator!) that was located above the rear tires. The Beetle was very popular in both Europe and the United States, where about 5 million were sold between 1949 and 1979. In the American market, an advertising campaign created by Bill Bernbach has achieved mythic status in the industry. Bernbach is credited with launching the Creative Revolution by "telling the truth" about cars and encouraging buyers to "Think Small."

After VW retooled its German plant for a successor to the Beetle, production was shifted to Brazil. The Beetle was absent from the U.S. market from 1979 until 1999, at which time the second-generation Beetle was launched. The United States was the primary target market for the New Beetle, which was produced at VW's plant in Puebla, Mexico. The designers retained the distinctive, iconic profile of the original so that the new version would be instantly recognizable. It also featured whimsical touches such as a flower vase on the dashboard; however, the launch ad campaign promised, "Less flower. More power."

Other automakers rushed to capitalize on the nostalgia craze that VW was tapping; the BMW Mini Cooper was one notable success. The New Beetle was especially popular with women, but it was discontinued in 2010. The third-generation Beetle went on sale in the fall of 2011. The new Bug was designed for the global market; besides the United States, China, Europe, and Mexico are expected to be key markets. The new car has a bigger engine and is more sporty in appearance than its predecessors. VW hopes to attract more male buyers while still appealing to women.

## Product Strategy: Passat

As noted at the beginning of the chapter, the first cars rolling off the line at VW's new Chattanooga plant were Passat sedans. Soon, however, the plant will also start producing a new seven-passenger SUV, thereby filling a large gap in VW's product line. This entails risks, as David Sargent, a vice president at J.D. Power and Associates, notes: "Brand-new plants with brand-new models historically have struggled to produce world-class quality. Not to say a plant can't do that, but it's a struggle."

The Chattanooga plant is also capable of producing diesel-powered cars; however, diesel versions of its current offerings account for only about one-quarter of VW's U.S. sales. Although diesel engines get higher mileage than gasoline engines, they are simply not popular with the majority of U.S. drivers. By contrast, diesels are very popular in Europe. However, it remains to be seen whether VW can change entrenched American attitudes toward diesels, especially since diesel models typically carry a price premium compared to their gasoline-powered counterparts. The issue took on new importance in 2014 as the price of oil dropped below $65 a barrel and gas prices fell at the pump.

By 2014, the business environment had shifted, creating new challenges for VW. For example, after several years of robust growth, sales in the United States began to decline. The story was the same in key emerging markets. In Brazil, Russia, India, and China, currency volatility, economic factors, and political turmoil resulted in steep sales declines. In China, for example, after several years of double-digit growth, growth slowed to less than 10 percent. Meanwhile, EU regulations regarding reductions in carbon emissions by 2020 required the investment of billions of euros.

Christoph Stürmer is a director at IHS Global Insight consultancy. Summarizing the strategic challenges facing Volkswagen, he said, "VW has to get it right. Get adjusted to American standards of what on-the-road quality is. It's a big challenge for a company so deep-dyed German."

## Discussion Questions

**16-7.** CEO Winterkorn intends to make VW the world's number 1 automaker by 2018. Do you think this is an attainable goal, or is it an "exaggerated" or "stretch" goal designed to motivate employees?

**16-8.** In VW's advertising, the "Das Auto" tagline encourages potential buyers to associate the brand with its German heritage. Is this the right approach for VW?

**16-9.** Which rivals present the strongest competitive threats to VW's strategic plans?

**16-10.** What are some of the risks inherent in VW's relentless drive to become the world's number 1 auto maker?

**Sources:** William Boston, "VW Strains to Keep Foot on Gas," *The Wall Street Journal* (December 11, 2014), pp. A1, A14; Chris Bryant, "Building Blocks to Cut Output Costs," *Financial Times* (May 20, 2013), p. 17; Dan Neil, "At Geneva, the Promise and Perils of Sharing," *The Wall Street Journal* (March 10/11, 2013), p. D9; John Reed, "Design Through Discipline," *Financial Times* (May 25, 2012), p. 10; Patrick Olsen, "Success Is Sweeter the 2nd Time for VW," *USA Today* (April 12, 2012), p. 3B; Ed Crooks, "Volkswagen Flags Up Its Plans for U.S. Market," *Financial Times* (May 26, 2011), p. 20; Chris Woodyard, "VW Takes Risks with 3G Beetle," *USA Today* (April 18, 2011), pp. 1A, 1B; James R. Healey, "2012 VW Beetle Gets Bigger, Ditches 'Girls' Car' Image," *USA Today* (April 18, 2011); Healey, "VW Plans to Be No. 1 Car Seller in the World by 2018," *USA Today* (September 3, 2010), pp. 1A, 1B; Healey, "Volkswagen Wants to Be the No. 1 Automaker," *USA Today* (November 30, 2009), pp. 1A, 1B; Stephen Power, "Aggressive Driver: Top Volkswagen Executive Tries U.S.-Style Turnaround Tactics," *The Wall Street Journal* (July 18, 2006), p. 1; Peter F. Drucker, *Innovation and Entrepreneurship: Practice and Principles* (New York: Harper & Row, 1985), p. 87.

# CASE 16-2
# IKEA

IKEA has been called "one of the most extraordinary success stories in the history of postwar European business." However, the first few years of the twenty-first century were difficult for IKEA, the $31 billion global furniture powerhouse based in Sweden. The euro's strength dampened financial results, as did an economic downturn in Central Europe. The company faces increasing competition from hypermarkets, "do-it-yourself" retailers such as Walmart, and supermarkets that are expanding into home furnishings. During his tenure as CEO from 1999 to 2009, Anders Dahlvig stressed three areas for improvement: product assortment, customer service, and product availability.

With stores in 40 countries, the company's success reflects founder Ingvar Kamprad's "social ambition" of selling a wide range of stylish, functional home furnishings at prices so low that the majority of people could afford to buy them (see Exhibit 16-11). The store

**Exhibit 16-11** IKEA currently has eleven stores in China; the Xu Hui store in Shanghai is one of the Swedish company's top performers by revenues. In keeping with IKEA's standardized global retail concept, the Chinese stores are spacious and clean. All locations feature restaurants where visitors can enjoy Swedish meatballs and other meal items. In some cases, the restaurants have also become a favorite meeting place for dating clubs that allow older Chinese to socialize.
**Source:** Doug Kanter/Bloomberg via Getty Images.

exteriors are painted bright blue and yellow, Sweden's national colors. Shoppers view furniture on the main floor in scores of realistic-looking settings arranged throughout the cavernous showrooms.

At IKEA, shopping is a self-service activity; after browsing and writing down the names of desired items, shoppers can pick up their furniture on the lower level. There, they find "flat packs" containing the furniture in kit form; one of the cornerstones of IKEA's low-cost strategy is having customers take their purchases home in their own vehicles and assemble the furniture themselves. The lower level of a typical IKEA store also contains a restaurant, a grocery store called the Swede Shop, a supervised play area for children, and a baby care room.

IKEA's unconventional approach to the furniture business has enabled it to rack up impressive growth in an industry in which overall sales have been flat. Sourcing furniture from a network of more than 1,600 suppliers in 55 countries helps the company maintain its low-cost, high-quality position. During the 1990s, IKEA expanded into Central and Eastern Europe. Because consumers in those regions have relatively little purchasing power, the stores offer a smaller selection of goods; some furniture is designed specifically for the cramped living styles typical in former Soviet bloc countries.

Throughout Europe, IKEA benefits from the perception that Sweden is a source of high-quality products and efficient service. Currently, Germany and the United Kingdom (UK) are IKEA's top two markets. The UK represents IKEA's fastest-growing market in Europe. Although Brits initially viewed the company's less-is-more approach as cold and "too Scandinavian," they were eventually won over. IKEA currently has 18 stores in the UK, and plans call for opening more in this decade. As Allan Young, creative director of London's St. Luke's advertising agency, noted, "IKEA is anticonventional. It does what it shouldn't do. That's the overall theme for all IKEA ads: liberation from tradition."

In 2005, IKEA opened two stores near Tokyo; more stores are on the way as the company expands in Asia. IKEA's first attempt to develop the Japanese market in the mid-1970s resulted in failure. Why? As Tommy Kullberg, former chief executive of IKEA Japan, explained, "In 1974, the Japanese market from a retail point of view was closed. Also, from the Japanese point of view, I do not think they were ready for IKEA, with our way of doing things, with flat packages and asking the consumers to put things together and so on." However, demographic and economic trends are much different today. After years of recession, consumers are seeking alternatives to paying high prices for quality goods. Also, IKEA's core customer segment—post–baby boomers in their thirties—grew nearly 10 percent between 2000 and 2010. In Japan, IKEA will offer home delivery and an assembly service option.

The coming years will bring big changes at IKEA. In 2013, Peter Agnefjäll became the company's new chief executive. He plans to continue the company's sustainability initiatives, including the possibility of leasing kitchens to consumers. As Steve Howard, chief sustainability officer, said, "We want a smarter consumption, and maybe people are less attached to ownership." However, some observers question IKEA's sustainability bona fides, noting that its low-priced furniture contributes to a "throw it away" mentality when a piece breaks. Howard responds to such criticism by noting that "People have needs to be met—they need wardrobes, sofas, kitchens. The most important thing is to meet those needs in the most sustainable way possible." For example, in France, one factory sources half its wood from recycled IKEA products that are ground up and repurposed as bookshelves, tables, and other new products.

## Discussion Questions

**16-11.** Review the characteristics of global and transnational companies in Chapter 1. Based on your reading of the case, would IKEA be described as a global firm or a transnational firm?

**16-12.** At the end of Chapter 11, it was noted that managers of IKEA stores have a great deal of discretion when it comes to setting prices. In terms of the ethnocentric/polycentric/regiocentric/geocentric (EPRG) framework, which management orientation is in evidence at IKEA?

**16-13.** What does it mean to say that, in terms of Porter's generic strategies, IKEA pursues a strategy of "cost focus"?

**Sources:** Richard Milne, "Against the Grain," *Financial Times* (November 14, 2012), p. 7; Milne, "IKEA Eyes Kitchen Recycling in Green Push," *Financial Times* (October 23, 2012), p. 19; Mei Fong, "IKEA Hits Home in China," *The Wall Street Journal* (March 3, 2006), pp. B1, B4; Richard Tomkins, "How IKEA Has Managed to Treat Us Mean and Keep Us Keen," *Financial Times* (January 14/January 15, 2006), p. 7; Kerry Capell, "IKEA: How the Swedish Retailer Became a Global Cult Brand," *BusinessWeek* (November 14, 2005), pp. 96–106; Theresa Howard, "IKEA Builds on Furnishings Success," *USA Today* (December 29, 2004), p. 3B; Mariko Sanchanta, "IKEA's Second Try at Japan's Flat-Pack Fans," *Financial Times* (March 4, 2004), p. 11; Paula M. Miller, "IKEA with Chinese Characteristics," *The China Business Review* (July–August, 2004), pp. 36–38; Christopher Brown-Humes, "An Empire Built on a Flat Pack," *Financial Times* (November 24, 2003), p. 8.

# CASE 16-3
# LEGO

The LEGO Company is a $4 billion global business built out of the humblest of materials: interlocking plastic toy bricks. From its base in Denmark, the family-owned LEGO empire has extended around the world and has at times included theme parks, clothing, and computer-controlled toys. Each year, the company produces about 15 billion molded plastic blocks as well as tiny human figures to populate towns and operate gizmos that spring from the imaginations of young people (see Exhibit 16-12). LEGO products, which are especially popular with boys, are available in more than 130 countries; in the key North American market, the company's overall share of the construction-toy market has been as high as 85 percent.

Kjeld Kirk Kristiansen, the grandson of the company's founder as well as the main shareholder, served as CEO from 1979 until 2004. Kristiansen says that LEGO products stand for "exuberance, spontaneity, self-expression, concern for others, and innovation." (The company's name comes from the Danish phrase *leg godt*, which means "play well.") Kristiansen also attributes his company's success to the esteem the brand enjoys among parents. "Parents consider LEGO not as just a toy company but as providing products that help learning and developing new skills," he says.

LEGO has always been an innovator. For example, Mybots was a $70 toy set that included blocks with computer chips embedded to provide lights and sound. A $200 Mindstorms Robotics Invention System allows users to build computer-controlled creatures. To further leverage the LEGO brand, the company also formed alliances with Walt Disney Company and Lucasfilms, creator of the popular *Star*

**Exhibit 16-12**
Source: AP Images.

*Wars* series. For several years, sales of licensed merchandise relating to the popular *Harry Potter* and *Star Wars* movie franchises sold extremely well.

After a disappointing Christmas 2003 season, LEGO was left with millions of dollars' worth of unsold goods. The difficult retail situation was compounded by the dollar's weakness relative to the Danish krone; LEGO posted a record loss of $166 million for 2003. The company then unveiled a number of new initiatives aimed at restoring profitability. A new line, Quattro, consisting of large, soft bricks, is targeted directly at the preschool market. Clikits is a line of pastel-colored bricks targeted at young girls who want to create jewelry.

In 2004, after LEGO had posted several years of losses, Jørgen Vig Knudstorp succeeded Kristiansen as LEGO's chief executive. Knudstorp convened a task force consisting of company executives and outside consultants to review the company's operations and business model. The task force discovered that LEGO's sources of competitive advantage—creativity, innovation, and superior quality—were also sources of weakness. The company had become overly complex, with 12,500 stock-keeping units (SKUs), a palette of 100 different block colors, and 11,000 suppliers.

Acknowledging that the company's forays into theme parks, children's clothing, and software games had been the wrong strategy, Knudstorp launched a restructuring initiative known as "Shared Vision." Within a few months, cross-functional teams collaborated to reduce the number of SKUs to 6,500; the number of color options was slashed by 50 percent. Production was outsourced to a Singaporean company with production facilities in Mexico and the Czech Republic, resulting in the elimination of more than 2,000 jobs.

Knudstorp also decided to focus on the company's retail customers, which include Toys 'R' Us, Metro, Karstadt, and Galeria. After surveying these customers, Knudstorp and his task force learned that the customers do not require express product deliveries. This insight prompted a change to once-weekly deliveries of orders that are placed in advance. The result: improved customer service and lower costs. In the three-year period from 2005 to 2008, on-time deliveries increased by 62 percent to 92 percent. LEGO also logged improvements in other key performance indicators, such as package quality and quantity. In 2008, LEGO was awarded the European Supply Chain Excellence Award in the category "Logistics and Fulfillment."

In terms of competitive advantage, Knudstorp has noted, "A bucket of bricks is the core of the core." Still, he adds, "There's more to being a global successful company than being able to build a plastic brick." Evidence of the company's magic touch can be found in LEGO Friends, a new theme targeting girls that has sold extremely well. Moreover, the company's forays into video games such as *Lego Batman 2*, children's books such as *The Lego Ideas Book*, and TV series on the Cartoon Network have proven to be successful as well. *The Lego Movie*, released in 2014, proved to be a global blockbuster with ticket sales of nearly $500 million.

## Discussion Questions

**16-14.** Jørgen Vig Knudstorp became CEO in 2004. Assess the key strategic decisions he has made, including outsourcing and divesting the theme parks.

**16-15.** LEGO's movie-themed products, keyed to popular film franchises such as *Harry Potter, Lord of the Rings*, and *Spider-Man*, include detailed construction plans. Do you think this is the right strategy?

**16-16.** Using Porter's generic strategies framework, assess LEGO in terms of the company's pursuit of competitive advantage.

**16-17.** What risk, if any, is posed by LEGO's movement into multimedia categories such as video games and television?

**Sources:** Clemens Bomsdorf, "Lego Building Up Its Mexico Plant," *The Wall Street Journal* (June 21–22, 2014), p. B4; Jens Hansegard, "What It Takes to Build a Lego Hobbit (and Gollum and More)," *The Wall Street Journal* (December 20, 2012), p. D1; Matt Richtel and Jesse McKinley, "Has Lego Sold Out?" *The New York Times* (December 23, 2012), p. SR4; Carlos Cordon, Ralf Seifert, and Edwin Wellian, "Case Study: LEGO," *Financial Times* (November 24, 2010); Kim Hjelmgaard, "Lego, Refocusing on Bricks, Builds an Image," *The Wall Street Journal* (December 24, 2009); David Robertson and Per Hjuler, "Innovating a Turnaround at LEGO," *Harvard Business Review* (September 2009); John Tagliabue, "Taking Their Blocks and Playing Toymaker Elsewhere," *The New York Times* (November 20, 2006), p. A4; Lauren Foster and David Ibison, "Spike the Robot Helps LEGO Rebuild Strategy," *Financial Times* (June 22, 2006), p. 18; Ian Austen, "Building a Legal Case, Block by Block," *The New York Times* (February 2, 2005), p. C6; Joseph Pereira and Christopher J. Chipello, "Battle of the Block Makers," *The Wall Street Journal* (February 4, 2004), pp. B1, B4; Clare MacCarthy, "Deputy Chief Sacked as LEGO Tries to Rebuild," *Financial Times* (January 9, 2004), p. 19; Majken Schultz and Mary Jo Hatch, "The Cycles of Corporate Branding: The Case of the LEGO Company," *California Management Review* 46, no. 1 (Fall 2003), pp. 6–26; Meg Carter, "Building Blocks of Success," *Financial Times* (October 30, 2003), p. 8.

## MyMarketingLab

Go to the Assignments section of your MyLab to complete these writing exercises.

**16-18.** How can a company measure its competitive advantage? How does a firm know if it is gaining or losing competitive advantage? Cite a global company and its source of competitive advantage.

**16-19.** Give an example of a company that illustrates each of the four generic strategies that can lead to competitive advantage: overall cost leadership, cost focus, differentiation, and focused differentiation.

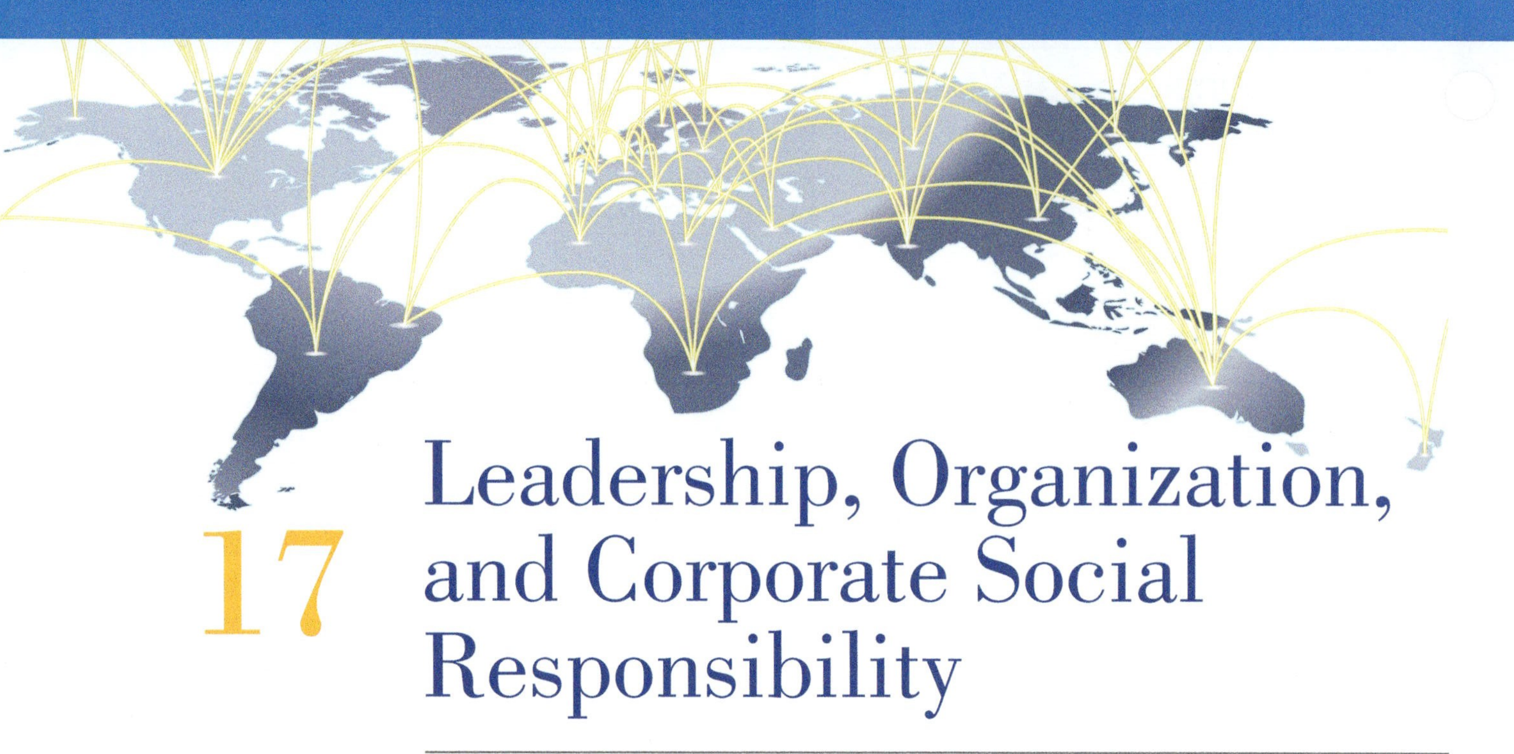

# 17 Leadership, Organization, and Corporate Social Responsibility

## LEARNING OBJECTIVES

**17-1** Identify the names and nationalities of the chief executives at five global companies discussed in the text.

**17-2** Describe the different organizational structures that companies can adopt as they grow and expand globally.

**17-3** Discuss the attributes of lean production and identify some of the companies that have been pioneers in this organizational form.

**17-4** List some of the lessons regarding corporate social responsibility that global marketers can take away from Starbucks' experience with Global Exchange.

## CASE 17-1
## A Changing of the Guard at Unilever

Unilever, the global food and consumer packaged goods powerhouse, markets a brand portfolio that includes such well-known names as Axe, Ben & Jerry's, Dove, Hellmann's, Lipton, and Rexona. The company has approximately 167,000 employees and annual sales of almost $59 billion; Unilever can trace its roots, in part, to the northern English town of Port Sunlight on the River Mersey. There, in 1888, Lever Brothers founder William Hesketh Lever created a garden village for the benefit of his employees.

Before retiring at the end of 2008, Unilever Group Chief Executive Patrick Cescau wanted to reconnect the company with its heritage of sustainability and concern for the environment (see Exhibit 17-1). These and other values reflect Unilever's philosophy of "doing well by doing good." One example: the "Campaign for Real Beauty," which was launched by managers at the company's Dove brand. To prepare for their first presentation to management, Dove team members videotaped interviews with teen girls who talked about the pressures they felt to conform to a certain look and body type. The interviewees included Cescau's daughter as well as the daughters of Unilever's directors. Later, when the CEO recalled watching the video, he explained, "It suddenly becomes personal. You realize your own children are impacted by the beauty industry, and how stressed they are by this image of unattainable beauty which is imposed on them every day." The Dove team was given the green light to launch a new advertising campaign based on

**Exhibit 17-1** Patrick Cescau (left) put corporate social responsibility at the top of his agenda during his tenure as CEO of Unilever. The company's current chief executive, Paul Polman (right), is building on Cescau's initiatives while expanding into key emerging markets.

**Sources:** Unilever/AFP/Newscom and Peter Cavanagh/Alamy.

this insight; in the years since, Dove has won numerous awards and accolades.

Cescau's vision of "doing well by doing good" manifested itself in other ways, too. For example, he guided the company's detergent business toward using fewer chemicals and less water, plastic, and packaging. In addition, he recognized that today's "conscience consumers" look to a company's reputation when deciding which brands to purchase.

Paul Polman, Cescau's successor, has built on another of the former chief executive's priorities: business opportunities in emerging markets such as India and China. However, Polman also took the top job in the middle of the recent global recession. To find out more about Unilever's commitment to global social responsibility while dealing with tough economic challenges, turn to Case 17-1 at the end of the chapter.

This chapter focuses on the integration of each element of the marketing mix into a total plan that addresses opportunities and threats in the global marketing environment. Cescau's achievements as the head of Unilever illustrate some of the challenges facing business leaders in the twenty-first century: They must be able to articulate a coherent global vision and strategy that integrate global efficiency, local responsiveness, and leverage. The leader is also the architect of an organizational design that is appropriate for the company's strategy. For large global enterprises such as ABB, GE, Koninklijke Philips, Tesco, Toyota, and Unilever, the leader must ensure that size and scale are assets that can be leveraged rather than encumbrances that slow response times and stifle innovation. Finally, the leader must ensure that the organization takes a proactive approach to corporate social responsibility.

## 17-1 Leadership

Global marketing demands exceptional leadership. As noted throughout this book, the hallmark of a global company is its capacity to formulate and implement global strategies that leverage worldwide learning, respond fully to local needs and wants, and draw on the talent and energy of every member of the organization. This daunting task requires global vision and sensitivity to local needs. Overall, the leader's challenge is to direct the efforts and creativity of everyone in the company toward a global effort that best utilizes organizational resources to exploit global opportunities. As Carly Fiorina, former CEO of Hewlett-Packard, said in her 2002 commencement address at the Massachusetts Institute of Technology:

> Leadership is not about hierarchy or title or status: It is about having influence and mastering change. Leadership is not about bragging rights or battles or even the accumulation of

> wealth; it's about connecting and engaging at multiple levels. It's about challenging minds and capturing hearts. Leadership in this new era is about empowering others to decide for themselves. Leadership is about empowering others to reach their full potential. Leaders can no longer view strategy and execution as abstract concepts, but must realize that both elements are ultimately about people.[1]

An important leadership task is articulating beliefs, values, policies, and the intended geographic scope of a company's activities. Using the mission statement or similar document as a reference and guide, members of each operating unit must address their immediate responsibilities and at the same time cooperate with functional, product, and country experts in different locations. However, it is one thing to spell out a vision and another thing entirely to secure commitment to it throughout the organization. As noted in Chapter 1, global marketing further entails engaging in significant business activities outside the home country. This means an exposure to different languages and cultures. In addition, global marketing involves the skillful application of specific concepts, insights, and strategies. Such endeavors may represent substantial change, especially in U.S. companies with a long tradition of a domestic focus. When the "go global" initiative is greeted with skepticism, the CEO must be a change agent who prepares and motivates employees.

Former Whirlpool CEO David Whitwam described his own efforts in this regard in the early 1990s after he had approved the acquisition of Royal Philips Electronics' European home appliance division:

> When we announced the Philips acquisition, I talked with our people, explained why it was so important. Most opposed the move. They thought, "We're spending a billion dollars on a company that has been losing money for 10 years? We're going to take resources we could use right here and ship them across the Atlantic because we think this is becoming a 'global' industry? What the hell does that mean?"[2]

Jack Welch encountered similar resistance at GE: "The lower you are in the organization, the less clear it is that globalization is great," he said. As Paolo Fresco, a former GE vice chairman, explained:

> To certain people, globalization is a threat without rewards. You look at the engineer for X-ray in Milwaukee and there is no upside on this one for him. He runs the risk of losing his job, he runs the risk of losing authority—he might find his boss is a guy who does not even know how to speak his language.[3]

In addition to "selling" their visions, top management at Whirlpool, GE, Nokia, Boeing, Tata Group, and other companies face the formidable task of building a cadre of globally oriented managers. Similar challenges face corporate leaders in all parts of the world. For example, Uichiro Niwa, former president of Japan's ITOCHU Corp., took steps to ensure that more of the trading company's $115 billion in annual transactions were conducted online.[4] He also radically changed the way he communicated with employees and began relying more on e-mail, a practice that until recently was virtually unknown in Japan. He also convened face-to-face meetings and conferences with employees to solicit suggestions and to hear complaints. This too represented a dramatic change in the way some Japanese companies were being led; traditionally, low-level employees were expected to accept the edicts of top management without questioning them.

---

[1] Carleton "Carly" S. Fiorina, Commencement Address, Massachusetts Institute of Technology, Cambridge, MA, June 2, 2002. See also "It's Death If You Stop Trying New Things," *Financial Times* (November 20, 2003), p. 8.

[2] William C. Taylor and Alan M. Webber, *Going Global: Four Entrepreneurs Map the New World Marketplace* (New York: Penguin Books USA, 1996), p. 12.

[3] Noel M. Tichy and Stratford Sherman, *Control Your Destiny or Someone Else Will* (New York: HarperBusiness, 1994), p. 227.

[4] Robert Guth, "Facing a Web Revolution, a Mighty Japanese Trader Reinvents Itself," *The Wall Street Journal* (March 27, 2000), p. B1.

## Top Management Nationality

Many globally minded companies realize that the best person for a top management job or board position is not necessarily someone born in the home country. Speaking of U.S. companies, Christopher Bartlett of the Harvard Business School has noted:

> Companies are realizing that they have a portfolio of human resources worldwide, that their brightest technical person might come from Germany, or their best financial manager from England. They are starting to tap their worldwide human resources. And as they do, it will not be surprising to see non-Americans rise to the top.[5]

The ability to speak foreign languages is one difference between managers born and raised in the United States and those born and raised elsewhere. For example, the U.S. Department of Education has reported that 200 million Chinese children are studying English; by contrast, only 24,000 American children are studying Chinese! Fluency in English is a prerequisite for managerial success in many global organizations, irrespective of the language of the headquarters country. For example, Yong Nam, CEO of LG, recently stipulated that English would be required throughout the company. He explained:

> English is essential. The speed of innovation that is required to compete in the world mandates that we must have seamless communication. We cannot depend on a small group of people who are holding the key to all communication throughout the world. That really impedes information sharing and decision making. I want everybody's wisdom instead of just a few.[6]

Sigismundus W. W. Lubsen, the former president and CEO of Quaker Chemical Corporation, is a good example of today's cosmopolitan executive. Born in the Netherlands and educated in Rotterdam as well as New York, Lubsen speaks Dutch, English, French, and German. He recalled, "I was lucky to be born in a place where if you drove for an hour in any direction, you were in a different country, speaking a different language. It made me very comfortable traveling in different cultures."[7] PepsiCo's Indra Nooyi is also bilingual (see Exhibit 17-2). Table 17-1 shows additional examples of corporate leaders who are not native to the headquarters country.

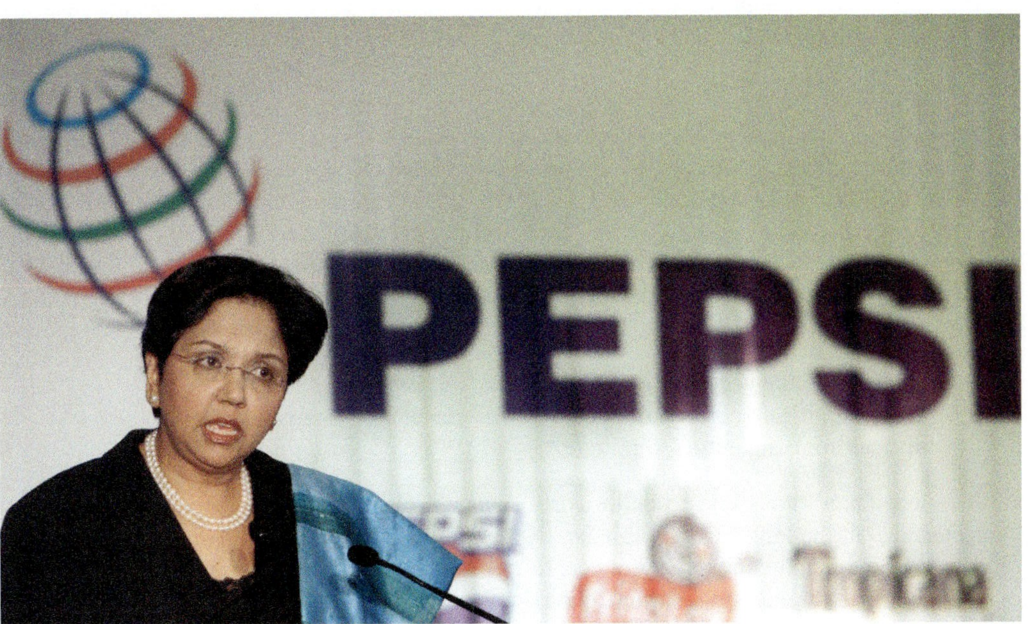


**Exhibit 17-2** Indra Nooyi, chair and chief executive of PepsiCo, is faced with rising commodity prices and weak demand for carbonated soft drinks in the United States. Despite these threats, Nooyi believes the snack-and-beverage giant's current strategy is on track. In recent quarters, the strongest results have come from PepsiCo's fast-growing international division. Snack sales are particularly strong in Mexico and Russia; international sales volume for beverage brands is also increasing, particularly in the Middle East, Argentina, China, and Brazil.
**Source:** Manish Swarup/AP Images.

[5]Kerry Peckter, "The Foreigners Are Coming," *International Business* (September 1993), p. 53.
[6]Evan Ramstad, "CEO Broadens Vistas at LG," *The Wall Street Journal* (May 21, 2008), pp. B1, B2.
[7]Kerry Peckter, "The Foreigners Are Coming," *International Business* (September 1993), p. 58.

**TABLE 17-1 Who's in Charge? Executives of 2015**

| Company (Headquarters Country) | Executive/Nationality | Position |
|---|---|---|
| 3M (United States) | Inge G. Thulin (Sweden) | CEO |
| ABB (Switzerland) | Joe Hogan (United States) | CEO |
| Chrysler (United States) | Sergio Marchionne (Italy) | CEO |
| Dow Chemical (United States) | Andrew Liveris (Australia) | CEO |
| Eastman Kodak (United States) | Antonio Perez (Spain) | Chairman and CEO |
| Electrolux (Sweden) | Keith McLoughlin (United States) | CEO |
| Molton Brown (Great Britain) | Amy Nelson-Bennett (United States) | CEO |
| Monsanto (United States) | Hugh Grant (United Kingdom–Scotland) | Chairman, CEO, and President |
| Nippon Sheet Glass (Japan) | Craig Naylor (United States) | President and CEO |
| Nissan Motor (Japan) | Carlos Ghosn (Brazil) | Chairman, President, and CEO |
| PepsiCo (United States) | Indra K. Nooyi (India) | CEO |
| Reckitt Benckiser (Great Britain) | Rakesh Kapoor (India) | CEO |
| Sony (Japan) | Howard Stringer (United Kingdom–Wales) | Chairman |
| Wolters Kluwer NV (Netherlands) | Nancy McKinstry (United States) | Chairman and CEO |

Generally speaking, Japanese companies have been reluctant to place non-Japanese nationals in top positions. For years, only Sony, Mazda, and Mitsubishi had foreigners on their boards. Recently, some Japanese companies have made hiring and promotion decisions aimed at increasing the diversity of top-management ranks. For example, Didier Leroy recently became the most-senior non-Japanese executive at Toyota; an American, Julie Hamp, is the company's first Western female senior executive.[8]

Similarly, after Renault SA bought a 36.8 percent stake in Nissan Motor, the French company installed a Brazilian, Carlos Ghosn, as president. An outsider, Ghosn moved aggressively to cut costs and make drastic changes in Nissan's structure. He also introduced two new words into Nissan's lexicon: *speed* and *commitment*. Ghosn's turnaround effort was so successful that his life story and exploits have been celebrated in *Big Comic Story*, a comic that is popular with Japan's salarymen.[9]

## Leadership and Core Competence

Core competence, a concept developed by global strategy experts C. K. Prahalad and Gary Hamel, was introduced in Chapter 16. In the 1980s, many business executives were assessed on their ability to reorganize their corporations. In the 1990s, Prahalad and Hamel believed instead that executives would be better judged on their abilities to identify, nurture, and exploit the core competencies that make growth possible. Simply put, **core competence** is something that an organization can do better than its competitors. Prahalad and Hamel note that a core competence has three characteristics:

- It provides potential access to a wide variety of markets.
- It makes a significant contribution to perceived customer benefits.
- It is difficult for competitors to imitate.

Few companies are likely to build world leadership in more than five or six fundamental competencies. In the long run, an organization derives its global competitiveness from its ability to bring high-quality, low-cost products to market faster than its competitors. To do this, an organization must be viewed as a portfolio of competencies rather than as a portfolio of businesses. In some instances, a company has the technical resources to build competencies, but key

[8]Kana Inagaki, "Rise of Leroy Signals Toyota's Global Goals," *Financial Times* (June 19, 2015), p. 17.
[9]Norihiko Shirouzu, "U-Turn: A Revival at Nissan Shows There's Hope for Ailing Japan Inc.," *The Wall Street Journal* (November 16, 2000), pp. A1, A10. See also Todd Zaun, "Look! Up in the Sky! It's Nissan's Chief Executive!" *The Wall Street Journal* (December 27, 2001), p. B1.

**TABLE 17-2 Responsibility for Global Marketing**

| Company (Headquarters Country) | Executive | Position/Title |
|---|---|---|
| Amway (United States) | Candace Matthews | Global Chief Marketing Officer |
| Apple (United States) | Greg Joswiak | Vice President of Worldwide iPod Product Marketing |
| Coca-Cola (United States) | Joseph Tripodi | Chief Marketing and Commercial Officer |
| Ford (United States) | Stephen Odell | Executive Vice President–Global Marketing |
| General Motors (United States) | Tim Mahoney | Global GM Marketing Operations Leader |
| Levi's (United States) | Rebecca Van Dyck | Global Chief Marketing Officer |
| L'Oréal (France) | Marc Menesguen | Global Chief Marketing Officer |
| McDonald's (United States) | Kevin Newell | Global Chief Brand Officer |
| Procter & Gamble (United States) | Marc Pritchard | Global Marketing Officer |
| SAP AG (Germany) | Martin Homlish | Global Chief Marketing Officer |
| Starbucks (United States) | Annie Young-Scrivner | Global Chief Marketing Officer |
| Warner Music (United States) | John Reid | Executive Vice President, Warner Music International |
| Yum! Brands (United States) | Muktesh Pant | Worldwide Chief Marketing Officer |

executives lack the vision to do so. Sometimes the vision is present, but is rigidly focused on existing competencies even as market conditions are changing rapidly.

For example, in the early 2000s Jorma Ollila, then chairman of Finland's Nokia, noted, "Design is a fundamental building block of the [Nokia] brand. It is central to our product creation and is a core competence integrated into the entire company."[10] The chairman was right—10 years ago. Design did help Nokia secure its position as the worldwide leader in handset sales. However, Apple's introduction of the game-changing iPhone in 2007 caught Nokia off guard. Nokia clung to its proprietary Symbian operating system even as smartphones running Google's Android operating system exploded in popularity. Nokia responded by launching new, mid-priced smartphone models; in addition, new CEO Steven Elop announced an alliance with Microsoft to develop new phones using Windows OS. Despite such changes, however, by early 2011 Nokia was issuing profit warnings. In 2014, Microsoft acquired Nokia's handset business and Elop was named executive vice president of the newly formed Devices Group.

Nokia's reversal of fortune at the hands of Apple and Google underscores the fact that today's executives must rethink the concept of the corporation if they wish to operationalize the concept of core competencies. In addition, the task of management must be viewed as building both competencies and the administrative means for assembling resources spread across multiple businesses.[11] Table 17-2 lists some of the individuals responsible for global marketing at select companies.

## 17-2 Organizing for Global Marketing

The goal in **organizing for global marketing** is to find a structure that enables the company to respond to relevant market environment differences while ensuring the diffusion of corporate knowledge and experience from national markets throughout the entire corporate system. The struggle between the value of centralized knowledge and coordination and the need for individualized response to the local situation creates a constant tension in the global marketing organization. A key issue in global organization is how to achieve a balance between autonomy and integration. Subsidiaries need autonomy to adapt to their local environments, but the business as a whole needs to be integrated in order to implement global strategy.[12]

[10]Neil McCartney, "Squaring Up to Usability at Nokia," *Financial Times—IT Review Telecom World* (October 13, 2003), p. 4.
[11]C. K. Prahalad and Gary Hamel, "The Core Competence of the Corporation," *Harvard Business Review* 68, no. 3 (May–June 1990), pp. 79–86.
[12]George S. Yip, *Total Global Strategy* (Upper Saddle River, NJ: Prentice Hall, 1992), p. 179.

When management at a domestic company decides to pursue international expansion, the issue of how to organize arises immediately. Who should be responsible for this expansion? Should product divisions operate independently or should an international division be established? Should individual countries' subsidiaries report directly to the company president or should a special corporate officer be appointed to take full-time responsibility for international activities? After the decision of how to organize initial international operations has been reached, a growing company is faced with a number of reappraisal points during the development of its international business activities. Should a company abandon its international division, and, if so, what alternative structure should be adopted? Should it form an area or regional headquarters? What should be the relationship among staff executives at corporate, regional, and subsidiary offices? Specifically, how should the company organize the marketing function? To what extent should regional and corporate marketing executives become involved in subsidiary marketing management?

Even companies with years of experience competing around the globe find it necessary to adjust their organizational designs in response to environmental changes. It is perhaps not surprising that, during his tenure at Quaker Chemical, Sigismundus Lubsen favored a global approach to organizational design over a domestic/international approach. He advised Peter A. Benoliel, his predecessor CEO, to have units in Holland, France, Italy, Spain, and England report to a regional vice president in Europe. "I saw that it would not be a big deal to put all of the European units under one common denominator," Lubsen recalled.[13]

As markets globalize and as Japan opens its own market to more competition from overseas, more Japanese companies are likely to break from traditional organization patterns. Many of the Japanese companies discussed in this text qualify as global or transnational companies because they serve world markets, source globally, or do both. Typically, however, knowledge is created at headquarters in Japan and then transferred to other country units. For example, Canon enjoys a strong reputation for world-class, innovative imaging products such as bubble-jet printers and laser printers. In the past two decades, Canon has shifted more control to subsidiaries, hired more non-Japanese staff and management personnel, and assimilated more innovations that were not developed in Japan. In 1996, for example, research and development (R&D) responsibility for software was shifted from Tokyo to the United States, responsibility for telecommunication products to France, and computer-language translation to Great Britain. As Canon president Fujio Mitarai explained, "The Tokyo headquarters cannot know everything. Its job should be to provide low-cost capital, to move top management between regions, and come up with investment initiatives. Beyond that, the local subsidiaries must assume total responsibility for management. We are not there yet, but we are moving step by step in that direction." Toru Takahashi, director of R&D, shared this view: "We used to think that we should keep research and development in Japan, but that has changed," he said. Despite these changes, Canon's board of directors includes only Japanese nationals.[14]

No single correct organizational structure exists for global marketing. Even within a particular industry, worldwide companies have developed different strategic and organizational responses to changes in their environments.[15] Still, it is possible to make some generalizations. Leading-edge global competitors share one key organizational design characteristic: Their corporate structure is flat and simple, rather than tall and complex. The message is clear: The world is complicated enough, so there is no need to add to the confusion with complex internal structuring. Simple structures increase the speed and clarity of communication and allow for the concentration of organizational energy and valuable resources on learning, rather than on controlling, monitoring, and reporting.[16] According to David Whitwam, former CEO of Whirlpool, "You must create an organization whose people are adept at exchanging ideas, processes, and systems across borders, people who are absolutely free of the 'not-invented-here' syndrome,

---

[13]Kerry Peckter, "The Foreigners Are Coming," *International Business* (September 1993), p. 58.
[14]William Dawkins, "Time to Pull Back the Screen," *Financial Times* (November 18, 1996), p. 12. See also Sumantra Ghoshal and Christopher A. Bartlett, *The Individualized Corporation* (New York: Harper Perennial, 1999), pp. 179–181.
[15]Christopher Bartlett and Sumantra Ghoshal, *Managing Across Borders: The Transnational Solution* (Boston: Harvard Business School Press, 1989), p. 3.
[16]Vladimir Pucik, "Globalization and Human Resource Management," in V. Pucik, N. Tichy, and C. Barnett (eds.), *Globalizing Management: Creating and Leading the Competitive Organization* (New York: J. Wiley & Sons, 1992), p. 70.

people who are constantly working together to identify the best global opportunities and the biggest global problems facing the organization."[17]

A geographically dispersed company cannot limit its knowledge to product, function, and the home territory. Company personnel must acquire knowledge of the complex set of social, political, economic, and institutional arrangements that exist within each international market. Many companies start with ad hoc arrangements such as having all foreign subsidiaries report to a designated vice president or to the president. Eventually, such companies establish an international division to manage their geographically dispersed new businesses. It is clear, however, that the international division in the multiproduct company is an unstable organizational arrangement. As a company grows, this initial organizational structure frequently gives way to various alternative structures.

In the fast-changing, competitive global environment of the twenty-first century, corporations will have to find new, more creative ways to organize. New forms of flexibility, efficiency, and responsiveness are required to meet the demands of globalizing markets. The need to be cost-effective, to be customer driven, to deliver the best quality, and to deliver that quality quickly are some of today's global realities. Recently, several authors have described new organizational designs that represent responses to today's competitive environment. These designs acknowledge the need to find more responsive and flexible structures, to flatten the organization, and to employ teams. There is also the recognition of the need to develop networks, to develop stronger relationships among participants, and to exploit technology. These designs reflect an evolution in approaches to organizational effectiveness. Early in the twentieth century, Frederick Taylor claimed that all managers had to see the world the same way. Then came the contingency theorists, who said that effective organizations design themselves to match their conditions. These two basic theories are reflected in today's popular management writings. As Henry Mintzberg observed, "To Michael Porter, effectiveness resides in strategy, while to Tom Peters it is the operations that count—executing any strategy with excellence."[18]

Kenichi Ohmae has written extensively on the implications of globalization on organization design. He recommends a type of "global superstructure" at the highest level that provides a view of the world as a single unit. The staff members at this level are responsible for ensuring that work is performed in the best location and coordinating efficient movement of information and products across borders. Below this level, Ohmae envisions organizational units assigned to regions "governed by economies of service and economies of scale in information." In Ohmae's view of the world, there are 30 regions with populations ranging from 5 million to 20 million people. For example, China would be viewed as several distinct regions; the same would be true of the United States. The first task of the CEO in such an organization is to become oriented to the single unit that is the borderless business sphere, much as an astronaut might view the earth from space. Then, zooming in, the CEO attempts to identify differences. As Ohmae explained:

> A CEO has to look at the entire global economy and then put the company's resources where they will capture the biggest market share of the most attractive regions. Perhaps as you draw closer from outer space you see a region around the Pacific Northwest, near Puget Sound, that is vibrant and prosperous… In parts of New England you will see regions that are strong centers for health care and biotechnology. As a CEO, that's where you put your resources and shift your emphasis.[19]

Your authors believe that successful companies, the real global winners, must have both good strategies and good execution.

## Patterns of International Organizational Development

Organizations vary in terms of the size and potential of targeted global markets and local management competence in different country markets. Conflicting pressures may arise from the need for product and technical knowledge; functional expertise in marketing, finance, and operations;

[17]Regina Fazio Maruca, "The Right Way to Go Global: An Interview with Whirlpool CEO David Whitwam," *Harvard Business Review* 72, no. 2 (March–April 1994), p. 137.
[18]Henry Mintzberg, "The Effective Organization: Forces and Forms," *Sloan Management Review* 32, no. 2 (Winter 1991), pp. 54–55.
[19]William C. Taylor and Alan M. Webber, *Going Global: Four Entrepreneurs Map the New World Marketplace* (New York: Penguin, 1996), pp. 48–58.

## THE CULTURAL CONTEXT

### Can New Leaders Reinvent Sony, the "Apple of the 1980s," in the Twenty-First Century?

MyMarketingLab SYNC • THINK • LEARN

Sony Corporation is a legend in the global consumer electronics industry. Its reputation for innovation and engineering has made it the envy of rivals. For decades, quality-conscious consumers paid premium prices for the company's Trinitron color televisions. In 1979, Sony created the personal stereo category with its iconic Walkman.

By the early 2000s, however, Sony's vaunted innovation and marketing machine was faltering. The company had not anticipated the rapid consumer acceptance of flat-panel, wide-screen TV sets, and the Sony Walkman was eclipsed by Apple's iPod and iTunes Music Store. In 2005, tumbling stock prices resulted in the resignation of chairman and CEO Nobuyuki Idei. Sir Howard Stringer, a Welsh-born American who had been knighted in 2000, was named as Idei's replacement.

One of Stringer's first priorities was to bridge the divide between Sony's media businesses, which included music, games, and motion pictures, and its hardware businesses. As Stringer himself declared, "We've got to get the relationship between content and devices seamlessly managed."

Management writers often use terms like *silos, stovepipes,* or *chimneys* to describe an organization in which autonomous business units operate with their own agendas and a minimum of horizontal interdependence. This was the situation at Sony, where the internal rivalries between different engineering units—the PC and Walkman groups, for example—were ingrained in the corporate culture and regarded as healthy. As Osamu Katayama, author of several books about Sony, notes, "Instead of working together, the managers of the different businesses fought to keep their independence."

Because Sony's consumer products businesses have historically accounted for a significant proportion of Sony's worldwide sales, breathing new life into the home entertainment and mobile products units was important. To do this, Sir Howard developed a restructuring plan: He cut 28,000 jobs, reduced the number of manufacturing sites, and eliminated some unprofitable products.

Cost cutting was only part of the story. Boosting revenues with new products was also crucial to Sony's recovery. Sir Howard was convinced that Sony's TV business would recover, thanks in part to the new Bravia line of HDTVs. As it turned out, however, the television business continued to lose money. The company also launched an e-book reader and, in 2006, the PlayStation 3 (PS3) game console.

After seven years, it was clear that Sir Howard's turnaround effort was still a work in progress. He had successfully negotiated Sony's withdrawal from a smartphone partnership with Sweden's Ericsson. He had restructured the TV business and ended an expensive LCD screen partnership with Samsung. Sony's Blu-ray DVD format had gained widespread acceptance. However, Sony, Sharp, Panasonic, and other Japanese manufacturers were all experiencing declining sales of traditional electronics products. Meanwhile, Apple and Samsung had risen to prominence in the competitive landscape once dominated by the Japanese.

In 2012, Sir Howard relinquished the chief executive role to Kazuo Hirai (see Exhibit 17-3). In 2013, Hirai presided over the launch of the Xperia Z smartphone, an event that provided tangible evidence of a reduction in divisional rivalries. New CFO Kenichiro Yoshida is trying to return the company to profitability by infusing employees with entrepreneurial spirit while trimming the bureaucracy and speeding up decision making.

**Sources:** Eric Pfanner and Takashi Mochizuki, "Sony Pares Down Before Rebuilding," *The Wall Street Journal* (November 17, 2014), pp. B1; B4; Daisuke Wakabayashi, "Japan's Electronics Under Siege," *The Wall Street Journal* (May 15, 2013), pp. B1, B4; Andrew Edgecliffe-Johnson and Jonathan Soble, "Channels to Choose," *Financial Times* (February 28, 2012), p. 9; Soble, "Sony Chief Looks to Secure Legacy," *Financial Times* (May 23, 2011); Yukari Iwatani Kane, "Sony Expects to Trim PS3 Losses, Plans More Games, Online Features," *The Wall Street Journal* (May 18, 2007), p. B4; Phred Dvorak, "Sony Aims to Cut Costs, Workers to Revive Its Electronics Business," *The Wall Street Journal* (September 23, 2005), p. A5; Dvorak, "Out of Tune: At Sony, Rivalries Were Encouraged; Then Came iPod," *The Wall Street Journal* (June 29, 2005), pp. A1, A6; Lorne Manly and Andrew Ross Sorkin, "Choice of Stringer Aims to Prevent Further Setbacks," *The New York Times* (March 8, 2005), pp. C1, C8.

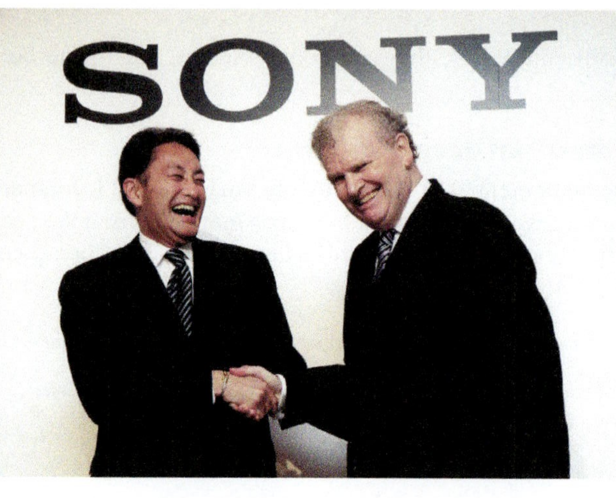


**Exhibit 17-3** In 2012, Kazuo Hirai was named president and CEO of Sony Corporation; Sir Howard Stringer was chairman. The new boss faced many challenges, as Japan's once-vaunted electronics industry had fallen behind in the fast-changing tech world. For example, Sony had lost its lead in flat-panel television technology to Samsung; meanwhile, the one-two punch of Apple's iPod/iTunes combination had upstaged Sony's Walkman personal stereo brand. Part of Sony's problem was that different divisions—e.g., Home Entertainment and Sound; Mobile Products and Communication; and Entertainment—did not work well together.

**Source:** © Hajime Takashi/Jana Press/ZUMAPRESS.com/Alamy.

and area and country knowledge. Because the constellation of pressures that shape organizations is never exactly the same, no two organizations pass through organizational stages in exactly the same way, nor do they arrive at precisely the same organizational pattern. Nevertheless, some general patterns hold.

A company engaging in limited export activities often has a small in-house export department as a separate functional area. Most domestically oriented companies undertake initial foreign expansion by means of foreign sales offices or subsidiaries that report directly to the company president or other designated company officer. This person carries out his or her responsibilities without assistance from a headquarters staff group. Many other design options are available to companies that seek to extend their reach internationally without creating separate divisions. For example, Des Moines, Iowa–based Meredith Corporation participates in international markets by means of licensing agreements developed and managed by the Corporate Development group, and further supported by various operating departments within the company (see Exhibit 17-4).

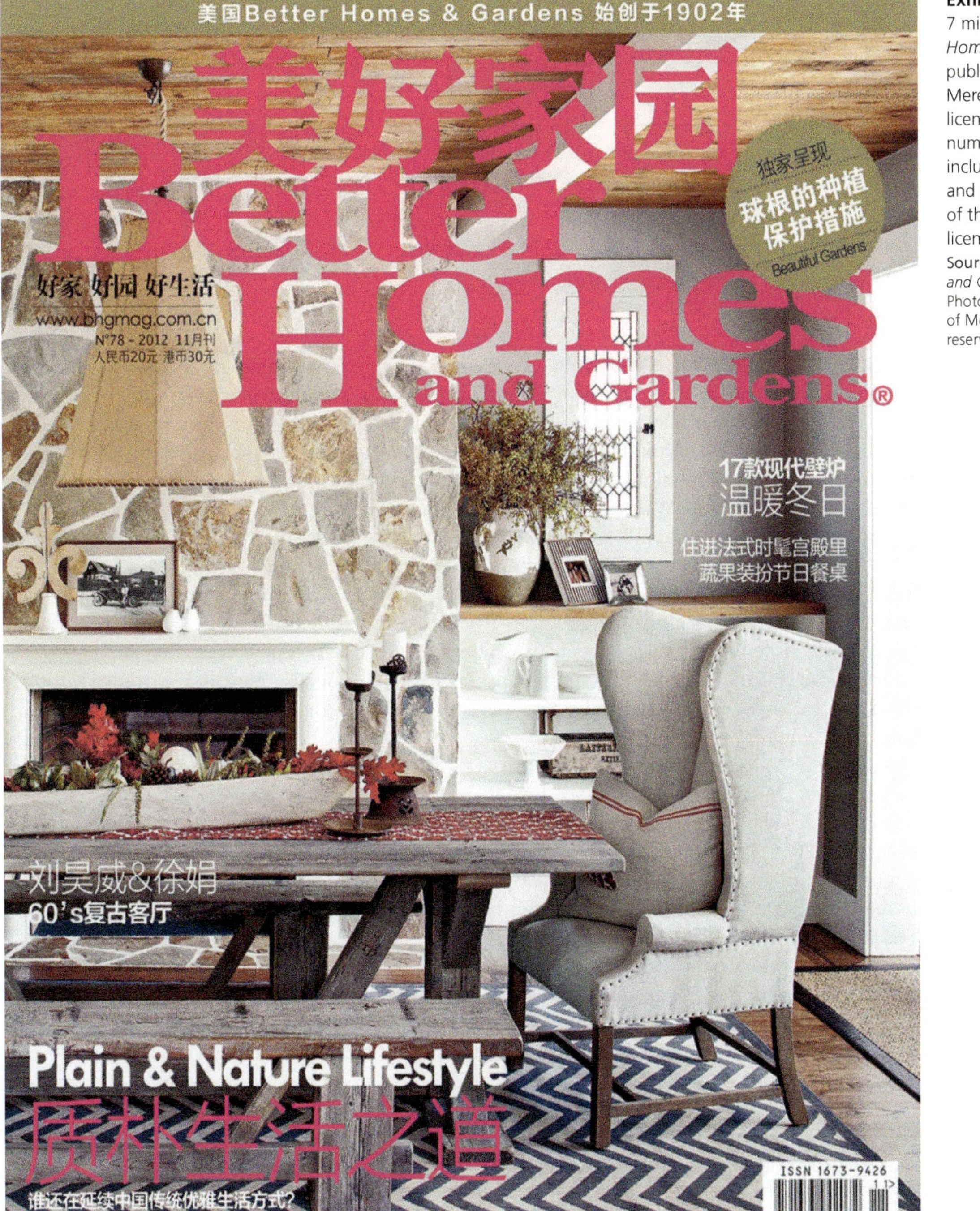


**Exhibit 17-4** With more than 7 million U.S. subscribers, *Better Homes and Gardens* is the flagship publication of Des Moines, Iowa–based Meredith Corporation. Meredith licenses *BH&G* and other titles in numerous international markets, including Europe, the Middle East, and Asia. At left is the Chinese edition of the magazine, published under license by SEEC Media.

**Source:** November 2012 *Better Homes and Gardens*® Magazine China edition. Photography by Edmund Barr. Photo courtesy of Meredith Corporation ©2012. 

FIGURE 17-1
**Functional Corporate Structure, Domestic Corporate Staff Orientation, International Division**

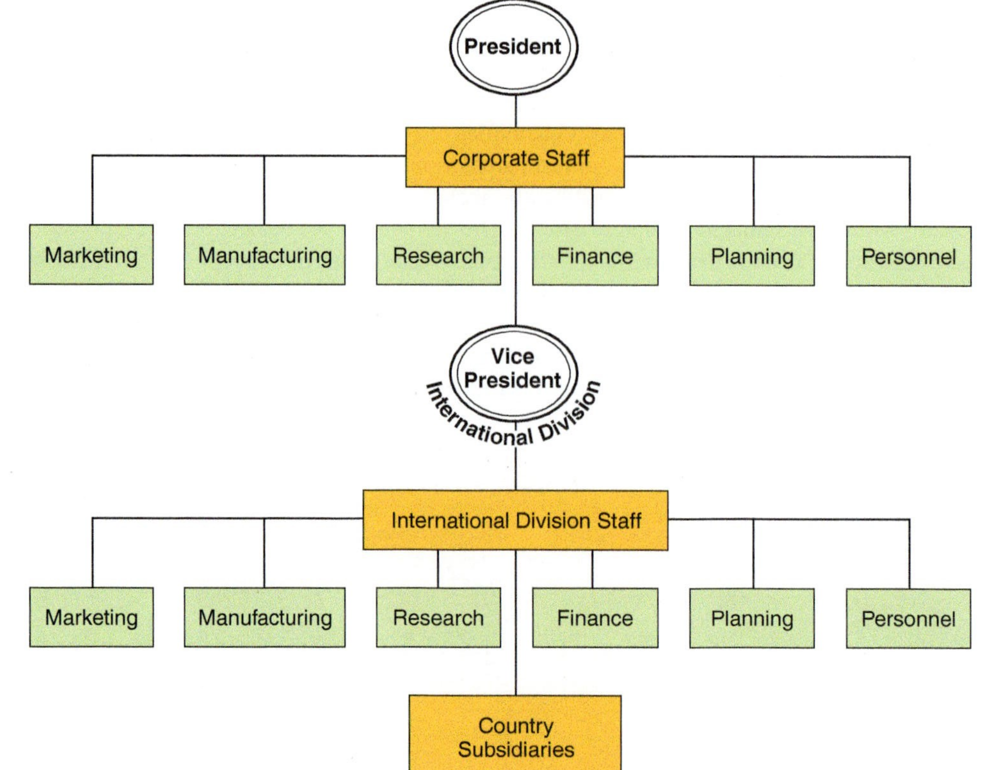


**INTERNATIONAL DIVISION STRUCTURE** As a company's international business grows, the complexity of coordinating and directing this activity extends beyond the scope of a single person. Pressure is created to assemble a staff that will have responsibility for coordination and direction of the growing international activities of the organization. Eventually, this process leads to the creation of the international division, as illustrated in Figure 17-1. Best Buy, Hershey, Levi Strauss, Under Armour, Walmart, and Walt Disney are some examples of companies whose structures include international divisions.

When Hershey announced the creation of its international division in 2005, J. P. Bilbrey, the division's senior vice president, noted that Hershey would no longer utilize the extension strategy of exporting its chocolate products from the United States. Instead, the company would tailor products to local markets and also manufacture locally. As Bilbrey explained, "We're changing our business model in Asia. The product was not locally relevant and it also got there at an unattractive cost."[20] Currently, international sales make up only 15 percent of Hershey's sales; the company's strategic goal is to boost that figure to 25 percent by 2017. China is the world's fastest-growing candy market, so it is no surprise that Hershey is ramping up efforts to penetrate the Middle Kingdom. Until recently, Hershey had only about a 2.2 percent share of China's chocolate market; by contrast, Mars commands 43 percent with its M&M's and Dove brands. In 2013, Hershey rolled out a new line of condensed-milk candies specifically targeting China's premium candy segment. Lancaster (as in "Lancaster, Pennsylvania," the company's hometown) is the English-language name; in Chinese, the brand is Yo-man (see Exhibit 17-5). Hershey has opened its second-largest R&D facility, Asia Innovation Center, in Shanghai.[21]

Several factors contribute to the establishment of an international division. First, top management's commitment to global operations has increased enough to justify an organizational unit headed by a senior manager. Second, the complexity of international operations requires a single organizational unit whose management has sufficient authority to make its own determinations on important issues such as which market-entry strategy to employ. Third, an

[20]Jeremy Grant, "Hershey Chews Over Growth Strategy," *Financial Times* (December 14, 2005), p. 23.
[21]Colum Murphy and Laurie Burkitt, "Hershey Launches New Brand in China," *The Wall Street Journal* (May 21, 2013), p. B8.

**Exhibit 17-5** Hershey has rolled out its new Lancaster brand in China. Flavors include Original Pure Nai Bei, Pure Nai Bei filled with Rich Nai Bei, and Pure Nai Bei with Strawberry. "Nai Bei" refers to a slow-cooking process using imported milk.

Lancaster is the first completely new brand launched outside the United States in Hershey's 120-year history.

**Source:** The Hershey Company.

international division is frequently formed when the firm has recognized the need for internal specialists to deal with the special demands of global operations. A fourth contributing factor is management's recognition of the importance of strategically scanning the global horizon for opportunities and aligning them with company resources rather than simply responding on an ad hoc basis to opportunities as they arise.

**REGIONAL MANAGEMENT CENTERS** When business is conducted in a single region that is characterized by similarities in economic, social, geographical, and political conditions, there is both justification and need for a management center. Thus, another stage of organizational evolution is the emergence of an area or regional headquarters as a management layer between the country organization and the international division headquarters. The increasing importance of the European Union (EU) as a regional market has prompted a number of companies to change their organizational structures by setting up regional headquarters there. In the mid-1990s, for example, Quaker Oats established its European headquarters in Brussels; Electrolux, the Swedish home appliance company, has also regionalized its European operations.[22] In 2012, Procter & Gamble (P&G) began to shift its global skin, cosmetics, and personal-care unit from Cincinnati to Singapore; Asia-Pacific countries account for about half of the $100 billion global skin-care market.[23] A regional center typically coordinates decisions on pricing, sourcing, and other matters. Executives at the regional center also participate in the planning and control of each country's operations with an eye toward applying company knowledge on a regional basis and optimally utilizing corporate resources on a regional basis. This organizational design is illustrated in Figure 17-2.

Regional management can offer a company several advantages. First, many regional managers agree that an on-the-scene regional management unit makes sense where there is a real need for coordinated, pan-regional decision making. Coordinated regional planning and control are becoming necessary as the national subsidiary continues to lose its relevance as an independent operating unit. Regional management can probably achieve the best balance of geographical, product, and functional considerations required to implement corporate objectives effectively. By shifting operations and decision making to the region, the company is better able to maintain an insider advantage.[24]

However, a major disadvantage of a regional center is its cost. The cost of a two-person office can be as much as half a million dollars per year. The scale of regional management must

[22] "... And Other Ways to Peel the Onion," *The Economist* (January 7, 1995), pp. 52–53.
[23] Emily Glazer, "P&G Unit Bids Goodbye to Cincinnati, Hello to Asia," *The Wall Street Journal* (May 11, 2012), p. B1.
[24] Allen J. Morrison, David A. Ricks, and Kendall Roth, "Globalization Versus Regionalization: Which Way for the Multinational?" *Organizational Dynamics* (Winter 1991), pp. 17–29.

FIGURE 17-2
**Functional Corporate Structure, Domestic Corporate Staff Orientation, International Division, Area Divisions**

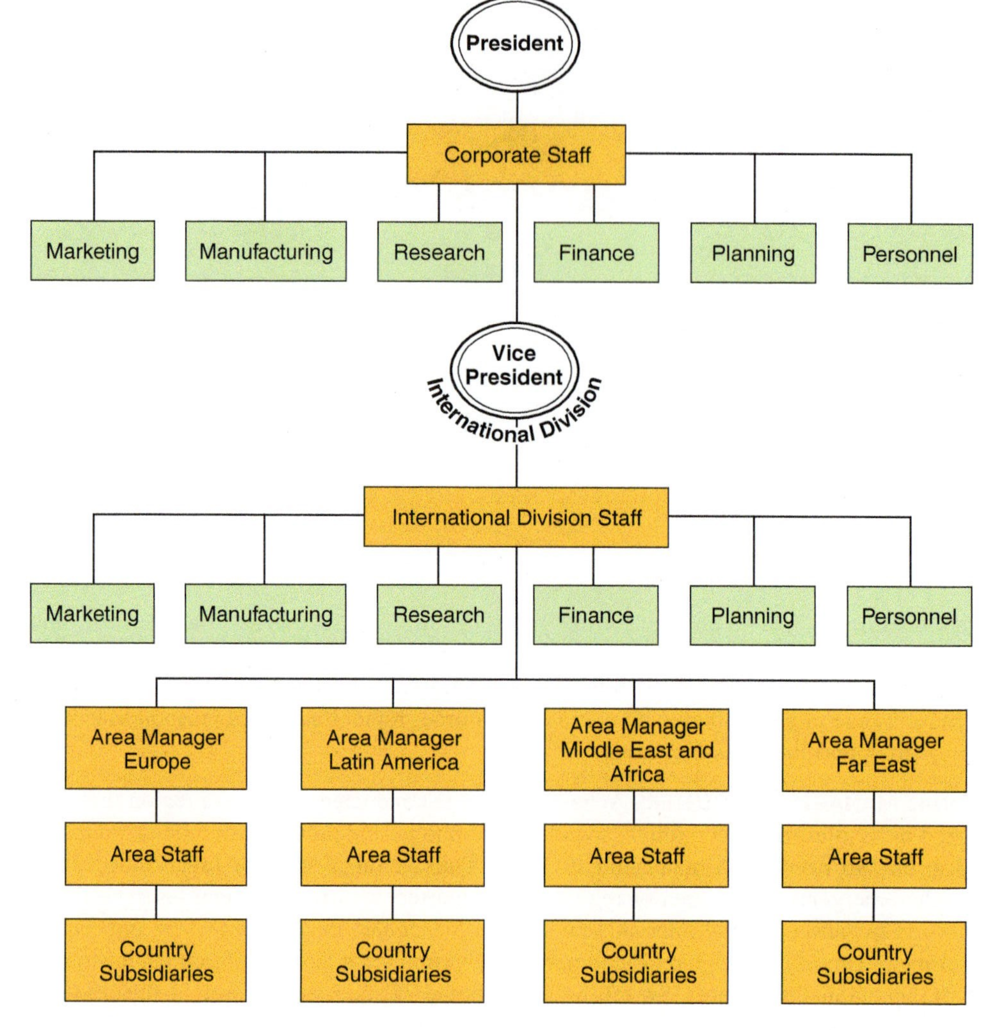


be in line with the scale of operations in a region. A regional headquarters is inappropriate if the size of the operations it manages is inadequate to cover the costs of the additional layer of management. The basic issue with regard to the regional headquarters is "Does it contribute enough to organizational effectiveness to justify its cost and the complexity of another layer of management?"

**GEOGRAPHICAL AND PRODUCT DIVISION STRUCTURES** As a company becomes more global, management frequently faces the dilemma of whether to organize by geography or by product lines. The geographically organized structure involves the assignment of operational responsibility for geographic areas of the world to line managers. The corporate headquarters retains responsibility for worldwide planning and control, and each area of the world—including the "home" or base market—is organizationally equal. For the company with French origins, for example, France is simply another geographic market under this organizational arrangement. This structure is most common in companies with closely related product lines that are sold in similar end-use markets around the world. For example, the major international oil companies utilize the geographical structure, which is illustrated in Figure 17-3. McDonald's organizational design integrates the international division and geographical structures. McDonald's U.S. has three geographical operating divisions, and McDonald's International has three.

When an organization assigns regional or worldwide product responsibility to its product divisions, manufacturing standardization can result in significant economies. For example, Whirlpool recently reorganized its European operations, switching from a geographic or country orientation to one based on product lines. One potential disadvantage of the product approach is that local input from individual country managers may be ignored, with the result that products will not be sufficiently tailored to local markets. The essence of the Ford 2000 reorganization

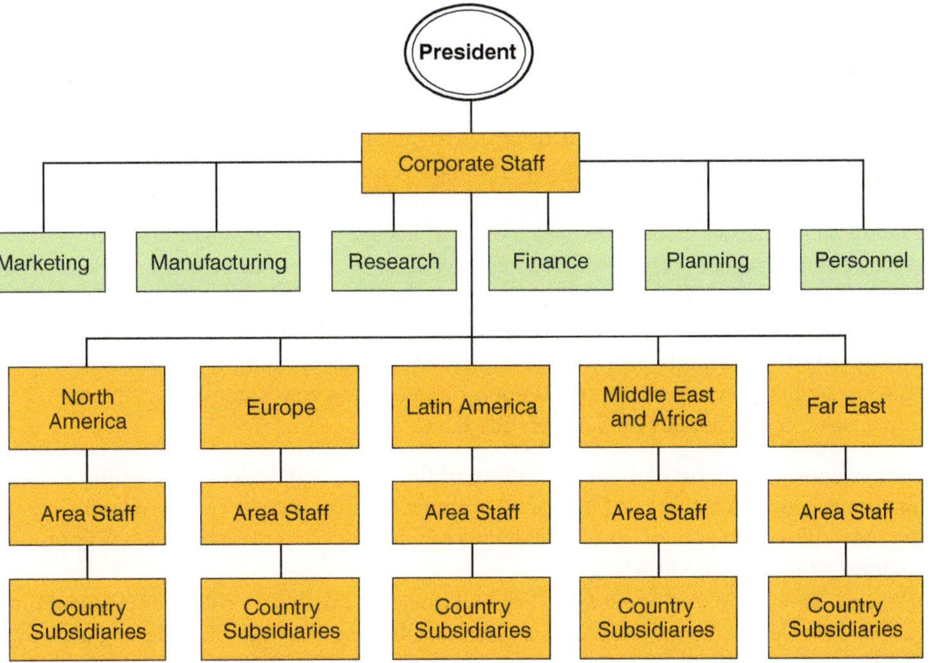


**FIGURE 17-3**
**Geographic Corporate Structure, World Corporate Staff Orientation, Area Divisions Worldwide**

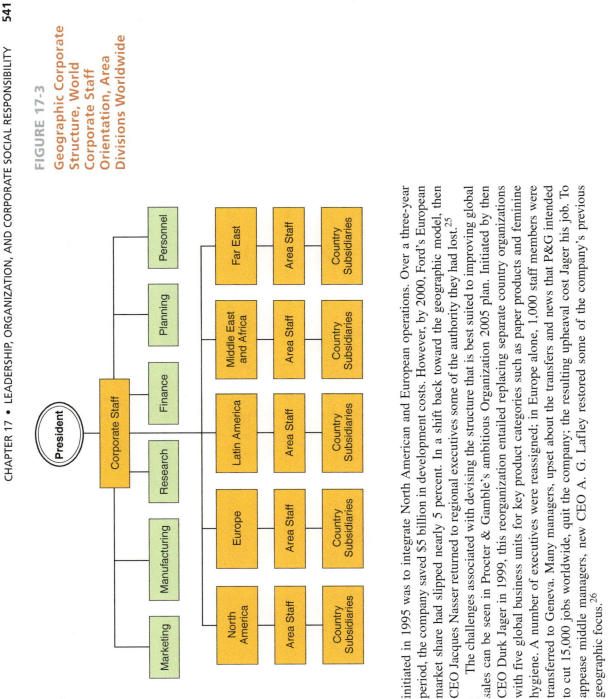

initiated in 1995 was to integrate North American and European operations. Over a three-year period, the company saved $5 billion in development costs. However, by 2000, Ford's European market share had slipped nearly 5 percent. In a shift back toward the geographic model, then CEO Jacques Nasser returned to regional executives some of the authority they had lost.[25]

The challenges associated with devising the structure that is best suited to improving global sales can be seen in Procter & Gamble's ambitious Organization 2005 plan. Initiated by then CEO Durk Jager in 1999, this reorganization entailed replacing separate country organizations with five global business units for key product categories such as paper products and feminine hygiene. A number of executives were reassigned; in Europe alone, 1,000 staff members were transferred to Geneva. Many managers, upset about the transfers and news that P&G intended to cut 15,000 jobs worldwide, quit the company; the resulting upheaval cost Jager his job. To appease middle managers, new CEO A. G. Lafley restored some of the company's previous geographic focus.[26]

> **"GE is managing its worldwide organization as a network, not a centralized hub with foreign appendages."[27]**
> Christopher A. Bartlett

**THE MATRIX DESIGN** In the fully developed large-scale global company, product or business, function, area, and customer know-how are simultaneously focused on the organization's worldwide marketing objectives. This type of total competence is a **matrix organization**. Management's task in the matrix organization is to achieve an organizational balance that brings together different perspectives and skills to accomplish the organization's objectives. In 1998, both Gillette and Ericsson announced plans to reorganize into matrix organizations. Ericsson's matrix is focused on three customer segments: network operators, private consumers, and commercial enterprises.[28] Gillette's matrix structure separates product-line management from geographical sales and marketing responsibility.[29] Likewise, Boeing has reorganized its commercial transport design and manufacturing engineers into a matrix organization built around five platform or aircraft model–specific groups. Previously, Boeing was organized along functional lines; the new design was expected to lower costs and quicken updates and problem solving. It was also

25Joann S. Lublin, "Division Problem: Place vs. Product: It's Tough to Choose a Management Model," *The Wall Street Journal* (June 27, 2001), pp. A1, A4.
26Emily Nelson, "Rallying the Troops at P&G: New CEO Lafley Aims to End Upheaval by Revamping Program of Globalization," *The Wall Street Journal* (August 31, 2000), pp. B1, B4.
27Claudia Deutsch, "At Home in the World," *The New York Times* (February 14, 2008), p. C1.
28"Ericsson to Simplify Business Structure," *Financial Times* (September 29, 1998), p. 21.
29Mark Maremont, "Gillette to Shut 14 of Its Plants, Lay Off 4,700," *The Wall Street Journal* (September 29, 1998), pp. A3, A15.

expected to unite essential design, engineering, and manufacturing processes between Boeing's commercial transport factories and component plants, enhancing product consistency.[30]

Why are executives at these and other companies implementing matrix designs? The matrix form of organization is well suited to global companies because it can be used to establish a multiple-command structure that gives equal emphasis to functional and geographical departments.

Professor John Hunt of the London Business School has suggested four considerations regarding the matrix organizational design. First, the matrix is appropriate when the market is demanding and dynamic. Second, employees must accept higher levels of ambiguity and understand that policy manuals cannot cover every eventuality. Third, in country markets where the command-and-control model persists, it is best to overlay matrices on only small portions of the workforce. Finally, management must be able to clearly state what each axis of the matrix can and cannot do. However, this must be accomplished without creating a bureaucracy.[31]

Having established that the matrix is appropriate, management can expect the matrix to integrate four basic competencies on a worldwide basis:

1. *Geographic knowledge.* An understanding of the basic economic, social, cultural, political, and governmental market and competitive dimensions of a country is essential. The country subsidiary is the major structural device employed today to enable the corporation to acquire geographical knowledge.
2. *Product knowledge and know-how.* Product managers with a worldwide responsibility can achieve this level of competence on a global basis. Another way of achieving global product competence is simply to duplicate product management organizations in domestic and international divisions, achieving high competence in both organizational units.
3. *Functional competence in such fields as finance, production, and, especially, marketing.* Corporate functional staff with worldwide responsibility contributes to the development of functional competence on a global basis. In some companies, the corporate functional manager, who is responsible for the development of his or her functional activity on a global basis, reviews the appointment of country subsidiary functional managers.
4. *A knowledge of the customer or industry and its needs.* Certain large and extremely sophisticated global companies have staff with the responsibility for serving industries on a global basis to assist the line managers in the country organizations in their efforts to penetrate specific customer markets.

Under this arrangement, instead of designating national organizations or product divisions as profit centers, both are responsible for profitability—the national organization for country profits and the product divisions for national and worldwide product profitability.

Figure 17-4 illustrates the matrix organization. This organizational chart starts with a bottom section that represents a single-country responsibility level, moves to representing the area or international level, and finally moves to representing global responsibility from the product divisions, to the corporate staff, to the chief executive at the top of the structure.

At Whirlpool, North American operations are organized in matrix form. Former CEO David Whitwam expected to extend this structure into Europe and other regional markets. Whirlpool managers from traditional functions such as operations, marketing, and finance also work in teams devoted to specific products, such as dishwashers or ovens. To encourage interdependence and integration, the cross-functional teams are headed by "brand czars," such as the brand chief for Whirlpool or Kenmore. As Whitwam explained, "The Whirlpool-brand czar still worries about the Whirlpool name. But he also worries about all the refrigerator brands that we make because he heads that product team. It takes a different mind-set."[32]

The key to successful matrix management is ensuring that managers are able to resolve conflicts and achieve integration of organization programs and plans. The mere adoption of a matrix design or structure does not create a matrix organization. The matrix organization requires fundamental changes in management behavior, organizational culture, and technical systems. In a matrix, influence is based on technical competence and interpersonal sensitivity,

---

[30]Paul Proctor, "Boeing Shifts to 'Platform Teams,'" *Aviation Week & Space Technology* (May 17, 1999), pp. 63–64.
[31]John W. Hunt, "Is Matrix Management a Recipe for Chaos?" *Financial Times* (January 12, 1998), p. 10.
[32]William C. Taylor and Alan M. Webber, *Going Global: Four Entrepreneurs Map the New World Marketplace* (New York: Penguin USA, 1996), p. 25.

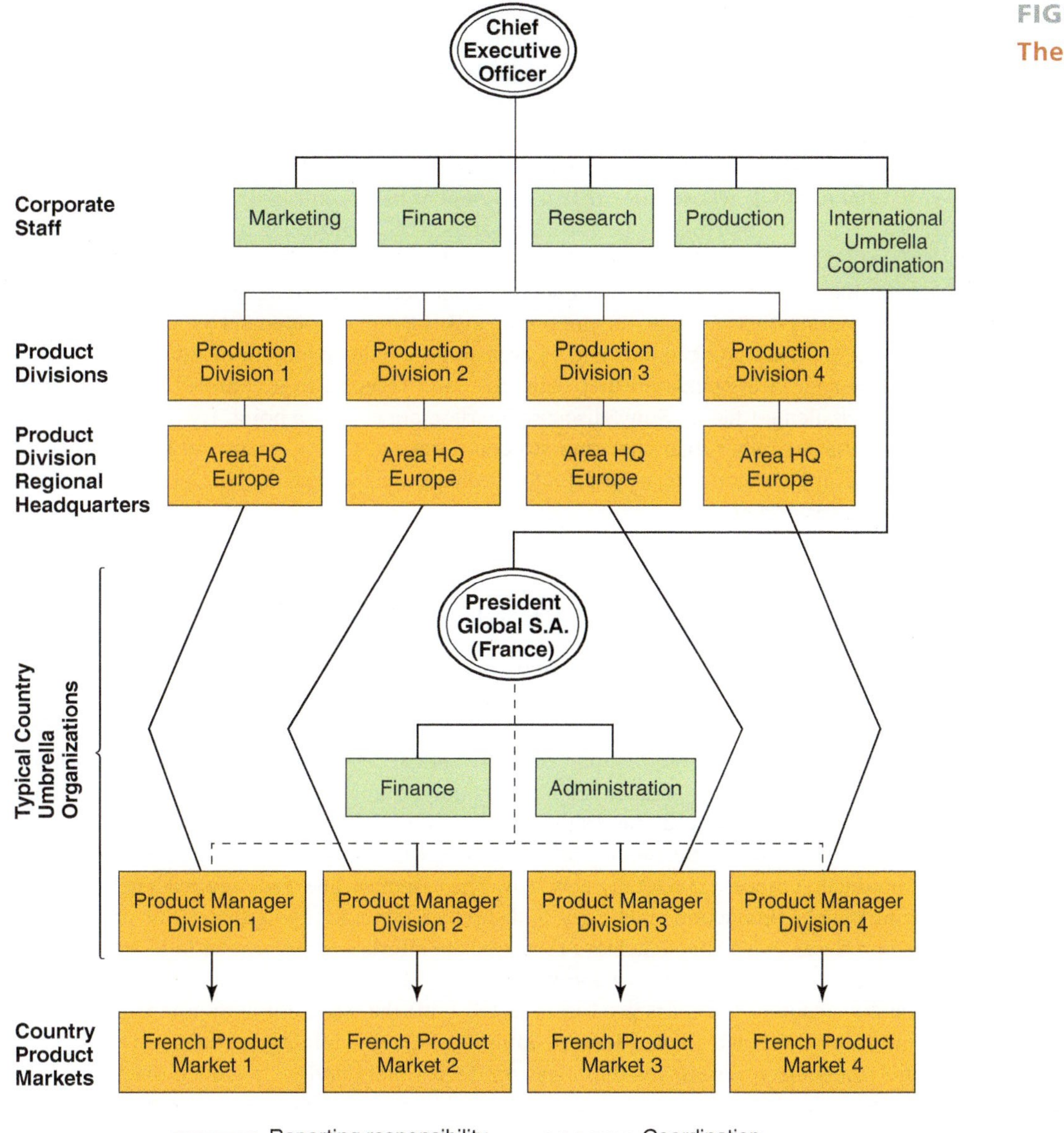


**FIGURE 17-4**
**The Matrix Structure**

not on formal authority. In a matrix culture, managers recognize the absolute need to resolve issues and choices at the lowest possible level and do not rely on higher authority.

Some companies are moving away from the matrix in response to changing competitive conditions. Heineken and EMI are two examples; ABB is another.[33] For nearly a decade, ABB was a matrix organized along regional lines. Local business units—factories that make motors or power generators, for example—reported both to a country manager and to a business area manager who set strategy for the whole world. This structure allowed ABB to execute global strategies while still thriving in local markets. However, in 1998, new chairman Göran Lindahl dissolved the matrix. As the chairman explained in a press release, "This is an aggressive move aimed at greater speed and efficiency by further focusing and flattening the organization. This step is possible now thanks to our strong, decentralized presence in all local and global markets around the world."

In January 2001, Lindahl stepped down and his successor, Jorgen Centerman, revamped the organizational structure yet again. The new design was intended to improve the focus on industries and large corporate customers; Centerman wanted to ensure that all of ABB's products

[33] Andrew Edgecliffe-Johnson, "Case Study: EMI," *Financial Times* (September 23, 2011), p. 4.

were designed to the same systems standards. However, in 2002, with the chief executive under pressure to sell assets, ABB's board replaced Centerman with Jürgen Dorman. Dorman stepped down in 2005 and was succeeded by Fred Kindle. Although ABB returned to profitability under his leadership, Kindle left after three years. The official reason: irreconcilable differences about leading the company. Michel Demaré, ABB's chief financial officer, was named interim CEO. Then, in fall 2008, Joe Hogan was selected as ABB's new CEO. Hogan, an American, was a 23-year veteran of GE whose most recent assignment had been running GE Healthcare. ABB's board was impressed by Hogan's performance at the U.S. industrial giant: During his eight years at GE Healthcare, the unit's sales more than doubled, from $7 billion to $18 billion. These results were due, in part, to several major acquisitions engineered by Hogan.[34]

In the twenty-first century, an important task of top management is to eliminate a one-dimensional approach to decisions and to encourage the development of multiple management perspectives and an organization that will sense and respond to a complex and fast-changing world. The challenges facing Sony, discussed earlier, are a case in point. By thinking in terms of changing behavior rather than changing structural design, management can free itself from the limitations of the structural chart and focus instead on achieving the best possible results with the available resources.

## 17-3 Lean Production: Organizing the Japanese Way

In the automobile industry, a comparison of early craft production processes, mass production, and modern "lean" production provides an interesting case study of the effectiveness of new organizational structures in the twenty-first century.[35] Dramatic productivity differences existed between craft and mass producers in the first part of the twentieth century. The mass producers—most notably Ford Motor Company—gained their substantial advantage by changing their value chains so that each worker was able to do far more work each day than the craft producers. The innovation that made this possible was the moving assembly line, which required the originators to conceptualize the production process in a totally new way. The assembly line also required a new approach to organizing people, production machinery, and supplies. By rearranging their value chain activities, the mass producers were able to achieve reductions in effort ranging from 62 to 88 percent over the craft producers. These productivity improvements provided an obvious competitive advantage.

The advantage of the mass producers lasted until the Japanese auto companies further revised the value chain and created **lean production**, thereby gaining for themselves the kinds of dramatic competitive advantages that mass producers had previously gained over craft producers. For example, the Toyota Production System (TPS), as the Japanese company's manufacturing methods are known, achieves efficiencies of about 50 percent over typical mass production systems. Even with the reduced assembly time, the lean producer's vehicles have significantly fewer defects than mass-produced vehicles. The lean producer is also using about 40 percent less factory space and maintaining only a fraction of the inventory stored by the mass producer. Again, the competitive advantages are obvious. Whether the strategy is based on differentiation or low cost, the lean producer has the advantage.

To achieve these gains at Toyota, production gurus Taiichi Ohno and Shigeo Shingo challenged several assumptions traditionally associated with automobile manufacturing. First, they made changes to operations within the auto company itself, such as reducing setup times for machinery. The changes also applied to operations within supplier firms and the interfaces between Toyota and its suppliers and to the interfaces with distributors and dealers. Ohno and Shingo's innovations have been widely embraced in the industry; as a result, individual producers' value chains have been modified, and interfaces between producers and suppliers have been optimized to create more effective and efficient value systems.

---

[34] Haig Simonian, "The GE Man Who Generated a Buzz," *Financial Times* (June 8, 2009).

[35] This section is adapted from the following sources: James P. Womack, Daniel T. Jones, and Daniel Roos, *The Machine That Changed the World: The Story of Lean Production* (New York: HarperCollins, 1990); Ranganath Nayak and John M. Ketteringham, *Breakthroughs!* (San Diego, CA: Pfeiffer, 1994), Chapter 9; and Michael Williams, "Back to the Past: Some Plants Tear Out Long Assembly Lines, Switch to Craft Work," *The Wall Street Journal* (October 24, 1994), pp. A1, A4.

**Exhibit 17-6** The Toyota Production System (TPS) is based on two concepts. First is *jidoka*, which involves visualizing potential problems. *Jidoka* also means that quality is built into the company's vehicles during the manufacturing process. "Just-in-time," the second pillar of the TPS, means that Toyota only produces what is needed, when it is needed, in the amount that is needed. Toyota's training programs ensure that all employees understand the Toyota Way. Future factory workers attend the Toyota Technical Skills Academy in Toyota City, Japan. Executive training takes place at the Toyota Institute.
**Source:** Ko Sasaki/Redux Pictures.

## Assembler Value Chains

Employee ability is emphasized in a lean production environment. Before being hired, people seeking jobs with Toyota participate in the Day of Work, a 12-hour assessment test to determine who has the right mix of physical dexterity, team attitude, and problem-solving ability. Once hired, workers receive considerable training to enable them to perform any job in their section of the assembly line or area of the plant, and they are assigned to teams in which all members must be able to perform the functions of all other team members. Workers are also empowered to make suggestions and to take actions aimed at improving quality and productivity. Quality control is achieved through *kaizen*, a devotion to continuous improvement that ensures that every flaw is isolated, examined in detail to determine the ultimate cause, and then corrected (see Exhibit 17-6).

Mechanization, and particularly flexible mechanization, is a hallmark of lean production. For example, a single assembly line in Georgetown, Kentucky, that produces Toyota's Camry sedan also produces the Sienna minivan. The Sienna and Camry share the same basic chassis and 50 percent of their parts. Of the 300 different stations on the line, only 26 stations require different parts to assemble minivans. Similarly, Honda has invested hundreds of millions of dollars to introduce flexible production technology in its U.S. plants. In an era of volatile gasoline prices and fluctuating exchange rates, production flexibility becomes a source of competitive advantage. For example, when the weak dollar put pressure on margins for vehicles imported into the United States, Honda shifted production of CR-V crossovers from the United Kingdom to a plant in Ohio. Within a matter of minutes, Honda can switch from producing Civic compacts to CR-V crossovers as demand or other market conditions dictate.[36]

In contrast to the lean producers, U.S. mass producers typically maintain operations with greater direct labor content, less mechanization, and much less flexible mechanization. They also divide their employees into a large number of discrete specialties with no overlap. Employee initiative and teamwork are not encouraged. In addition, quality control is expressed as an acceptable number of defects per vehicle.

Even when the comparisons are based on industry averages, the Japanese lean producers continue to enjoy substantial productivity and quality advantages. Again, these advantages put the lean producers in a better position to exploit low-cost or differentiation strategies. They are getting better productivity out of their workers and machines, and they are making better use of their factory floor space. The relatively small size of the repair area reflects the higher quality of their products. A high number of "suggestions per employee" provides some insight into why lean producers outperform

[36]Kate Linebaugh, "Honda's Flexible Plants Provide Edge," *The Wall Street Journal* (September 23, 2008), p. B1.

**EMERGING MARKETS BRIEFING BOOK**

## Western Business Executives Scold China

MyMarketingLab SYNC • THINK • LEARN

What happened when the chief executives of some of the world's biggest global companies got a chance to meet face-to-face with China's Premier Wen Jiabao? They gave him an earful, that's what. The CEOs, Jürgen Hambrecht of BASF and Peter Loescher of Siemens, were accompanying Germany chancellor Angela Merkel on a four-state visit. The criticisms reflected broader concerns among Western business and government leaders about China's business environment.

One issue is bidding procedures that appear to discriminate against foreign companies. For example, government procurement practices in China often favor local producers. Market access is another issue; CEO Hambrecht expressed frustration that foreign companies are forced to transfer technology to their Chinese partners in exchange for the opportunity to do business. Hambrecht said, "That does not exactly correspond to our views of a partnership."

GE's Jeff Immelt is another well-known CEO who has directed criticism at Beijing. At a private meeting in Rome with Italian business leaders, Immelt expressed his concern about China's increasingly protectionist tendencies. He reportedly told the group, "I am not sure that, in the end, they want any of us to win, or any of us to be successful." While acknowledging China's strategic importance to GE, Immelt also made it clear that the Middle East, Africa, and Latin America are emerging as key world markets. "The[y] don't all want to be colonized by the Chinese. They want to develop themselves," he said.

Manufacturing executives are not the only ones speaking out about China. Google CEO Eric Schmidt has also made his voice heard. Addressing the Council on Foreign Relations in New York recently, Schmidt expressed concern about Beijing's ongoing efforts to censor the Internet. For much of 2010, Google and the Chinese government clashed over issues concerning filtering content accessed via search engines. Beijing is also struggling to keep control over new media. In one instance, a Chinese woman was sent to a labor camp for retweeting a message of which the authorities disapproved. Using fewer than 140 characters, Dick Costolo, CEO of Twitter, tweeted his objections to the case. He wrote, "Dear Chinese Government, year-long detentions for sending a sarcastic tweet are neither the way forward nor the future of your great people."

**Sources:** Mark Millan, "Twitter CEO Chides China," *CNN Tech* (November 19, 2010); Qichen Zhang, "Google CEO Criticizes Chinese Internet Censorship," *OpenNet Initiative* (November 11, 2010); Jamil Anderlini, "German Industrialists Attack China," *Financial Times* (July 18, 2010); Guy Dinmore and Geoff Dyer, "Immelt Hits Out at China and Obama," *Financial Times* (July 1, 2010).

mass producers. First, they invest a great deal more in the training of their workers. They also rotate all workers through all jobs for which their teams are responsible. Finally, all workers are encouraged to make suggestions, and management acts on those suggestions. These changes to the value chain translate into major improvements in the value of the lean producers' products.

It should come as no surprise that many of the world's automakers are studying lean production methods and introducing them in both existing and new plants throughout the world. In 1999, for example, General Motors (GM) announced plans to spend nearly $500 million to overhaul its Adam Opel plant in Germany. Pressure for change came from several sources, including increasingly intense rivalry in Europe's car market, worldwide overcapacity, and a realization that price transparency in the euro zone will exert downward pressure on prices. GM's goal was to transform the plant into a state-of-the-art lean production facility with a 40 percent workforce reduction. As GM Europe president Michael J. Burns said at the time, "Pricing is more difficult today. . . . You have to work on product costs, structural costs . . . everything."[37]

### Downstream Value Chains

The differences between lean producers and U.S. mass producers in the way they deal with their respective dealers, distributors, and customers are as dramatic as the differences in the way they deal with their suppliers. U.S. mass producers follow the basic industry model and maintain an "arm's-length" relationship with dealers that is often characterized by a lack of cooperation and even open hostility. There is often no sharing of information because there is no incentive to do so. Frequently the manufacturer is trying to force on the dealer models the dealer knows will not sell. The dealer, in turn, is often trying to pressure the customer into buying models he or she does not want. All parties are trying to keep from the others information about what they really want. This does little to ensure that the industry is responsive to market needs.

[37]Joseph B. White, "GM Plans to Invest $445 Million, Cut Staff," *The Wall Street Journal* (May 27, 1999), p. A23.

The problem starts with the market research, which is often in error. It is compounded by lack of feedback from dealers regarding real customer desires. It continues to worsen when the product-planning divisions make changes to the models without consulting the marketing divisions or the dealers. This process invariably results in production of models that are unpopular and almost impossible to sell. The manufacturer then uses incentives and other schemes, such as making a dealer accept one unpopular model for every five hot-selling models it orders, to persuade the dealers to accept the unpopular models. The dealer then has the problem of persuading customers to buy the unpopular models.

Within the mass assembler's value chain, the linkage between the marketing elements and the product planners is broken. The external linkage between the sales divisions and the dealers is also broken. The production process portion of the value chain is broken as well in that it relies on the production of thousands of models that won't sell and that will then sit on dealer lots, at enormous cost, while the dealer works to find customers. Within the dealerships, there are even more problems. The relationship between the salesperson and the customer is based on sparring and trying to outsmart each other on price. When the salesperson gets the upper hand, the customer gets stung. It is very much like the relationship between the dealer and the manufacturer. Each is withholding information from the other in the hope of outsmarting the other. Too often, salespeople do not investigate customers' real needs and try to find the best product to satisfy those needs. Rather, they provide only as much information as is needed to close the deal. Once the deal is closed, the salesperson has virtually no further contact with the customer. No attempt is made to optimize the linkage between dealers and manufacturers or the linkage between dealers and customers.

The contrast with the lean producer is again striking. In Japan, the dealer's employees are true product specialists. They know their products and deal with all aspects of the products, including financing, service, maintenance, insurance, registration and inspection, and delivery. A customer deals with one person in the dealership, and that person takes care of everything from the initial contact through eventual trade-in and replacement and all the problems in between. Further, dealer representatives are included on the manufacturer's product development teams and provide continuous input regarding customer desires. The linkages between dealers, marketing divisions, and product development teams are totally optimized.

The stress caused by large inventories of unsold cars is also absent. A car is not built until there is a customer order for it. Each dealer has only a stock of models for the customer to view. Once the customer has decided on the car he or she wants, the order is sent to the factory and in a matter of a couple of weeks, the salesperson delivers the car to the customer's house.

Once a Japanese dealership gets a customer, it is absolutely determined to hang on to that customer for life. It is also determined to acquire all of that customer's family members as customers. A joke among the Japanese says that the only way to escape the salesperson who sold a person a car is to leave the country. Japanese dealers maintain extensive databases on actual and potential customers. These databases deal with demographic data and preference data. Customers are encouraged to help keep the information in the database current, and they do so. This elaborate store of data becomes an integral part of the market research effort and helps ensure that products match customer desires. The fact that there are no inventories of unpopular models because every car is custom ordered for each customer and the fact that the dealer has elaborate data on the needs and desires of its customers change the whole nature of the interaction between the customer and the dealer. The customer literally builds the car she or he wants and can afford. There is no need for the salesperson and the customer to try to outsmart each other.

The differences between U.S. mass producers and Japanese lean producers reflect their fundamental differences in business objectives. The U.S. producers focus on short-term income and return on investment. Today's sale is a discrete event that is not connected to upstream activities in the value chain and has no value in tomorrow's activities. Efforts are made to reduce the cost of the sales activities. In contrast, the Japanese see the process in terms of the long-term perspective. There are two major goals of the sales process. The first is to maximize the income stream from each customer over time. The second is to use the linkage with the production processes to reduce production and inventory costs and to maximize quality and therefore differentiation.

## 17-4 Ethics, Corporate Social Responsibility, and Social Responsiveness in the Globalization Era

Today's chief executive must be a proactive steward of the reputation of the company he or she is leading. This entails, in part, understanding and responding to the concerns and interests of a variety of stakeholders. A **stakeholder** is any group or individual that is affected by, or takes an interest in, the policies and practices adopted by an organization (see Exhibit 17-7).[38] Top management, employees, customers, persons or institutions that own the company's stock, and suppliers constitute a company's *primary stakeholders. Secondary stakeholders* include the media, the general business community, local community groups, and **nongovernmental organizations (NGOs)**. The latter focus on human rights, political justice, and environmental issues; examples include Global Exchange, Greenpeace, Oxfam, and others. **Stakeholder analysis** is the process of formulating a "win-win" outcome for all stakeholders.[39]

The leaders of global companies must practice **corporate social responsibility (CSR)**, which can be defined as a company's obligation to pursue goals and policies that are in society's best interests. A key issue becomes: Whose interests come first? How does a company find the balance between competing points of view? As Peter Brabeck, chairman and CEO of Nestlé, summarizes the situation, "The unique role of business is to create social, economic and environmental value for the countries where we operate." [40]

Organizations can demonstrate their commitment to CSR in a variety of ways, including cause-marketing efforts or a commitment to sustainability (see Exhibit 17-8). In some companies, such policies play an important internal role with primary stakeholders, especially employees drawn from the ranks of Generation Y. As Kevin Havelock, president of Unilever U.S., has noted:

> We are seeing, particularly with the new generation of young businesspeople and young marketers, that they are only attracted to companies that fit with their own value set. And the value set of the new generation is one that says this company must take a positive and

**Exhibit 17-7** U2 singer Bono and Bobby Shriver are cofounders of Product (RED)™, a partnership with several well-known global companies to raise money to fight disease in Africa. Apple, American Express, Emporio Armani, Converse, Gap, and Motorola are all offering (RED)-themed merchandise and services to their customers. The partners are demonstrating their commitment to corporate social responsibility by pledging to donate a percentage of the profits generated to the Global Fund to Fight AIDS, Tuberculosis, and Malaria. To launch its (RED) line, Gap's advertising campaign used celebrities and one-word headlines consisting of verbs that end in "-red." For example, one ad featured the word "INSPI(RED)" superimposed over a photo of director Steven Spielberg wearing a Product (RED) leather jacket.
Source: Tony Cenicola/Redux Pictures.

---

[38]The English term *stakeholder* is sometimes hard to convey in different languages, especially in developing countries. See Neil King, Jr., and Jason Dean, "Untranslatable Word in U.S. Aide's Speech Leaves Beijing Baffled," *The Wall Street Journal* (December 7, 2005), pp. A1, A8.

[39]Archie B. Carroll and Ann K. Buchholtz, *Business and Society: Ethics and Stakeholder Management*, 5th ed. (Cincinnati: South-Western, 2003).

[40]Haig Simonian, "Nestlé Charts Low-Income Territory," *Financial Times* (July 14, 2006), p. 15.

The world keeps
getting smaller.
Leave a small footprint.
The 2013 XV Crosstrek. It's a natural choice for any direction you're headed. As the most fuel-efficient all-wheel-drive crossover in America* with 33 MPG† and a Partial Zero Emissions Vehicle built in a zero-landfill plant, it'll take you more places, more responsibly than ever. Love. It's what makes a Subaru, a Subaru.
SUBARU
Confidence in Motion
XV Crosstrek.™ Well-equipped at $21,995††


**Exhibit 17-8** The Subaru nameplate is synonymous with the company's Symmetrical All-Wheel Drive and Partial Zero Emissions Vehicle (PZEV) engineering. The company's U.S. assembly plant, Subaru of Indiana Automotive, Inc., has won awards for its zero landfill approach to manufacturing. Subaru, a unit of Japan's Fuji Heavy Industries, is enjoying strong demand in North America for its new Crosstrek hatchback and revamped Forester SUV. The Indiana plant currently produces 200,000 vehicles per year; plans call for increasing annual capacity to 300,000 vehicles by 2016.
**Source:** Subaru of America.

global view on the global environment.... The ethical positions we take on brands like Dove, the positions we take on not using [fashion] models of size zero across any of our brands, the positions we take in terms of adding back to communities ... these all underpin an attractive proposition for marketers.[41]

Similarly, Starbucks founder and CEO Howard Schultz's enlightened human resources policies have played a key part in the company's success. Partners, as the company's employees are known, who work 20 hours or more per week are offered health benefits; partners can also take

[41]Jack Neff, "Unilever, P&G War Over Which Is Most Ethical," *Advertising Age* (March 3, 2008), p. 67.

advantage of an employee stock option plan known as Bean Stock. As noted on the company's Web site:

> Consumers are demanding more than "product" from their favorite brands. Employees are choosing to work for companies with strong values. Shareholders are more inclined to invest in businesses with outstanding corporate reputations. Quite simply, being socially responsible is not only the right thing to do; it can distinguish a company from its industry peers.

Schultz takes advantage of every opportunity to repeat his message. In interviews and personal appearances, CSR is a constant theme. Here's a typical example, from a 2005 interview with *Financial Times*:

> Perhaps we have the opportunity to be a different type of global company, a global brand that can build a different model, a company that is a global business, that makes a profit, but at the same time demonstrates a social conscience and gives back to the local market.[42]

"Coke has become a whipping boy for globalization, just as Nike and McDonald's have been for years."[43]

Tom Pirko, president, BevMark.

As noted in Chapter 1, one of the forces restraining the growth of global business and global marketing is resistance to globalization. In a wired world, a company's reputation can quickly be tarnished if activists target its policies and practices. The antiglobalization movement constitutes an important secondary stakeholder for global companies; the movement takes a variety of forms and finds expression in various ways. In developed countries, the movement's concerns and agenda include cultural imperialism (e.g., the French backlash against McDonald's), the loss of jobs due to offshoring and outsourcing (e.g., the furniture industry in the United States), and a distrust of global institutions (e.g., anti-World Trade Organization [WTO] protesters in Hong Kong).

In developing countries, globalization's opponents accuse companies of undermining local cultures, placing intellectual property rights ahead of human rights, promoting unhealthy diets and unsafe food technologies, and pursuing unsustainable consumption.[44] Environmental degradation and labor exploitation are also key issues (see Exhibit 17-9).

In a socially responsible firm, employees conduct business in an ethical manner. In other words, they are guided by moral principles that enable them to distinguish between right and wrong. At many companies, a formal statement or **code of ethics** summarizes core ideologies, corporate values, and expectations. GE, Boeing, and United Technologies Corp. are some of the American companies offering training programs that specifically address ethics issues. For many years, Jack Welch, the legendary former CEO of GE, challenged his employees to take an informal "mirror test." The challenge: "Can you look in the mirror every day and feel proud of what you're doing?"[45] Today, GE uses more formal approaches to ethics and compliance; it has produced training videos and instituted an online training program, and also provides employees with a 64-page guide to ethical conduct titled *The Spirit & The Letter*. The document provides guidance on potentially illegal payments, security and crisis management, and other issues. At Johnson & Johnson, the ethics statement is known as "Our Credo"; first introduced in 1943, the Credo has been translated into dozens of languages for Johnson & Johnson employees around the world (see Figure 17-5 and the Appendix at the end of this chapter).

As we have seen, the issue of corporate social responsibility becomes complicated for the global company with operations in multiple markets. When the chief executive of a global firm in a developed country or government policymakers attempt to act in "society's best interests,"

---

[42]John Murray Brown and Jenny Wiggins, "Coffee Empire Expands Reach by Pressing Its Luck in Ireland," *Financial Times* (December 15, 2005), p. 21.
[43]Andrew Ward, "Coke Struggles to Defend Positive Reputation," *Financial Times* (January 6, 2006), p. 15.
[44]Terrence H. Witkowski, "Antiglobal Challenges to Marketing in Developing Countries: Exploring the Ideological Divide," *Journal of Public Policy and Marketing* 24, no. 1 (Spring 2005), pp. 7–23.
[45]Stratford Sherman and Noel Tichy, *Control Your Destiny or Someone Else Will* (New York: HarperBusiness, 2001), Chapter 9, "The Mirror Test."

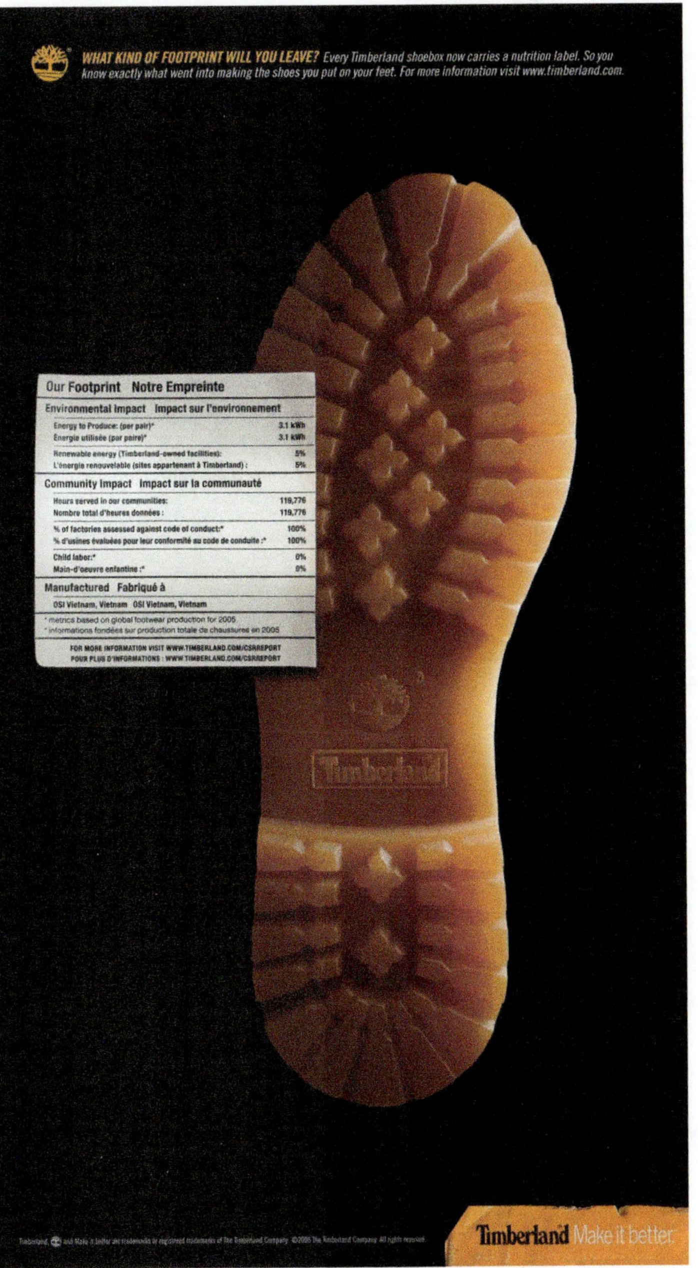


**Exhibit 17-9** The Timberland Company, based in Stratham, New Hampshire, is best known for its popular hiking boots and work boots. Timberland is a truly global brand; each year, the company sells outdoor gear, accessories, and apparel (2012 revenue was $1.4 billion) through a network of 200 franchised and company-owned stores as well as department and sporting goods stores.

However, the company stands for more than just rugged authenticity; Timberland is a mission-centered company as well. CEO Jeff Swartz, the grandson of Timberland's founder, is deeply concerned with social justice issues. In 2006, Timberland unveiled a "nutritional label" on its footwear boxes as a means of communicating its CSR commitment to consumers. The label (in both English and French) addresses issues of interest to many consumers, including "Percent of factories assessed against Code of Conduct—100%" and "Child labor—0%."

**Source:** Used with permission of Timberland.

the question arises: Which society? That of the home-country market (see Exhibit 17-10)? Other developed countries? Developing countries? For example, in the late 1990s, in an effort to address the issue of child labor, the U.S. government threatened trade sanctions against the garment industry in Bangladesh. Thousands of child workers lost their jobs, and their plight worsened. Whose interests were served by this turn of events? In addition, as noted in Chapter 1, companies that do business around the globe may be in different stages of evolution. Thus, a multinational firm may rely on individual country managers to address CSR issues on an ad hoc basis, while a global or transnational firm may create a policy at headquarters.

Consider the following:

- Nike came under fire from critics who alleged poor working conditions in the factories that made the company's athletic shoes.
- Walmart has become the target of criticism for a variety of reasons. Well-publicized lawsuits put the company's compensation policies in the public spotlight. Activists

**FIGURE 17-5**

**Johnson & Johnson Credo**

As management guru Jim Collins notes in his book Built to Last, Johnson & Johnson's (J&J) credo is a "codified ideology" that guides managerial actions. J&J operationalizes the credo in various ways, including its organizational structure and its planning and decision-making processes. The credo also serves as a crisis management guide. For example, during the Tylenol crisis of the early 1980s, J&J's adherence to the credo enabled the company to mount a swift, decisive, and transparent response.

Source: Courtesy of Johnson & Johnson.

**Our Credo**

We believe our first responsibility is to the doctors, nurses and patients,
to mothers and fathers and all others who use our products and services.
In meeting their needs everything we do must be of high quality.
We must constantly strive to reduce our costs
in order to maintain reasonable prices.
Customers' orders must be serviced promptly and accurately.
Our suppliers and distributors must have an opportunity
to make a fair profit.

We are responsible to our employees,
the men and women who work with us throughout the world.
Everyone must be considered as an individual.
We must respect their dignity and recognize their merit.
They must have a sense of security in their jobs.
Compensation must be fair and adequate,
and working conditions clean, orderly and safe.
We must be mindful of ways to help our employees fulfill
their family responsibilities.
Employees must feel free to make suggestions and complaints.
There must be equal opportunity for employment, development
and advancement for those qualified.
We must provide competent management,
and their actions must be just and ethical.

We are responsible to the communities in which we live and work
and to the world community as well.
We must be good citizens – support good works and charities
and bear our fair share of taxes.
We must encourage civic improvements and better health and education.
We must maintain in good order
the property we are privileged to use,
protecting the environment and natural resources.

Our final responsibility is to our stockholders.
Business must make a sound profit.
We must experiment with new ideas.
Research must be carried on, innovative programs developed
and mistakes paid for.
New equipment must be purchased, new facilities provided
and new products launched.
Reserves must be created to provide for adverse times.
When we operate according to these principles,
the stockholders should realize a fair return.

Johnson & Johnson

targeted the company, urging management to pay higher wages to hourly employees. A documentary film titled *The High Cost of Low Prices* examined the social repercussions of the retailer's presence in American communities. Two separate Web sites—WakeUpWalMart.com and WalMartWatch.com—were established by organizations representing U.S. labor unions.

- As retail gasoline prices soared in the United States following the devastation of Hurricane Katrina, BP, Royal Dutch Shell, and other companies were accused of price gouging. The American Petroleum Institute, the industry's trade group, launched a national TV advertising campaign aimed at explaining its business and urging conservation.[46]
- CEO pay in the United States is rising faster than average salaries and much faster than inflation. One study found that in 2004, CEOs were paid 431 times more than the average worker.

What is the best way for a global firm to respond to such issues? Table 17-3 provides several examples. Using Starbucks as a case study, Paul A. Argenti explains how global companies can work collaboratively with NGOs to arrive at a "win-win" outcome. As previously noted, with no external prompting, Starbucks CEO Schultz uses enlightened compensation and benefits packages to attract and retain employees. Despite the fact that Starbucks is widely admired for such forward-thinking management policies, Global Exchange pressed the company to further demonstrate its commitment to social responsibility by selling Fair Trade coffee. Schultz was faced with three options: ignore Global Exchange's demands, fight back, or capitulate. In

[46]Jean Halliday, "Slick: Big Oil Tries Image Makeover," *Advertising Age* (November 7, 2005), pp. 1, 56.

**Exhibit 17-10** New Balance Athletic Shoe, Inc., is the only major footwear company in the United States that manufactures athletic shoes domestically. Management believes that creating jobs at home is an important aspect of corporate citizenship. As a company spokesman has noted, if maximizing profit were the sole objective, it would be more advantageous to source shoes in low-wage countries. This corporate image print ad encourages other U.S. companies to follow New Balance's example.
**Source:** Courtesy of New Balance Athletic Shoe, Inc.

the end, Schultz pursued a middle ground: He agreed to offer Fair Trade coffee in Starbucks' company-owned U.S. stores. He also launched several other initiatives, including establishing long-term, direct relationships with suppliers. Argenti offers seven lessons from the Starbucks case study:[47]

- Realize that socially responsible companies are likely targets but also attractive candidates for collaboration.
- Don't wait for a crisis to collaborate.
- Think strategically about relationships with NGOs.
- Recognize that collaboration involves some compromise.

[47]Paul A. Argenti, "Collaborating with Activists: How Starbucks Works with NGOs," *California Management Review* 47, no. 1 (Summer 2004), pp. 91–116.

**TABLE 17-3 Global Marketing and Corporate Social Responsibility**

| Company (Headquarters Country) | Nature of CSR Initiative |
|---|---|
| IKEA (Sweden) | IKEA's primary carpet supplier in India monitors subcontractors to ensure that they do not employ children (see Exhibit 17-11). IKEA also helps lower-caste Indian women reduce their indebtedness to moneylenders. In an effort to create a more child-friendly environment in Indian villages, IKEA sponsors "bridge schools" to increase literacy so young people—including girls and untouchables—can enroll in regular schools.* |
| Avon (USA) | The company's Breast Cancer Awareness Crusade has raised hundreds of millions of dollars for cancer research. The money funds research in 50 countries. |
| Subaru (Japan) | Subaru's assembly plant in Indiana is the first "zero landfill" auto plant in the United States. More than 99 percent of the packaging taken in by the plant is recycled. Subaru also partners with key organizations such as the Leave No Trace Center for Outdoor Ethics and United By Blue, the ocean-friendly apparel brand. |

*Edward Luce, "IKEA's Grown-Up Plan to Tackle Child Labor," *Financial Times* (September 15, 2004), p. 7.

- Appreciate the value of the NGOs' independence.
- Understand that building relationships with NGOs takes time and effort.
- Think more like an NGO by using communication strategically.

In an article in *Business Ethics Quarterly*, Arthaud-Day proposed a three-dimensional framework for analyzing the social behavior of international, multinational, global, and transnational firms; these different stages of development constitute the first dimension.[48] The second dimension of the model includes CSR's three "content domains": human rights, labor, and the environment. These are the universal concerns for global companies established by the United Nations Global Compact. The third dimension in Arthaud-Day's framework

**Exhibit 17-11** In India's carpet belt, IKEA operationalizes the concept of corporate global responsibility by sponsoring bridge schools. The school programs are intended to reduce child labor in India's carpet industry by preparing village children to enroll in mainstream schools. To date, the bridge school program has helped an estimated 21,000 children learn to read and write.
**Source:** Pallava Bagla/Corbis.

[48]Marne Arthaud-Day, "Transnational Corporate Social Responsibility: A Tri-Dimensional Approach to International CSR Research," *Business Ethics Quarterly* 15, no. 1 (January 2005), pp. 1–22.

consists of three perspectives. The *ideological dimension* of CSR pertains to the things a firm's management believes it should be doing. The *societal dimension* consists of the expectations held by the firm's external stakeholders. The *operational dimension* includes the actions and activities actually taken by the firm. The interaction between the dimensions can result in several conflict scenarios. Conflict may arise if there is an incongruity between those things a company's leadership believes it should be doing and the expectations of stakeholders. Conflict can also arise when there is an incongruity between those things a company's leadership believes it should be doing and the things it actually is doing. A third scenario is conflict that arises from an incongruity between society's expectations and actual corporate practices and activities.

## Summary

To respond to the opportunities and threats in the global marketing environment, organizational leaders must develop a global vision and strategy. Leaders must also be able to communicate that vision throughout the organization and build *core competencies* on a worldwide basis. Global companies are increasingly realizing that the "right" person for a top job is not necessarily a home-country national.

In *organizing* for the global marketing effort, the goal is to create a structure that enables the company to respond to significant differences in international market environments and to extend valuable corporate knowledge. Alternatives include an international division structure, regional management centers, geographical structure, regional or worldwide product division structure, and the *matrix organization*. Whichever form of organization is chosen, balance between autonomy and integration must be established. Many companies are adopting the organizational principle of *lean production* that was pioneered by Japanese automakers.

Many global companies are paying attention to the issue of *corporate social responsibility (CSR)*. A company's *stakeholders* may include *nongovernmental organizations (NGOs)*; *stakeholder analysis* can help identify others. Consumers throughout the world expect that the brands and products they buy and use are marketed by companies that conduct business in an ethical, socially responsible way. Socially conscious companies should include human rights, labor, and environmental issues in their agendas. These values may be spelled out in a *code of ethics*. Ideological, societal, and organizational perspectives can all be brought to bear on CSR.

**MyMarketingLab**

To complete the problems with the ✪, go to EOC Discussion Questions in the MyLab.

## Discussion Questions

✪ **17-1.** Are top executives of global companies likely to be home-country nationals?

✪ **17-2.** In a company involved in global marketing, which activities should be centralized at headquarters and which should be delegated to national or regional subsidiaries?

**17-3.** "A matrix structure integrates four competencies on a worldwide scale." Explain.

**17-4.** In the automobile industry, how does "lean production" differ from the traditional assembly-line approach?

✪ **17-5.** Identify some of the ways the global companies discussed in this text demonstrate their commitment to CSR.

## CASE 17-1 CONTINUED (REFER TO PAGE 528)

# Unilever

After Cescau was elevated to the top job, Unilever's board streamlined the company's management structure. Now there is a single chief executive; previously, there had been one in Rotterdam and one in London. Cescau asserted that, with a single chief executive, the need for consensus was replaced by speed at making decisions. As noted, many of those decisions concerned "doing good." However, some observers were skeptical of Cescau's determination to operationalize a responsible business philosophy. Cescau recalled, "The company was not doing well. There was an article saying that I was draping myself in a flag of corporate social responsibility to excuse poor performance. I was so angry with that."

Cescau's commitment was put to the test in 2008, his final year as CEO. Greenpeace launched an advertising campaign alleging that Unilever's purchases of Indonesian palm oil were contributing to rain forest destruction. Palm oil, a key ingredient in Dove soap, Magnum ice cream bars, and Vaseline lotion, comes from oil palm trees that grow in Indonesia and Malaysia. Unilever is the world's biggest palm oil customer, buying about 1.4 million tons each year. Rising world prices for the commodity prompted Indonesian farmers to cut down large swaths of old-growth rain forest and plant fast-growing oil palms. Specifically, Greenpeace identified the operations of Sinar Mas, an Indonesian company that is a major palm oil supplier, as contributing to deforestation.

The media strategy for the Greenpeace campaign included newspaper ads in London and a video on YouTube. Fliers parodied Unilever's Campaign for Real Beauty; for example, they showed pictures of orangutans juxtaposed with the headline "Gorgeous or gone?" John Sauven, executive director of Greenpeace, explained why his organization had targeted Unilever: "Everyone has heard of those brands. They are the public face of the company" (see Exhibit 17-12).

Cescau responded by calling for a moratorium on rain forest destruction by Indonesian oil producers. The Unilever chief also pledged that his company would buy palm oil only from producers who could prove that the rain forest had not been sacrificed in the production process. The move allied Unilever with the Roundtable on Sustainable Palm Oil (RSPO), an organization that certifies palm oil producers. A Unilever spokesperson also indicated that the proposed change in Unilever's palm oil sourcing strategy had been in the works for months. Nevertheless, Greenpeace and other NGOs claimed victory.

Unilever brought its message to the public with a print ad campaign featuring the headline "What you buy in the supermarket can change the world." The body copy outlined Unilever's pledge that "by 2015 all our palm oil will come from sustainable sources." The ads ended with the tagline "Small actions, big difference." By 2011, however, only about 2 percent of Unilever's palm oil purchases were coming from traceable sources. Even so, as chief procurement officer Marc Engel said, "I'm not aware of anyone else who has made that commitment, particularly on our scale." In an effort to achieve its goals, Unilever began buying GreenPalm certificates, which are sold by growers certified by the RSPO.

"Doing well" is also part of the leadership equation at Unilever. Cescau understood the importance of improving Unilever's

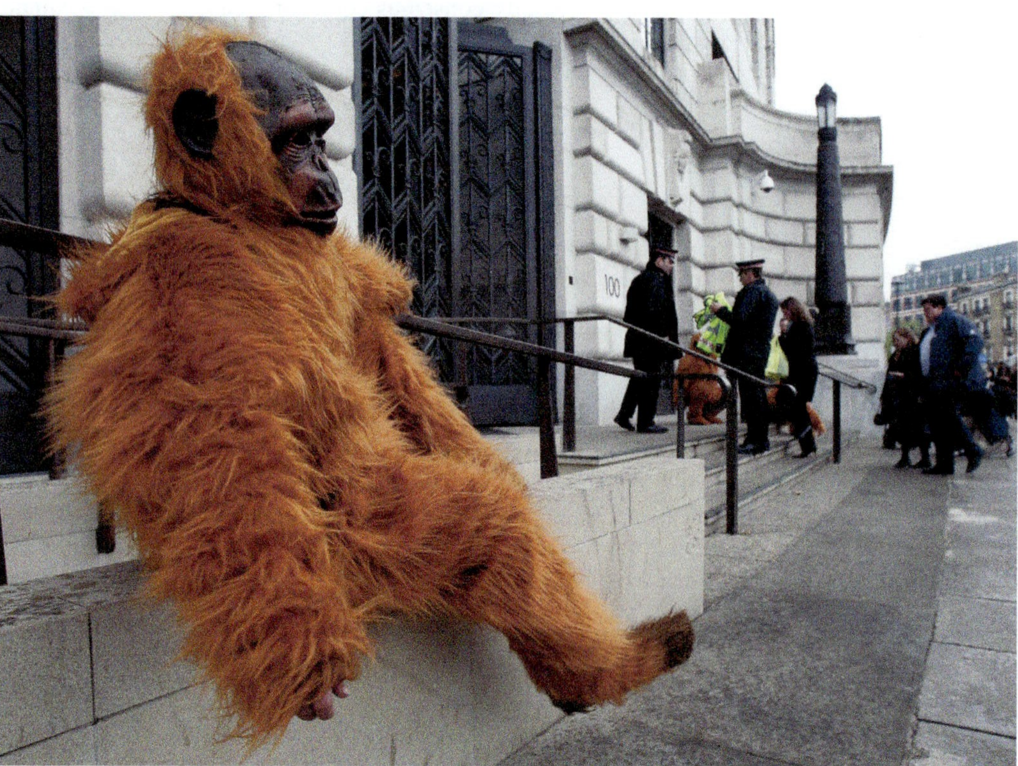


**Exhibit 17-12** Unilever has been targeted by activist groups concerned about sustainability issues. For example, palm oil is a key ingredient in several of Unilever's brands; however, orangutan habitat in Indonesia has been cleared to make room for oil palm plantations. Greenpeace and other NGOs have staged protests; here, an activist dressed as an orangutan is shown outside Unilever House in London. Unilever has pledged that, by 2020, all its palm oil will come from sustainable sources.
**Source:** REUTERS/Stephen Hird (BRITAIN).

profitability. To this end, he continued a restructuring drive that was initiated by his predecessor, cochairman Niall FitzGerald. Specific actions included reducing Unilever's bureaucracy by removing several management layers. Cescau also reduced the top management head count from 25 people to 7 and narrowed the vertical distance between management and marketing. In addition, the company shed hundreds of brands and closed dozens of factories in France, Germany, and elsewhere. In Cescau's view, the new, leaner structure would translate into a more rapid response to changing market trends and consumer preferences and ensure quicker rollouts of new products.

Cescau also bet heavily on emerging markets to jump-start sales growth. Rising incomes mean that many people purchase consumer packaged goods for the first time. One scenario: As increasing numbers of people in developing countries buy their first washing machines, they will need to buy laundry detergent. To capitalize on such trends, Cescau shifted budgetary resources out of mature markets such as Europe; those funds were then used to support research in India and other emerging markets. Brand managers were instructed to innovate by taking a "clean slate" approach to developing new products for emerging markets. As Steph Carter, packaging director for deodorant brands, noted, "Traditionally, we would have taken existing products and then tried to fathom how to adapt them for the developing world. Our thinking has changed."

## The Polman Era Begins

Paul Polman took over as CEO in January 2009; a former Nestlé executive, he is the first outsider to lead Unilever in its 80-year history. In his first months on the job, Polman initiated a shift in Unilever's core strategy. In the past, the company generated sales growth by increasing prices. Noting that this was the wrong strategy for recessionary times, Polman said the new priority would be to increase sales volumes. The change entailed some risk: Holding the line on prices could put pressure on margins, given the trend of rising costs for the agricultural commodities that are key ingredients in Unilever's products.

Polman was also keenly aware that many budget-conscious shoppers were choosing less expensive, private-label supermarket products instead of well-known name brands. Polman vowed to improve product quality across the board and to boost marketing and advertising spending. To support the increased investment, he accelerated some of the cost-cutting measures that his predecessor had initiated. For example, the timetable for planned factory closures and job cuts was moved up; Polman also froze executive salaries and changed the bonus policy. He established 30-day action plans for managers of brands with flagging sales. He also replaced about one-third of Unilever's top 100 executives, including the chief marketing officer.

When it comes to demonstrating Unilever's commitment to its customers, Polman sends clear signals to his employees. He spends about 50 percent of his time on the road, with regular stops in Asia, Latin America, and, of course, Europe. In a recent interview, he noted that he meets with consumers in every country that he visits. Polman believes strongly that the leader must set an example from the top of the organization.

That passion is evident in a flurry of marketing activities orchestrated by Polman. One is the quick pace of new-product rollouts, especially in emerging markets. For example, Unilever's home care unit was the first to market with liquid laundry detergent in China; it also introduced a dishwashing liquid in Turkey in less than 30 days. In addition, innovation has become a key element for shoring up the value proposition of Unilever's brands, with existing brands such as Surf laundry detergent getting an upgrade in the African market.

Driving growth in the personal-care category is another priority for Polman. By itself, the global deodorant segment represents an estimated $17 billion in annual sales. To tap into that market, the Dove brand has been extended to men's products. Dove for Men has been rolled out in dozens of countries. Meanwhile, Dove's product managers devised a new strategy for persuading women to switch deodorant brands. Dove Ultimate Go Sleeveless resulted from company research designed to discover insights about consumer attitudes toward underarms. What the researchers learned is that 93 percent of women think their armpits are not attractive. Dove Ultimate Go Sleeveless is formulated with moisturizers that, the company claims, will result in nicer-looking underarms after just a few days' use.

The ice cream and beverage unit is also on the move. Unilever's Magnum brand premium ice cream bars are the world's top-selling ice cream novelty. Although Magnum enjoys great popularity in Europe, it was not introduced in the United States until 2011. Häagen-Dazs and Mars were already entrenched in the market; undaunted, the Magnum marketing team is confident its brand will stand out. One manager explained that an important part of the brand's equity is the loud cracking sound heard when someone bites through Magnum's thick chocolate shell. It must be helping: In the first year, Magnum rang up $100 million in sales in the United States.

## Renewing the Commitment to Sustainability

Even as he oversees these and other marketing activities, Polman is making sure that former CEO Cescau's commitment to corporate social responsibility is maintained. Summarizing his views on sustainability and environmental impact, Polman said:

> [T]he road to well-being doesn't go via reduced consumption. It has to be done via more responsible consumption. . . . So that's why we're taking such a stand on moving the world to sustainable palm oil. That's why we work with small-hold farmers, to be sure that people who don't have sufficient nutrition right now have a chance to have a better life.

In 2012, Unilever announced plans to build a $100 million palm oil processing plant in Indonesia. Having a company-controlled plant near the source should make the task of tracing oil to sustainable sources easier. It is currently common practice at processing plants to combine oil from different sources—both sustainable and not—in the same vat. That makes it difficult to trace any individual batch of oil to its origins. Marc Engel, the procurement officer, draws an analogy between palm oil processing and crude oil processing used to make gasoline. "When you actually want to know where the gas in your car is coming from—from which oil well—it's very hard to see," he says. To hedge its bets, Unilever has also invested in Solazyme, a California-based company that produces oil from algae. What kind of potential does this technology hold? "We've made all kinds of food products," says Solazyme CEO and cofounder Jonathan Wolfson. "We've used the oil for frying. We've made mayonnaises, ice creams. And they work, taste good and are functional."

### Discussion Questions

**17-6.** If a company such as Unilever has to make trade-offs between being a good corporate citizen and making a profit, which should be the higher priority?

**17-7.** Assess Cescau's response to the Greenpeace palm oil protest. Was it appropriate? What type of relationships should Unilever cultivate with Greenpeace and other NGOs in the future?

**17-8.** Do you think that a streamlined management structure and emphasis on emerging markets will enable current CEO Polman to lead Unilever to improved performance?

**Sources:** Paul Sonne, "Unilever Takes Palm Oil in Hand," *The Wall Street Journal* (April 24, 2012), p. B3; Louise Lucas, "Growing Issue for Palm Oil Producers," *Financial Times* (May 23, 2011), p. 22; Ellen Byron, "Unilever Takes on the Ugly Underarm," *The Wall Street Journal* (March 30, 2011), p. B1; Sonne, "To Wash Hands of Palm Oil, Unilever Embraces Algae," *The Wall Street Journal* (September 7, 2010), p. B1; Lucas, "Investors Skeptical as Unilever Pursues Bold Growth Plan," *Financial Times* (November 16, 2010), p. 20; Stefan Stern, "The Outsider in a Hurry to Shake Up His Company," *Financial Times* (April 5, 2010); Jenny Wiggins, "Unilever Vows to Focus on Cheaper Products," *Financial Times* (August 7, 2009), p. 17; Wiggins, "Unilever's New Chief Prepares to Brew Up Changes," *Financial Times* (February 6, 2009), p. 15; Michael Skapinker, "Taking a Hard Line on Soft Soap," *Financial Times* (July 7, 2008), p. 12; Aaron O. Patrick, "After Protests, Unilever Does an About-Face on Palm Oil," *The Wall Street Journal* (May 2, 2008), p. B1.

## MyMarketingLab

Go to the Assignments section of your MyLab to complete these writing exercises.

**17-9.** Identify some of the factors that lead to the establishment of an international division as an organization increases its global business activities.

**17-10.** Identify and explain the three dimensions that provide different perspectives on CSR.

# Appendix

## Johnson & Johnson Credos: Brazil, Russia, India, and China

### Nosso Credo

Cremos que nossa primeira responsabilidade é para com os médicos, enfermeiras e pacientes,
para com as mães, pais e todos os demais que usam nossos produtos e serviços.
Para atender suas necessidades, tudo o que fizermos deve ser de alta qualidade.
Devemos constantemente nos esforçar para reduzir nossos custos,
a fim de manter preços razoáveis.
Os pedidos de nossos clientes devem ser pronta e corretamente atendidos.
Nossos fornecedores e distribuidores devem ter a oportunidade
de auferir um lucro justo.

Somos responsáveis por nossos empregados,
homens e mulheres que conosco trabalham em todo o mundo.
Todos devem ser considerados em sua individualidade.
Devemos respeitar sua dignidade e reconhecer o seu mérito.
Eles devem se sentir seguros em seus empregos.
A remuneração pelo seu trabalho deve ser justa e adequada
e o ambiente de trabalho limpo, ordenado e seguro.
Devemos ter em mente maneiras de ajudar nossos empregados
a atender as suas responsabilidades familiares.
Os empregados devem se sentir livres para fazer sugestões e reclamações.
Deve haver igual oportunidade de emprego, desenvolvimento
e progresso para os qualificados.
Devemos ter uma administração competente,
e suas ações devem ser justas e éticas.

Somos responsáveis perante as comunidades nas quais vivemos e trabalhamos,
bem como perante a comunidade mundial.
Devemos ser bons cidadãos – apoiar boas obras sociais e de caridade
e pagar corretamente os tributos.
Devemos encorajar o desenvolvimento do civismo e a melhoria da saúde e da educação.
Devemos manter em boa ordem
as propriedades que temos o privilégio de usar,
protegendo o meio ambiente e os recursos naturais.

Nossa responsabilidade final é para com os acionistas.
Os negócios devem proporcionar lucros adequados.
Devemos experimentar novas idéias.
Pesquisas devem ser levadas avante. Programas inovadores desenvolvidos
e os erros corrigidos.
Novos equipamentos devem ser adquiridos, novas fábricas construídas
e novos produtos lançados.
Reservas devem ser criadas para enfrentar tempos adversos.
Ao operarmos de acordo com esses princípios,
nossos acionistas devem
receber justa recompensa.

Johnson & Johnson

### Наше Кредо

Наша основная ответственность – перед врачами и медицинскими сестрами,
перед пациентами, перед отцами и матерями, перед всеми,
кто пользуется нашей продукцией и услугами. В соответствии с их
потребностями мы должны обеспечивать высокие стандарты качества во всем,
что мы делаем. Мы должны постоянно стремиться к снижению затрат,
чтобы поддерживать приемлемый уровень цен. Заказы клиентов должны
выполняться точно и в срок. Наши поставщики и дистрибьюторы
должны иметь возможность получать достойную прибыль.

Мы несем ответственность перед нашими сотрудниками,
мужчинами и женщинами, которые работают у нас по всему миру.
Мы должны ценить индивидуальность в каждом из них.
Мы должны уважать их достоинство и признавать их заслуги:
нам важно поддерживать в них чувство уверенности в завтрашнем дне.
Вознаграждение должно быть справедливым и соразмерным,
а условия труда обеспечивать чистоту, порядок и безопасность.
Нам важно, чтобы сотрудники имели возможность заботиться о семье.
Сотрудники должны чувствовать, что они могут свободно
выступать с предложениями и замечаниями.
У всех квалифицированных специалистов должны быть
равные возможности для получения работы, развития и продвижения.
Мы должны обеспечивать компетентное управление,
действия руководителей должны быть справедливыми и этичными.

Мы несем ответственность перед обществом,
в котором живем и работаем, а также перед мировым сообществом.
Мы должны выполнять свой гражданский долг:
поддерживать добрые начинания и благотворительные акции,
честно платить налоги. Мы должны содействовать улучшениям
в социальной сфере, здравоохранении и образовании.
Мы должны бережно относиться к вверенной нам собственности,
сохраняя природные ресурсы и защищая окружающую среду.

И, наконец, мы несем ответственность перед нашими акционерами.
Бизнес должен приносить существенную прибыль.
Мы должны экспериментировать с новыми идеями,
вести научно-исследовательскую работу,
внедрять инновации, учиться на своих ошибках.
Мы должны приобретать новое оборудование, обеспечивать современные
условия работы и выводить на рынок новую продукцию.
Мы должны быть готовы к сложным ситуациям и иметь резервы
для их решения. Придерживаясь этих принципов,
мы обеспечим нашим акционерам достойный доход.

### हमारी नीति

हम यह मानते हैं कि हमारी पहली जिम्मेदारी डाक्टरों, नर्सों, रोगीयों, माताओं, पिताओं तथा
उन सभी लोगों के प्रति है जो हमारे उत्पादनों और सेवाओं का उपयोग करते हैं।
उनकी आवश्यकताओं की पूर्ति के लिए जो कुछ भी हम करें, वह उत्तम दर्जे का हो।
हमें अपने उत्पादनों की कीमत घटाने की लगातार कोशिश करनी चाहिए
ताकि वे उचित कीमतों में उपलब्ध हों।
ग्राहकों की माँगे सही तौर पर तथा तत्परता से पूरी की जानी चाहिए।
हमारे विक्रेताओं और वितरकों को उचित लाभ मिलने का अवसर मिले।

हम अपने उन स्त्री और पुरुष कर्मचारियों के प्रति
जिम्मेदार हैं जो हमारे साथ संसार के हर देश में काम करते हैं।
हर व्यक्ति को व्यक्तिगत रूप से देखा जाय।
हमें उनकी प्रतिष्ठा और योग्यता का आदर करना चाहिए।
उन्हें अपनी नौकरी की सुरक्षा का विश्वास रहे।
उनका वेतन उचित और पर्याप्त हो।
काम करने का वातावरण स्वच्छ, सुव्यवस्थित और सुरक्षित हो।
पारिवारिक जिम्मेदारियाँ निभानेके लिए हमें अपने कर्मचारियोंको दक्षतापूर्वक मार्ग दिखाने चाहिए।
कर्मचारियों को उनके सुझाव और शिकायतें उचित ढंग से प्रस्तुत करने की स्वतंत्रता हो।
योग्य लोगों को सेवा, प्रगति और विकास का समान अवसर मिले।
हमारा व्यवस्थापन निपुण हो और प्रबंधकों की कृति उचित और न्यायपूर्ण हो।

हम जिस समाज में रहते और काम करते हैं और जिस विश्व समाज के हम भाग हैं
उस समाज के प्रति हमारी जिम्मेदारी है।
हमें अच्छा नागरिक होना चाहिए - दान, धर्म और दूसरे अच्छे कार्यों में
भाग लेना चाहिए तथा अपने हिस्से के कर बराबर देते रहना चाहिए।
हम नगर-सुधार, स्वास्थ्य और शिक्षा को प्रोत्साहित करें।
वातावरण और नैसर्गिक उपलब्धियों को सुरक्षित रखते हुए, जिस संपत्ति का उपयोग
करने का हमें सुअवसर मिला है इसे हम अच्छी तरह संभाल कर रखें।

हमारी आखरी जिम्मेदारी भागधारकों के प्रति है।
व्यापार में पर्याप्त लाभ होना चाहिए।
हमें नये-नये विचारों को अमल में लाना चाहिए।
अनुसंधान किए जाए, आन्वेषिक योजनाओं का विकास किया जाए और
भूलों से हुई हानि का मूल्य चुकाया जाए।
नये यंत्र खरिदे जाए, नई सुविधाएँ उपलब्ध हों और नये उत्पादनों का
निर्माण किया जाए ताकि बुरे दिनों के लिए प्रबंध हो।
यदि हम उन सिद्धान्तों के अनुसार कार्य करते हैं तो
भागधारकों को पर्याप्त लाभ मिल सकता है।

जॉन्सन ॲण्ड जॉन्सन

### 我们的信条

我们相信我们首先要对医生、护士和病人，
对父母亲以及所有使用我们的产品和接受我们服务的人负责。
为了满足他们的需求，我们所做的一切都必须是高质量的。
我们必须不断地致力于降低成本，以保持合理的价格。
客户的订货必须迅速而准确地供应。
我们的供应商和经销商应该有机会获得合理的利润。

我们要对世界各地和我们一起共事的男女同仁负责。
每一位同仁都应视为独立的个体。
我们必须维护他们的尊严，赞赏他们的优点。
要使他们对其工作有一种安全感。
薪酬必须公平合理，
工作环境必须清洁、整齐和安全。
我们必须设法帮助员工履行他们对家庭的责任。
必须让员工在提出建议和申诉时畅所欲言。
对于合格的人必须给予平等的聘用、发展和升迁的机会，
我们必须具备称职的管理人员，
他们的行为必须公正并符合道德。

我们要对我们所生活和工作的社会，对整个世界负责。
我们必须做好公民－支持对社会有益的活动和慈善事业，
缴纳我们应付的税款。
我们必须鼓励全民进步，促进健康和教育事业。
我们必须很好地维护我们所使用的财产，
保护环境和自然资源。

最后，我们要对全体股东负责。
企业经营必须获取可靠的利润。
我们必须尝试新的构想，
必须坚持研究工作，开发革新项目，
承担错误的代价并加以改正。
必须购置新设备，提供新设施，推出新产品。
必须设立储备金，以备不时之需。
如果我们依照这些原则进行经营，
股东们就会获得合理的回报。

Johnson & Johnson

Source: Courtesy of Johnson & Johnson.

# Glossary

The chapter number(s) follow(s) the definition.

**80/20 rule** In behavioral market segmentation, the rule of thumb that 20 percent of a company's products or customers account for 80 percent of revenues or profits. (7)

**acquisition** A market-entry strategy that entails investing in assets outside the home country. (12)

**adaptation approach** Management's use of highly localized marketing programs in different country markets. (1)

**adaptation strategy** A global market approach that involves changing elements of design, function, or packaging in response to needs or conditions in particular country markets. (10)

**adopter categories** In the adoption process developed by Everett Rogers, a typology of buyers at different stages of the "adoption" or product life cycle. The categories are innovators, early adopters, early majority, late majority, and laggards. (4)

**adoption process** A model developed by Everett Rogers that describes the "adoption" or purchase decision process. The stages consist of awareness, interest, evaluation, trial, and adoption. (4)

**ad valorem duty** A duty that is expressed as a percentage of the value of goods. (8)

**advertising** Any sponsored, paid message that is communicated through a nonpersonal channel. Advertising is one of the four variables in the promotion mix. (13)

**advertising appeal** The communications approach that relates to the motives of the target audience. (13)

**advertising organization** A corporation or holding company that includes one or more "core" advertising agencies, as well as units specializing in direct marketing, marketing services, public relations, or research. (13)

**advocacy advertising** A form of corporate advertising in which a company presents its point of view on a particular issue. (13)

**aesthetics** A shared sense within a culture of what is beautiful as opposed to not beautiful and what represents good taste as opposed to tastelessness. (4)

**agent** An intermediary who negotiates transactions between two or more parties but does not take title to the goods being purchased or sold. (12)

**Andean Community** A customs union comprised of Bolivia, Colombia, Ecuador, Peru, and Venezuela. (3)

**antidumping duties** Duties imposed on products whose prices government officials deem too low. (8)

**arbitration** A negotiation process between two or more parties to settle a dispute outside of the court system. (5)

**art direction** The visual presentation of an advertisement. (13)

**art director** An ad agency "creative" with general responsibility for the overall look of an advertisement. The art director chooses graphics, pictures, type styles, and other visual elements. (13)

**Association of Southeast Asian Nations (ASEAN)** A trade bloc comprised of Brunei, Cambodia, Indonesia, Malaysia, Laos, Myanmar, the Philippines, Singapore, Thailand, and Vietnam. (3)

**attitude** In culture, a learned tendency to respond in a consistent way to a given object or entity. (4)

**balance of payments** The record of all economic transactions between the residents of a country and the rest of the world. (2)

**barter** The least complex and oldest form of bilateral, nonmonetized countertrade consisting of a direct exchange of goods or services between two parties. (11)

**behavior segmentation** The process of performing market segmentation utilizing user status, usage rate, or some other measure of product consumption. (7)

**belief** In culture, an organized pattern of knowledge that an individual holds to be true about the world. (4)

**benefit segmentation** The process of segmenting markets on the basis of the benefits sought by buyers. (7)

**big idea** A concept that can serve as the basis for a memorable, effective advertising message. (13)

**bill of exchange** A written order from one party directing a second party to pay to the order of a third party. (8)

**Bluetooth** Technology that permits access to the Internet from a cell phone when the user is within the range of a hotspot. (15)

**brand** A representation of a promise by a particular company about a particular product; a complex bundle of images and experiences in the customer's mind. (10)

**brand equity** The reflection of the brand's value to a company as an intangible asset. (10)

**brand extensions** A strategy that uses an established brand name as an umbrella when entering new businesses or developing new product lines that represent new categories to the company. (10)

**brand image** A single, but often complex, mental image about both the physical product and the company that markets it. (10)

**bribery** The corrupt business practice of demanding or offering some type of consideration—typically a cash payment—when negotiating a cross-border deal. (5)

**BRICS** Brazil, Russia, India, China, and South Africa; the five fastest-growing markets that represent important opportunities. (2)

**broadband** A digital communication system with sufficient capacity to carry multiple voice, data, or video channels simultaneously. (15)

**business-to-business (b-to-b or B2B) marketing** Marketing products and services to other companies and organizations. Contrasts with business-to-consumer (b-to-c or B2C) marketing. (12)

**business-to-consumer (b-to-c or B2C) marketing** Marketing products and services to people for their own use. Contrasts with business-to-business (b-to-b or B2B) marketing. (12)

**Byrd Amendment** Law that calls for antidumping revenues to be paid to U.S. companies harmed by imported goods sold at below-market prices. (11)

**call centers** Sophisticated telephone operations that provide customer support and other services to in-bound callers from around the world. May also provide outsourcing services such as telemarketing. (8)

**call option** The right to buy a specified amount of foreign currency at a fixed price, up to the option's expiration date. (2)

**capital account** In a country's balance of payments, the record of all long-term direct investment, portfolio investment, and other short- and long-term capital flows. (2)

**CARICOM (Caribbean Community and Common Market)** Formed in 1973, a free trade area whose members include Antigua and Barbuda, Bahamas, Barbados, Belize, Dominica, Grenada, Guyana, Haiti, Jamaica, Montserrat, St. Kitts and Nevis, St. Lucia, St. Vincent and the Grenadines, and Trinidad and Tobago. (3)

**cartel** A group of separate companies or countries that collectively set prices, control output, or take other actions to maximize profits. (5)

**catalog** A magazine-style publication that features photographs, illustrations, and extensive information about a company's products. (14)

**category killer** A store that specializes in a particular product category and offers a vast selection at low prices. (12)

**Central American Integration System** A customs union comprised of El Salvador, Honduras, Guatemala, Nicaragua, Costa Rica, and Panama. (3)

**centrally planned capitalism** An economic system characterized by command resource allocation and private resource ownership. (2)

**centrally planned socialism** An economic system characterized by command resource allocation and state resource ownership. (2)

**CFR (cost and freight)** A contract in which the seller is not responsible for risk or loss at any point outside the factory. (11)

***chaebol*** In South Korea, a type of corporate alliance group composed of dozens of companies and centered around a central bank or holding company and dominated by a founding family. (9)

**changing the rules of engagement** A strategy for creating competitive advantage that involves breaking these rules and refusing to play by the rules set by industry leaders. (16)

**channel of distribution** An organized network of agencies and institutions that, in combination, perform all the activities required to link producers with users to accomplish the marketing task. (12)

**characteristics of innovations** One element of Everett Rogers' diffusion of innovations framework. The other elements in the framework are the five-stage innovation adoption process and innovation adopter categories. (4)

**cherry picking** In distribution, a situation in which a channel intermediary such as a distributor accepts new lines only from manufacturers whose products and brands already enjoy strong demand. (12)

**CIF (cost, insurance, freight) named port** The Incoterm for a contract requiring the seller to retain responsibility and liability for goods until they have physically passed over the rail of a ship. (11)

**civil-law country** A country in which the legal system reflects the structural concepts and principles of the Roman Empire in the sixth century. (5)

**click-through rate** The percentage of visitors to an Internet site who click on an advertisement link presented on the computer screen. (15)

**cluster analysis** In market research, a quantitative data analysis technique that groups variables into clusters that maximize within-group similarities and between-group differences. Can be used in psychographic segmentation. (6)

**co-branding** A variation of combination branding in which two or more different company or product brands are featured prominently on product packaging or in advertising. (10)

**code of ethics** A formal statement that summarizes a company's core ideologies, corporate values, and expectations. (17)

**collectivist culture** In Geert Hofstede's social values typology, a culture in which group cohesiveness and harmony are emphasized. A shared concern for the well-being of all members of society is also evident. (4)

**combination branding** A strategy in which a corporate name is combined with a product brand name; also called tiered or umbrella branding. (10)

**Common Agricultural Policy (CAP)** Legislation adopted by European countries after World War II to aid and protect the interests of farmers. (8)

**common external tariff (CET)** A tariff agreed upon by members of a preferential trading bloc. Implementation of a CET marks the transition from a free trade area to a customs union. (3)

**common-law country** A country in which the legal system relies on past judicial decisions (cases) to resolve disputes. (5)

**common market** A preferential trade agreement that builds on the foundation of economic integration provided by a free trade area and a customs union. (3)

**Common Market of the South (Mercosur)** A customs union comprised of Argentina, Brazil, Paraguay, Uruguay, and Venezuela. (3)

**compensation trading (buyback)** A countertrade deal typically involving the sale of plant equipment or technology licensing in which the seller or licensor agrees to take payment in the form of the products produced using the equipment or technology for a specified number of years. (11)

**competitive advantage** The result of a match between a firm's distinctive competencies and the factors critical for creating superior customer value in an industry. (1, 16)

**concentrated global marketing** The target market strategy that calls for creating a marketing mix to reach a niche segment of global consumers. (7)

**confiscation** Governmental seizure of a company's assets without compensation. (5)

**conjoint analysis** In market research, a quantitative data analysis technique that can be used to gain insights into the combination of product features that will be attractive to potential buyers. (6)

**consumer panel** Primary data collection using a sample of consumers or households whose behavior is tracked over time; frequently used for television audience measurement. (6)

**consumer sales promotions** Promotion designed to make consumers aware of a new product, to stimulate nonusers to sample an existing product, or to increase overall consumer demand. (14)

**containerization** In physical distribution, the practice of loading oceangoing freight into steel boxes measuring 20 feet, 40 feet, or longer. (12)

**content site** A Web site that provides news and entertainment and supports a company's PR efforts. (15)

**continuous innovation** A product that is "new and improved" and requires little research and development (R&D) expenditure to develop, causes minimal disruption in existing consumption patterns, and requires the least amount of learning on the part of buyers. (10)

**contract manufacturing** A licensing arrangement in which a global company provides technical specifications to a subcontractor or local manufacturer. (9)

**convenience stores** A form of retail distribution that offers some of the same products as supermarkets, but the merchandise mix is limited to high-turnover convenience products. (12)

**convergence** The aspect of the digital revolution that pertains to the merging, overlapping, or coming together of previously distinct industries or product categories. (15)

**cooperative exporter** An export organization of a manufacturing company retained by other independent manufacturers to sell their products in some or all foreign markets. (8)

**copy** The words that are the spoken or written communication elements in advertisements. (13)

**copyright** The establishment of ownership of a written, recorded, performed, or filmed creative work. (5)

**core competence** Something that an organization can do better than its competitors. (17)

**corporate advertising** Advertising that is not designed to directly stimulate demand for a specific product. Image advertising and advocacy advertising are two types of corporate advertising. (13)

**corporate social responsibility (CSR)** A company's obligation and commitment to the pursuit of goals and policies that are in society's best interests. (17)

**cost-based pricing** Pricing based on an analysis of internal costs (e.g., materials, labor, etc.) and external costs. (11)

**cost-based transfer pricing** A transfer pricing policy that uses costs as a basis for setting prices in intracorporate transfers. (11)

**cost focus** In Michael Porter's generic strategies framework, one of four options for building competitive advantage. When a firm that serves a small (niche) market has a lower cost structure than its competitors, it can offer customers the lowest prices in the industry. (16)

**cost leadership** A competitive advantage based on a firm's position as the industry's low-cost producer. (16)

**counterfeiting** The unauthorized copying and production of a product. (5)

**counterpurchase** A monetized countertrade deal in which the seller agrees to purchase products of equivalent value that it must then sell in order to realize revenue from the original deal. (11)

**countertrade** An export transaction in which a sale results in product flowing in one direction to a buyer, and a separate stream of products and services, often flowing in the opposite direction. (11)

**countervailing duties (CVDs)** Additional duties levied to offset subsidies granted in the exporting country. (8)

**country and market concentration** A market expansion strategy that involves targeting a limited number of customer segments in a few countries. (9)

**country and market diversification** The corporate market expansion strategy of a global, multibusiness company. (9)

**country concentration and market diversification** A market expansion strategy in which a company serves many markets in a few countries. (9)

**country diversification and market concentration** A market expansion strategy whereby a company seeks out the world market for a product. (9)

**country-of-origin effect** Perceptions of, and attitudes toward, products or brands on the basis of the country of origin or manufacture. (10)

**coupon** A sales promotion tool consisting of a printed certificate that entitles the bearer to a price reduction or some other value-enhancing consideration when purchasing a particular product or service. (14)

**creative execution** In advertising, the way an appeal or selling proposition is presented. Creative execution is the "how," and creative strategy is the "what." (13)

**creative strategy** A statement or concept of what a particular advertising message or campaign will say. (13)

**culture** A society's ways of living transmitted from one generation to another. Culture's manifestations include attitudes, beliefs, values, aesthetics, dietary customs, and language. (4)

**current account** A record of all recurring trade in merchandise and services, private gifts, and public aid transactions between countries. (2)

**customer relationship management (CRM)** The process of storing and analyzing data collected from customer "touchpoints" for the purpose of identifying a firm's best customers and serving their needs as efficiently, effectively, and profitably as possible. (6)

**customer strategy** A sales representative's plan for collecting and analyzing information about the needs of each customer or prospect. (14)

**customs union** A preferential trade bloc whose members agree to seek a greater degree of economic integration than is provided by a free trade agreement. In addition to reducing tariffs and quotas, a customs union is characterized by a common external tariff (CET). (3)

**cybersquatting** The practice of registering a particular domain name for the express purpose of reselling it to the company that should rightfully use it. (15)

**data warehouse** A database, part of a company's MIS, that is used to support management decision making. (6)

**Defense Advanced Research Projects Agency (DARPA)** Agency that created a computer network that could maintain lines of communication in the event of a war. (15)

**delivered duty paid (DDB)** A type of contract in which the seller has agreed to deliver the goods to the buyer at the place the buyer names in the country of import, with all costs, including duties, paid. (11)

**demand conditions** In Michael Porter's framework for national competitive advantage, conditions that determine the rate and nature of improvement and innovations by the firms in the nation. (16)

**demographic segmentation** The process of segmenting markets on the basis of measurable characteristics such as country, income, population, age, or some other measure. (7)

**department store** A category of retail operations characterized by multiple sections or areas under one roof, each representing a distinct merchandise line and staffed with a limited number of salespeople. (12)

**devaluation** The decline in value of a currency relative to other currencies. (2)

**developed countries** Countries that can be assigned to the high-income category. (2)

**developing countries** Countries that can be assigned to the upper ranks of the low-income category, the lower-middle-income category, or the upper-middle-income category. (2)

**differentiated global marketing** A strategy that calls for targeting two or more distinct market segments with multiple marketing mix offerings. (7)

**differentiation** In Porter's generic strategies framework, one of four options for building competitive advantage. Differentiation advantage is present when a firm serves a broad market and its products are perceived as unique; this allows the firm to charge premium prices compared with the competition. (16)

**diffusion of innovations** A framework developed by Everett Rogers to explain the way that new products are adopted by a culture over time. The framework includes the five-stage innovation adoption process, characteristics of innovations, and innovation adopter categories. (4)

**digital revolution** The paradigm shift resulting from technological advances allowing for the digitization (i.e., conversion to binary code) of analog sources of information, sounds, and images. (15)

**direct mail** A direct marketing technique that uses the postal service as a vehicle for delivering an offer to prospects targeted by a marketer. (14)

**direct marketing** Any communication with a consumer or business recipient that is designed to generate a response in the form of an order, a request for further information, and/or a visit to a store or other place of business. (14)

**discontinuous innovation** A new product that, when it is widely adopted, creates new markets and new consumption patterns. (10)

**discount retailers** A category of retail operations that emphasizes low merchandise prices. (12)

**discriminatory procurement policies** Policies that can take the form of government rules and administrative regulations, as well as formal or informal company policies that discriminate against foreign suppliers. (8)

**disruptive technology** A technology that redefines product or industry performance and enables new markets to emerge. (15)

**distribution** One of the four Ps of the marketing mix; the physical flow of goods through channels. (12)

**distribution channels** A barrier to entry into an industry created by the need to create and establish new channels. (12)

**distributor** A channel intermediary, frequently a wholesaler, that aggregates products from manufacturers and delivers them to retail channel members. (12)

**domestic company** A company that limits the geographic scope of its resource commitment and marketing activities to opportunities in the home country. (1)

**domestic market** A company's "home turf," generally the country or countries in which the organization's headquarters is located. (1)

**double-diamond framework** A framework for understanding national competitive advantage in terms of a "double diamond" instead of the single diamond found in Michael Porter's national advantage model. (16)

**draft** A payment instrument that transfers all the risk of non-payment onto the exporter-seller. (8)

**dumping** The sale of a product in an export market at a price lower than that normally charged in the domestic market or country of origin. (8, 11)

**duties** Rate schedule; can sometimes be thought of as a tax that punishes "individuals for making choices of which their governments disapprove." (8)

**dynamically continuous innovation** An intermediate category of newness that is somewhat disruptive and requires a moderate amount of learning on the part of consumers. (10)

**e-commerce** The general exchange of goods and services using the Internet or a similar online network as a marketing channel. (15)

**Economic Community of West African States (ECOWAS)** An association of 16 nations that includes Benin, Burkina Faso, Cape Verde, Gambia, Ghana, Guinea, Guinea-Bissau, Ivory Coast, Liberia, Mali, Mauritania, Niger, Nigeria, Senegal, Sierra Leone, and Togo. (3)

**economic freedom index** A table of country rankings based on key economic variables such as trade policy, taxation policy, government consumption, monetary policy, capital flows, and foreign investment, etc. (2)

**economic union** A highly evolved form of cross-border economic integration involving reduced tariffs and quotas, a common external tariff, reduced restrictions on the movement of labor and capital, and the creation of unified economic policies and institutions such as a central bank. (3)

**economies of scale** The decline in per-unit product costs as the absolute volume of production per period increases. (16)

**efficient consumer response (ECR)** An MIS tool that enables retailers to work more closely with vendors to facilitate stock replenishment. (6)

**electronic data interchange (EDI)** An MIS tool that allows a company's business units to submit orders, issue invoices, and conduct business electronically with other company units as well as with outside companies. (6)

**electronic point of sale (EPOS)** Purchase data gathered by checkout scanners that help retailers identify product sales patterns and the extent to which consumer preferences vary with geography. (6)

**emic analysis** Global market research that analyzes a country in terms of its local system of meanings and values. (6)

**emotional appeal** In advertising, an appeal intended to evoke an emotional response (as opposed to an intellectual response) that will direct purchase behavior. (13)

**enabling conditions** Structural market characteristics whose presence or absence can determine whether the marketing model can succeed. (7)

**environmental sensitivity** A measure of the extent to which products must be adapted to the culture-specific needs of different country markets. Generally, consumer products show a higher degree of environmental sensitivity than industrial products. (4)

**EPRG framework** A developmental framework for analyzing organizations in terms of four successive management orientations: ethnocentric, polycentric, regiocentric, and geocentric. (1)

**equity stake** Market-entry strategy involving foreign direct investment for the purpose of establishing partial ownership of a business. (9)

**ethnocentric orientation** The first level in the EPRG framework: the conscious or unconscious belief that one's home country is superior. (1)

**ethnocentric pricing** The practice of extending a product's home-country price to all country markets. Also known as extension pricing. (11)

**etic analysis** Global market research that analyzes a country from an outside perspective. (6)

**euro zone** Sixteen countries that use the euro: Austria, Belgium, Cyprus, Finland, Ireland, the Netherlands, France, Germany, Greece, Italy, Luxembourg, Malta, Portugal, Slovakia, Slovenia, and Spain. (3)

**expanded Triad** The dominant economic centers of the world: the Pacific region, North America, and Europe. (2)

**expatriate** An employee who is sent from his or her home country to work abroad. (14)

**export broker** A broker who receives a fee for bringing together the seller and the overseas buyer. (8)

**export commission representative** Representative assigned to all or some foreign markets by the manufacturer. (8)

**export distributor** An individual or organization that has the exclusive right to sell a manufacturer's products in all or some markets outside the country of origin. (8)

**export management company (EMC)** Term used to designate an independent export firm that acts as the export department for more than one manufacturer. (8)

**export marketing** Exporting using the product offered in the home market as a starting point and modifying it as needed to meet the preferences of international target markets. (8)

**export merchants** Merchants who seek out needs in foreign markets and make purchases in world markets to fill these needs. (8)

**export price escalation** The increase in an imported product's price due to expenses associated with transportation, currency fluctuations, etc. (11)

**export selling** Exporting without tailoring the product, the price, or the promotional material to suit individual country requirements. (8)

**express warranty** A written guarantee that assures a buyer that he or she is getting what was paid for or provides recourse in the event that a product's performance falls short of expectations. (10)

**expropriation** Governmental seizure of a company's assets in exchange for compensation that is generally lower than market value. (5)

**extension approach** Management's use of domestic country marketing programs and strategies when entering new country markets. (1)

**extension strategy** A global strategy of offering a product virtually unchanged (i.e., "extending" it) in markets outside the home country. (10)

**ex-works (EXW)** A type of contract in which the seller places goods at the disposal of the buyer at the time specified in the contract. (11)

**factor analysis** In market research, a computerized quantitative data analysis technique that is used to perform data reduction. Responses from questionnaires that contain multiple items about a product's benefits serve as input; the computer generates factor loadings that can be used to create a perceptual map. (6)

**factor conditions** A country's endowment with resources. (16)

**FAS (free alongside ship) named port** The Incoterm for a contract that calls for the seller to place goods alongside, or available to, the vessel or other mode of transportation and pay all charges up to that point. (11)

**femininity** In Geert Hofstede's social values framework, the extent to which the social roles of men and women overlap in a culture. (4)

**first-mover advantage** Orthodox marketing wisdom suggesting that the first company to enter a country market has the best chance of becoming the market leader. (7)

**five forces model** Model developed by Michael Porter that explains competition in an industry: the threat of new entrants, the threat of substitute products or services, the bargaining power of buyers, the bargaining power of suppliers, and the competitive rivalry among current members of the industry. (16)

**flagship model** A model of competitive advantage developed by Alan Rugman and Joseph D'Cruz that describes how networked business systems can create competitive advantage in global industries. (16)

**FOB (free on board) named port** The Incoterm for a contract in which the responsibility and liability of the seller do not end until the goods have actually been placed aboard a ship. (11)

**focus** The concentration of resources on a core business or competence. (1)

**focused differentiation** In Michael Porter's generic strategies framework, one of four options for building competitive advantage. When a firm serves a small (niche) market and its products are perceived as unique, the firm can charge premium prices. (16)

**focus group** Primary data collection method involving a trained moderator who facilitates discussion among the members of a group at a specially equipped research facility. (6)

**foreign consumer culture positioning (FCCP)** A positioning strategy that seeks to differentiate a product, brand, or company by associating it with its country or culture of origin. (7)

**Foreign Corrupt Practices Act (FCPA)** A law that makes it illegal for U.S. corporations to bribe an official of a foreign government or political party to obtain or retain business. (5)

**foreign direct investment (FDI)** The market-entry strategy in which companies invest in or acquire plants, equipment, or other assets outside the home country. (9)

**foreign purchasing agents** Purchasing agents who operate on behalf of, and are compensated by, an overseas customer. (8)

**foreign sales corporation (FSC)** Provision in the U.S. tax code that allowed American exporters to exclude 15 percent of international sales from reported earnings. (8)

**form utility** The availability of the product processed, prepared, in proper condition, and/or ready to use. (12)

**forward market** A mechanism for buying and selling currencies at a preset price for future delivery. (2)

**franchising** A contract between a parent company–franchisor and franchisee that allows the franchisee to operate a business developed by the franchisor in return for a fee and adherence to franchise-wide policies and practices. This is an appropriate entry strategy when barriers to entry are low yet the market is culturally distant in terms of consumer behavior or retailing structures. (9, 12)

**free carrier (FCA)** The Incoterm for a contract where transfer from seller to buyer is effected when the goods are delivered to a specified carrier at a specified destination. (11)

**free trade agreement (FTA)** An agreement that leads to the creation of a free trade area (also abbreviated FTA). A FTA represents a relatively low level of economic integration. (3)

**free trade area (FTA)** A preferential trade bloc whose members have signed a free trade agreement (also abbreviated FTA) that entails reducing or eliminating tariffs and quotas. (3)

**free trade zone (FTZ)** A geographical entity that may include a manufacturing facility and a warehouse. (8)

**freight forwarders** Specialists in traffic operations, customs clearance, and shipping tariffs and schedules. (8)

**full ownership** Market-entry strategy involving foreign direct investment for the purpose of establishing 100 percent control of a business. (9)

**General Agreement on Tariffs and Trade (GATT)** The organization established at the end of World War II to promote free trade; also, the treaty signed by member nations. (3)

**generic strategies** Michael Porter's model describing four different options for achieving competitive advantage: cost leadership, product differentiation, cost focus, focused differentiation. (16)

**geocentric orientation** The fourth level in the EPRG framework: the understanding that the company should seek market opportunities throughout the world. Management also recognizes that country markets may be characterized by both similarities and differences. (1)

**geocentric pricing** The practice of using both extension and adaptation pricing policies in different country markets. (11)

**global advertising** An advertising message whose art, copy, headlines, photographs, taglines, and other elements have been developed expressly for their worldwide suitability. (13)

**global brand** A brand that has the same name and a similar image and positioning throughout the world. (10)

**global brand leadership** The act of allocating brand-building resources globally with the goal of creating global synergies and developing a global brand strategy that coordinates and leverages country brand strategies. (10)

**global company** A company exhibiting a geocentric orientation that pursues marketing opportunities in all parts of the world using one of two strategies: either serving world markets by exporting goods manufactured in the home- country market or by sourcing products from a variety of different countries with the primary goal of serving the home-country market. Global operations are integrated and coordinated. (1)

**global competition** A success strategy in which a firm takes a global view of competition and sets about maximizing profits worldwide, rather than on a country-by-country basis. (16)

**global consumer culture positioning (GCCP)** A positioning strategy that seeks to differentiate a product, brand, or company as a symbol of, or association with, a global culture or a global market segment. (4, 7)

**global elite** A global market segment comprised of well-traveled, affluent consumers who spend heavily on prestige or luxury products and brands that convey an image of exclusivity. (7)

**global industry** An industry in which competitive advantage can be achieved by integrating and leveraging operations on a worldwide scale. (1)

**global marketing** The commitment of organizational resources to pursuing global market opportunities and responding to environmental threats in the global marketplace. (1)

**global marketing strategy (GMS)** A firm's blueprint for pursuing global market opportunities that addresses four issues: whether a standardization approach or a localization approach will be used; whether key marketing activities will be concentrated in relatively few countries or widely dispersed around the globe; the guidelines for coordinating marketing activities around the globe; and the scope of global market participation. (1)

**global market research** The project-specific gathering and analysis of data on a global basis or in one or more markets outside the home country. (6)

**global market segmentation** The process of identifying specific segments of potential customers with homogeneous attributes who are likely to exhibit similar buying behavior irrespective of their countries of residence. (7)

**global positioning system (GPS)** A digital communication system that uses satellite feeds to determine the geographic position of a mobile device. (15)

**global product** A product that satisfies the wants and needs of buyers in all parts of the world. (10)

**global retailing** Engaging in or owning retail operations in multiple national markets. (12)

**global strategic partnerships (GSPs)** A sophisticated market-entry strategy via an alliance with one or more business partners for the purpose of serving the global market. (9)

**global teens** A global market segment comprised of persons 12 to 19 years old whose shared interests in fashion, music, and youthful lifestyle issues shape purchase behavior. (7)

**gray market goods** Products that are exported from one country to another without authorization from the trademark owner. (11)

**greenfield investment** A market-entry strategy that entails foreign direct investment in a factory, retail outlet, or some other form of new operations in a target country. Also known as greenfield operations. (9)

**gross domestic product (GDP)** A measure of a nation's economic activity calculated by adding consumer spending ($C$), investment spending ($I$), government purchases ($G$), and net exports ($NX$): $C + I + G + NX = \text{GDP}$. (2)

**gross national income (GNI)** A measure of a nation's economic activity that includes gross domestic product (GDP) plus income generated by nonresident sources. (2)

**Group of Eight (G-8)** Eight nations—the United States, Japan, Germany, France, Great Britain, Canada, Italy, and Russia—whose representatives meet regularly to deal with global economic issues. (2)

**Group of Seven (G-7)** Seven nations—the United States, Japan, Germany, France, Great Britain, Canada, and Italy—whose representatives meet regularly to deal with global economic issues. (2)

**Group of Twenty (G-20)** Twenty nations whose representatives meet regularly to discuss global economic and financial issues. Objectives include restoring global economic growth and strengthening the global financial system. (2)

**Gulf Cooperation Council (GCC)** An association of oil-producing states that includes Bahrain, Kuwait, Oman, Qatar, Saudi Arabia, and the United Arab Emirates. (3)

**hard discounter** A retailer that sells a tightly focused selection of goods at very low prices, often relying heavily on private brands. (12)

**harmonization** The coming together of varying standards and regulations that affect the marketing mix. (3)

**Harmonized Tariff System (HTS)** A system in which importers and exporters have to determine the correct classification number for a given product or service that will cross borders. (8)

**hedging** An investment made to protect a company from possible financial losses due to fluctuating currency exchange rates. (2)

**hierarchy of effects** A model of consumer response that shows the stages—cognitive, affective, and conative—that individuals move through when considering purchasing a product or service. (4)

**high-context culture** A culture in which a great deal of information and meaning reside in the context of communication, including the background, associations, and basic values of the communicators. (4)

**high-income country** A country in which per capita gross national income (GNI) is $12,746 or greater. (2)

**hypercompetition** A strategy framework developed by Richard D'Aveni that views competition and the quest for competitive advantage in terms of the dynamic maneuvering and strategic interactions by hypercompetitive firms in an industry. (16)

**hypermarket** A category of retail operations characterized by very large-scale facilities that combine elements of discount store, supermarket, and warehouse club approaches. (12)

**hypertext markup language (HTML)** A format language that controls the appearance of Web pages. (15)

**hypertext transfer protocol (HTTP)** A protocol that enables hypertext files to be transferred across the Internet. (15)

**image advertising** A type of corporate advertising that informs the public about a major event, such as a name change, merger, etc. (13)

**incipient market** A market in which demand will materialize if particular economic, demographic, political, or sociocultural trends continue. (6)

**Incoterms** Internationally accepted terms of trade that impact prices. (11)

**individualist culture** In Geert Hofstede's social values typology, a society in which each member is primarily concerned with his or her interests and those of the immediate family. (4)

**infomercial** A form of paid television programming in which a particular product is demonstrated, explained, and offered for sale to viewers who call a toll-free number shown on the screen. (14)

**information technology (IT)** An organization's processes for creating, storing, exchanging, using, and managing information. (6)

**information utility** The availability of answers to questions and general communication about useful product features and benefits. (12)

**innovation** The process of endowing resources with a new capacity to create value. (10)

**innovator's dilemma** Executives become so committed to a current, profitable technology that they fail to provide adequate levels of investment in new, apparently riskier technologies. (15)

**integrated circuit (IC)** The silicon chip that gave modern form to the transistor and represented a milestone in the digital revolution. (15)

**integrated marketing communications (IMC)** An approach to the promotion element of the marketing mix that values coordination and integration of a company's marketing communication strategy. (13)

**interactive television (ITV)** Allows television viewers to interact with the programming content that they are viewing. (14)

**intermodal transportation** The aspect of physical distribution that involves transferring shipping containers between land and water transportation modes. (12)

**international brand** A brand that is available throughout a particular world region. Also known as an international product. (10)

**international company** A company that pursues market opportunities outside the home country via an extension strategy. (1)

**international law** The body of international law that pertains to noncommercial disputes between nations. (5)

**Internet** A network of computer networks across which e-mail and other digital files can be sent. (15)

**intranet** An electronic system that allows authorized company personnel or outsiders to share information electronically in a secure fashion while reducing the amount of paper generated. (6)

**inventory management** The distribution activity that ensures companies carry the optimum amount of manufacturing components or finished goods. The objective is to avoid running out of stock without incurring excessive inventory carrying costs. (12)

**Islamic law** A legal system used in the Middle East that is based on a comprehensive code known as *sharia*. (5)

**joint venture** A market-entry strategy in which two companies share ownership of a newly created business entity. (9, 12)

**jurisdiction** The aspect of a country's legal environment that deals with a court's authority to rule on particular types of controversies arising outside of a nation's borders or exercise power over individuals or entities from different countries. (5)

***keiretsu*** In Japan, an enterprise alliance consisting of businesses that are joined together in mutually reinforcing ways. (9)

**latent market** An undiscovered market segment in which demand for a product would materialize if an appropriate product were offered. (6)

**law of one price** A market in which all customers have access to the best product at the best price. (11)

**lean production** An extremely effective, efficient, and streamlined manufacturing system such as the Toyota Production System. (17)

**least-developed countries (LDCs)** Terminology adopted by the United Nations to refer to the 50 countries that rank lowest in per capita gross national product (GNP). (2)

**legal environment** A nation's system of laws, courts, attorneys, legal customs, and practices. (5)

**letter of credit (L/C)** A payment method in export/import in which a bank substitutes its creditworthiness for that of the importer-buyer. (8)

**leverage** Some type of advantage—for example, experience transfers, know-how, or scale economies—that a company enjoys by accumulating experience in multiple country markets. (1)

**licensing** A contractual market-entry strategy whereby one company makes an asset available to another company in exchange for royalties or some other form of compensation. (9, 12)

**line extension** A variation of an existing product such as a new flavor or new design. (10)

**local brand** A brand that is available in a single country market. Also known as a local product. (10)

**local consumer culture positioning** A positioning strategy that seeks to differentiate a product, brand, or company in terms of its association with local culture, local production, or local consumption. (7)

**localization (adaptation) approach** The pursuit of global market opportunities using an adaptation strategy of significant marketing mix variations in different countries. (1)

**logistics** The management process that integrates the activities of various suppliers and distribution intermediaries to ensure an efficient flow of goods through a firm's supply chain. (12)

**logistics management** The management activity responsible for planning, implementing, and controlling the flow of components and finished goods between the point of origin and the point of assembly or final consumption. (12)

**long-term orientation (LTO)** The fifth dimension in Geert Hofstede's social values framework, LTO is a reflection of a society's concern with immediate gratification versus persistence and thrift over the long term. (4)

**loose bricks** A strategy for creating competitive advantage by taking advantage of a competitor whose attention is narrowly focused on a market segment or geographic area to the exclusion of others. (16)

**low-context culture** A culture in which messages and knowledge are more explicit and words carry most of the information in communication. (4)

**lower-middle-income country** A country with gross national income (GNI) per capita between $1,046 and $4,125. (2)

**low-income country** A country with per capita gross national income (GNI) of less than $1,045. (2)

**Maastricht Treaty** The 1991 treaty that set the stage for the transition from the European monetary system to an economic and monetary union. (3)

**Madrid Protocol** A system of trademark protection that allows intellectual property registration in multiple countries with a single application and fee. (5)

**management information system (MIS)** A system that provides managers and other decision makers with a continuous flow of information about company operations. (6)

**manufacturer's export agent (MEA)** One who can act as an export distributor or as an export commission representative. (8)

**market** People or organizations with needs and wants and both the ability and the willingness to buy. (2)

**market-based transfer price** A transfer pricing policy that sets prices for intracorporate transactions at levels that are competitive in the global market. (11)

**market capitalism** An economic system characterized by market allocation of resources and private resource ownership. (2)

**market-entry strategy** The manner in which company management decides to pursue market opportunities outside the home country. (9)

**market expansion strategy** The particular combination of product-market and geographic alternatives that management chooses when expanding company operations outside the home country. (9)

**market holding strategy** A pricing strategy that allows management to maintain market share; prices are adjusted up or down as competitive or economic conditions change. (11)

**marketing** An organizational function and a set of processes for creating, communicating, and delivering value to customers and for managing customer relationships in ways that benefit the organization and its stakeholders. (1)

**marketing mix** The four factors—product, price, place, and promotion—that represent strategic variables controlled by the marketer. (1)

**marketing model drivers** Key elements or factors that must be taken into account when evaluating countries as potential target markets. (7)

**market penetration pricing strategy** A pricing strategy that calls for setting price levels that are low enough to quickly build market share. (11)

**market research** The project-specific, systematic gathering of data in the search scanning mode. (6)

**market segmentation** An effort to identify and categorize groups of customers and countries according to common characteristics. (7)

**market skimming** A pricing strategy designed to reach customers willing to pay a premium price for a particular brand or for a specialized product. (11)

**market socialism** An economic system characterized by limited market resource allocation within an overall environment of state ownership. (2)

**masculinity** In Geert Hofstede's social values framework, the extent to which a culture's male population is expected to be assertive, competitive, and concerned with material success. (4)

**Maslow's needs hierarchy** A classic framework for understanding how human motivation is linked to needs. (10)

**matrix organization** A pattern of organization design in which management's task is to achieve an organizational balance that brings together different perspectives and skills to accomplish the organization's objectives. (17)

**merchandise trade** In balance of payments statistics, entries that pertain to manufactured goods. (2)

**mobile advertising** Persuasive or informative communication that uses a smartphone or other handheld device as the channel. (15)

**mobile commerce (m-commerce)** Conducting commercial transactions using wireless handheld devices such as cell phones and tablets. (15)

**mobile music** Music that is purchased and played on a cell phone. (15)

**multidimensional scaling (MDS)** In market research, a quantitative data analysis technique that can be used to create perceptual maps. MDS helps marketers gain insights into consumer perceptions when a large number of products or brands are available. (6)

**multinational company** A company that pursues market opportunities outside the home-country market via an adaptation strategy (i.e., different product, price, place, and/or promotion strategies than used in the domestic market). In a typical multinational, country managers are granted considerable autonomy; there is little integration or coordination of marketing activities across different country markets. (1)

**multisegment targeting** A marketing strategy that entails targeting two or more distinct market segments with multiple marketing mix offerings. (7)

**national advantage** Strategy guru Michael Porter's competitive advantage framework for analysis at the nation-state level. The degree to which a nation develops competitive advantage depends on four elements: factor conditions, demand conditions, the presence of related and supporting industries, and the nature of firm strategy. (16)

**nationalization** Broad transfer of industry management and ownership in a particular country from the private sector to the government. (5)

**nature of firm strategy, structure, and rivalry** In Michael Porter's framework for national competitive advantage, the fourth determinant of a national "diamond." (16)

**negotiated transfer price** A transfer pricing policy that establishes prices for intracorporate transactions on the basis of the organization's affiliations. (11)

**newly industrializing economies (NIEs)** Upper-middle-income countries with high rates of economic growth. (2)

**niche** A single segment of the global market. (7)

**nongovernmental organization (NGO)** A secondary stakeholder that focuses on human rights, political justice, and environmental issues. (17)

**nontariff barriers (NTBs)** Any restriction besides taxation that restricts or prevents the flow of goods across borders, ranging from "buy local" campaigns to bureaucratic obstacles that make it difficult for companies to gain access to some individual country and regional markets. (1, 8)

**normal trade relations (NTR)** A trading stratus under World Trade Organization (WTO) rules that entitles a country to low tariff rates. (8)

**North American Free Trade Agreement (NAFTA)** A free trade area encompassing Canada, the United States, and Mexico. (3)

**"not invented here" (NIH) syndrome** An error made in choosing a strategy by ignoring decisions made by subsidiary or affiliate managers. (10)

**observation** A method of primary data collection using trained observers who watch and record the behavior of actual or prospective customers. (6)

**offset** A countertrade deal in which a government recoups hard-currency expenditures by requiring some form of cooperation from the seller, such as importing products or transferring technology. (11)

**one-to-one marketing** An updated framework for direct marketing that calls for treating each customer in a distinct way based on his or her previous purchase history or past interactions with the company. (14)

**operating system** A software code that provides basic instructions for a computer. (15)

**option** In foreign currency trading, a contract confirming the right to buy or sell a specific amount of currency at a fixed price. (2)

**order processing** The aspect of physical distribution that includes order entry, order handling, and order delivery. (12)

**organic growth** In global retailing, a market expansion strategy whereby a company uses its own resources to open a store on a greenfield site or to acquire one or more existing retail facilities or sites from another company. (12)

**Organization for Economic Cooperation and Development (OECD)** A group of 33 nations that work together to aid in the development of economic systems based on market capitalism and pluralistic democracy. (2)

**organizing** The goal of creating a structure that enables the company to respond to significant differences in international market environments and to extend valuable corporate knowledge. (17)

**outlet mall** A grouping of outlet stores. (12)

**outlet store** A category of retail operations that allows marketers of well-known consumer brands to dispose of excess inventory, out-of-date merchandise, or factory seconds. (12)

**outsourcing** Shifting jobs or work assignments to another company to cut costs. When the work moves abroad to a low-wage country such as India or China, the term *offshoring* is sometimes used. (8)

**paid search advertising** An Internet communication tactic in which companies pay to have their ads appear when users type certain search terms. (15)

**parallel importing** The act of importing goods from one country to another without authorization from the trademark owner. Parallel import schemes exploit price differentials among country markets. (11)

**patent** A formal legal document that gives an inventor the exclusive right to make, use, and sell an invention for a specified period of time. (5)

**pattern advertising** A communication strategy that calls for developing a basic pan-regional or global concept for which copy, artwork, or other elements can be adapted as required for individual country markets. (13)

**peer-to-peer (p-to-p) marketing** A marketing model whereby individual consumers market products to other individuals. (12)

**peoplemeter** An electronic device used by companies such as Nielsen to collect national television audience data. (6)

**personal computer (PC)** A compact, affordable computing device whose advent marked the next phase of the digital revolution. (15)

**personal interview** Primary data collection via interactive communication (face-to-face, telephone, etc.) that allows interviewers to ask "why"-type questions. (6)

**personal selling** One of four variables in the promotion mix; face-to-face communication between a prospective buyer and a company sales representative. (14)

**personal selling philosophy** A sales representative's commitment to the marketing concept coupled with a willingness to take on the role of problem solver or partner in helping customers. The first step in the strategic/consultative selling model. (14)

**physical distribution** All activities involved in moving finished goods from manufacturers to customers. Includes order processing, warehousing, inventory management, and transportation. (12)

**place utility** The availability of a product or service in a location that is convenient to a potential customer. (12)

**platform** A core product design element or component that can be quickly and cheaply adapted to various country markets. (10)

**political environment** The set of governmental institutions, political parties, and organizations that are the expression of the people in the nations of the world. (5)

**political risk** The risk of a change in political environment or government policy that would adversely affect a company's ability to operate effectively and profitably. (5)

**polycentric orientation** The second level in the EPRG framework: the view that each country in which a company does business is unique. In global marketing, this orientation results in high levels of marketing mix adaptation, often implemented by autonomous local managers in each country market. (1)

**polycentric pricing** The practice of setting different price levels for a given product in different country markets. Also known as adaptation pricing. (11)

**positioning** The act of differentiating a product or brand in the minds of customers or prospects relative to competing products or brands. (7)

**positioning by attribute or benefit** A positioning strategy that seeks to differentiate a company, product, or brand in terms of one or more specific benefits (e.g., reliability) offered to buyers. (7)

**positioning by competition** A positioning strategy that seeks to differentiate a company, product, or brand by comparing it to the competition. (7)

**positioning by quality/price** A positioning strategy that seeks to differentiate a product, brand, or company in terms of expensiveness/exclusivity, acceptable quality/good value, etc. (7)

**positioning by use or user** A positioning strategy that seeks to differentiate a product by associating it with users whose expertise or accomplishments potential buyers admire. (7)

**power distance** In Geert Hofstede's social values typology, the cultural dimension that reflects the extent to which it is acceptable for power to be distributed unequally in a society. (4)

**preferential tariff** A reduced tariff rate applied to imports from certain countries. (8)

**preferential trade agreement (PTA)** A trade agreement between a relatively small number of signatory nations, often on a regional or subregional basis. Different levels of economic integration can characterize such trade agreements. (3)

**presentation plan** In personal selling, the heart of the presentation strategy. The plan has six stages: approach, presentation, demonstration, negotiation, closing, and servicing the sale. (14)

**presentation strategy** Setting objectives for each sales call and establishing a presentation plan to meet those objectives. (14)

**price fixing** Secret agreements between representatives of two or more companies to set prices. (11)

**price transparency** Euro-denominated prices for goods and services that enable consumers and organizational buyers to comparison shop across Europe. (11)

**primary data** In market research, data gathered through research pertaining to the particular problem, decision, or issue under study. (6)

**product** One of the four Ps of the marketing mix: a good, service, or idea with tangible and/or intangible attributes that collectively create value for a buyer or user. (10)

**product adaptation–communication extension** A strategy of extending, with minimal change, the basic home-market communications strategy while adapting the product to local use or preference conditions. (10)

**product-communication adaptation (dual adaptation)** A dual-adaptation strategy that uses a combination of marketing conditions. (10)

**product-communication extension** A strategy for pursuing opportunities outside the home market. (10)

**product extension–communications adaptation** The strategy of marketing an identical product by adapting the marketing communications program. (10)

**product invention** In global marketing, developing new products with the world market in mind. (10)

**product market** A market defined in terms of a particular product category (e.g., in the automotive industry, "the SUV market," "the sports car market," etc.). (7)

**product placement** A marketing communication tool that involves a company paying a fee to have one or more products and brand names appear in popular television programs, movies, and other types of performances. (14)

**product saturation level** The percentage of customers or households that own a product in a particular country market; a measure of market opportunity. (2)

**product strategy** In personal selling, a sales representative's plan for selecting and positioning products that will satisfy customer needs. The third step in the strategic/consultative selling model. (14)

**product transformation** When a product that has been introduced into multiple country markets via a product extension–communication adaptation strategy serves a different function or use than originally intended. (10)

**pro forma invoice** A document that sets an export/import transaction into motion. The document specifies the amount and the means by which an exporter-seller wants to be paid; it also specifies the items to be purchased. (8)

**promotion site** A Web site that provides marketing communications about a company's goods or services. (15)

**psychographic segmentation** The process of assigning people to market segments on the basis of their attitudes, interests, opinions, and lifestyles. (7)

**publicity** Communication about a company or product for which the company does not pay. (13)

**public relations (PR)** One of four variables in the promotion mix. Within an organization, the department or function responsible for evaluating public opinion about, and attitudes toward, the organization and its products and brands. PR personnel also are responsible for fostering goodwill, understanding, and acceptance among a company's various constituents and the public. (13)

**purchasing power parity (PPP)** A concept that permits adjustment of national income measurements in various countries to reflect what a unit of each country's currency can actually buy. (2)

**put option** The right to sell a specified number of foreign currency units at a fixed price, up to the option's expiration date. (2)

**quota** Government-imposed limit or restriction on the number of units or the total value of a particular product or product category that can be imported. (8)

**rational appeal** In advertising, an appeal to the target audience's logic and intellect. (13)

**regiocentric orientation** The third level in the EPRG framework: the view that similarities as well as differences characterize specific regions of the world. In global marketing, a regiocentric orientation is evident when a company develops an integrated strategy for a particular geographic area. (1)

**regulatory environment** Governmental and nongovernmental agencies and organizations that enforce laws or establish guidelines for conducting business. (5)

**related and supporting industries** In Michael Porter's framework for national competitive advantage, one of the four determinants of a national "diamond." (16)

**relationship strategy** In personal selling, a sales representative's game plan for establishing and maintaining high-quality relationships with prospects and customers. The second step in the Strategic/Consultative Selling Model. (14)

**restrictive administrative and technical regulations** Regulations that can create barriers to trade; they may take the form of antidumping, size, or safety and health regulations. (8)

**revaluation** The strengthening of a country's currency. (2)

**rules of origin** A system of certification that verifies the country of origin of a shipment of goods. (3)

**sales agent** An agent who works under contract rather than as a full-time employee. (14)

**sales promotion** One of the four elements of the promotion mix. A paid, short-term communication program that adds tangible value to a product or brand. (14)

**sampling** A sales promotion technique that provides potential customers with the opportunity to try a product or service at no cost. (14)

**secondary data** Existing data in personal files, published sources, and databases. (6)

**self-reference criterion (SRC)** The unconscious human tendency to interpret the world in terms of one's own cultural experience and values. (4)

**selling proposition** In advertising, the promise or claim that captures the reason for buying the product or the benefit that product ownership confers. (13)

**services trade** The buying and selling of intangible, experience-based economic output. (2)

**shopping mall** A group of stores in one place, typically with one or more large department stores serving as anchors and with easy access and free parking. (12)

**short message service (SMS)** A globally accepted wireless standard for sending alphanumeric messages of up to 160 characters. (15)

**short-term orientation** One of the dimensions in Geert Hofstede's social values typology. Contrasts with long-term orientation. (4)

**single-column tariff** A schedule of duties in which the rate applies to imports from all countries on the same basis; the simplest type of tariff. (8)

**smartphone** A phone that offers some of the capabilities of computers, such as a Web browser. (15)

**social values typology** A study by Dutch organizational anthropologist Geert Hofstede that classifies national cultures according to five dimensions: individualism versus collectivism, masculinity versus femininity, power distance, uncertainty avoidance, and long-term orientation versus short-term orientation. (4)

**sourcing decision** A strategic decision that determines whether a company makes a product itself or buys products from other manufacturers as well as where it makes or buys its products. (8)

**Southern African Development Community (SADC)** An association whose member states are Angola, Botswana, Democratic Republic of Congo, Lesotho, Malawi, Mauritius, Mozambique, Namibia, Seychelles, South Africa, Swaziland, Tanzania, Zambia, and Zimbabwe. (3)

**sovereignty** A country's supreme and independent political authority. (5)

**special economic zone (SEZ)** A geographic entity that offers manufacturers simplified customs procedures, operational flexibility, and a general environment of relaxed regulations. (8)

**specialty retailer** A category of retail operations characterized by a more narrow focus than a department store and offering a relatively narrow merchandise mix aimed at a particular target market. (12)

**sponsorship** A form of marketing communication that involves payment of a fee by a company to have its name associated with a particular event, team or athletic association, or sports facility. (14)

**spreadsheet** A software application in the form of an electronic ledger that automatically calculates the effect of changes made to figures entered in rows and columns. (15)

**stakeholder** Any group or individual that is affected by, or takes an interest in, the policies and practices adopted by an organization. (17)

**stakeholder analysis** The process of formulating a "win-win" outcome for all stakeholders. (17)

**standardized (extension) approach** The pursuit of a global market opportunity using an extension strategy of minimal marketing mix variation in different countries. (1)

**standardized global marketing** A target market strategy that calls for creating the same marketing mix for a broad mass market of potential buyers. (7)

**strategic alliance** A partnership among two or more firms created to minimize risk while maximizing leverage in the marketplace. (9)

**strategic/consultative selling model** A five-step framework for approaching the personal selling task: personal selling philosophy, relationship strategy, product strategy, customer strategy, and presentation strategy. (14)

**strategic intent** A competitive advantage framework developed by strategy experts Gary Hamel and C. K. Prahalad. (16)

**strategic international alliances** A form of mutually beneficial collaboration among two or more companies doing business globally. The goal is to leverage complementary resources and competencies in order to achieve competitive advantage. (9)

**streaming audio** Transmission that allows users to listen to Internet radio stations. (15)

**streaming media** The transmission of combined audio and video content via a broadband network. (15)

**streaming video** A sequence of moving images sent in compressed form via the Internet and displayed on a computer screen. (15)

**subculture** Within a culture, a small group of people with their own shared subset of attitudes, beliefs, and values. (4)

**subsidies** Direct or indirect financial contributions or incentives that benefit producers. (8)

**supercenter** A category of retail operations that combines elements of discount stores and supermarkets in a space that occupies about half the size of a hypermarket. (12)

**supermarket** A category of retail operations characterized by a departmentalized, single-story retail establishment that offers a variety of food and nonfood items on a self-service basis. (12)

**superstore** A store that specializes in selling vast assortments of a particular product category in high volumes at low prices. (12)

**supply chain** A group of firms that perform support activities by generating raw materials, converting them into components or finished goods, and making them available to buyers. (12)

**survey research** Primary data collection via questionnaire-based studies designed to generate qualitative responses, quantitative responses, or both. (6)

**sustaining technologies** Incremental or radical innovations that improve product performance. (15)

**switch trading** A transaction in which a professional switch trader, switch trading house, or bank steps into a simple barter arrangement or other countertrade arrangement in which one of the parties is not willing to accept all the goods received in the transaction. (11)

**targeting** The process of evaluating market segments and focusing marketing efforts on a country, region, or group of people. (7)

**tariffs** The rules, rate schedules (duties), and regulations of individual countries affecting goods that are imported. (8)

**telematics** A car's ability to exchange information about its location or mechanical performance via a wireless Internet connection. (15)

**teleshopping** Round-the-clock programming exclusively dedicated to product demonstration and selling. (14)

**temporary surcharge** Surcharges introduced from time to time to provide additional protection for local industry and, in particular, in response to balance of payments deficits. (8)

**tiered branding** A strategy in which a corporate name is combined with a product brand name; also called combination or umbrella branding. (10)

**time utility** The availability of a product or service when desired by a customer. (12)

**trade deficit** A negative number in the balance of payments showing that the value of a country's imports exceeds the value of its exports. (2)

**trademark** A distinctive mark, motto, device, or emblem that a manufacturer affixes to a particular product or package to distinguish it from goods produced by other manufacturers. (5)

**trade mission** A state- or federally sponsored show outside the home country organized around a product, a group of products, an industry, or an activity at which company personnel can learn about new markets as well as competitors. (8)

**trade sales promotion** Promotion designed to increase product availability in distribution channels. (14)

**trade show** A gathering of company representatives organized around a product, a group of products, or an industry, at which company personnel can meet with prospective customers and gather competitor intelligence. (8)

**trade surplus** A positive number in the balance of payments showing that the value of a country's exports exceeds the value of its imports. (2)

**transaction site** A cyberspace retail operation that allows customers to purchase goods and services. (15)

**Transatlantic Trade and Investment Partnership (TTIP)** A proposed free-trade area that includes the United States and the EU. (3)

**transfer pricing** The pricing of goods, services, and intangible property bought and sold by operating units or divisions of a company doing business with an affiliate in another jurisdiction. (11)

**transistor** A "solid state amplifier" that replaced vacuum tubes in electronics products; it was a milestone in the digital revolution. (15)

**transnational company** A company exhibiting a geocentric orientation that pursues marketing opportunities in all parts of the world. However, a transnational company differs from a global company by fully integrating and coordinating two strategies: both sourcing products from a variety of different countries and serving multiple country markets across most world regions. (1)

**Trans-Pacific Partnership (TPP)** A proposed 12-nation free-trade area that includes Japan and the United States. (3)

**transparency** Openness in business dealings, financial disclosures, pricing, or other situations where the goal is to remove layers of secrecy or other obstacles to clear the way for understanding and decision making. (3)

**Triad** The three regions of Japan, Western Europe, and the United States, which represent the dominant economic centers of the world. (2)

**two-column tariff** General duties plus special duties indicating reduced rates determined by tariff negotiations with other countries. (8)

**uncertainty avoidance** In Geert Hofstede's social values framework, the extent to which members of a culture are uncomfortable with unclear, ambiguous, or unstructured situations. (4)

**uniform resource locator (URL)** An Internet site's address on the World Wide Web. (15)

**upper-middle-income country** A country with gross national income (GNI) per capita between $4,126 and $12,745. (2)

**usage rate** In behavioral market segmentation, an assessment of the extent to which a person uses a product or service. (7)

**user status** In behavioral market segmentation, an assessment of whether a person is a present user, potential user, nonuser, former user, etc. (7)

**value** A customer's perception of a firm's product or service offering in terms of the ratio of benefits (product, place, promotion) relative to price. This ratio can be represented by the value equation $V = B/P$. (1)

**value chain** The various activities that a company performs (e.g., research and development, manufacturing, marketing, physical distribution, and logistics) in order to create value for customers. (1)

**value equation** $V = B/P$, where $V$ stands for "perceived value," $B$ stands for "product, price, and place," and $P$ stands for "price." (1)

**value network** The cost structure in a particular industry that dictates the margins needed to achieve profitability. A broadly defined industry (e.g., computers) may have parallel value networks, each with its own metrics of value. (15)

**values** In culture, enduring beliefs or feelings that a specific mode of conduct is personally or socially preferable to another mode of conduct. (4)

**variable import levies** A system of levies applied to certain categories of imported agricultural products. (8)

**Voice over Internet Protocol (VoIP)** Technology that allows the human voice to be digitized and broken into data packets that can be transmitted over the Internet and converted back into normal speech. (15)

**warehousing** The aspect of physical distribution that involves the storage of goods. (12)

**Wi-Fi (wireless fidelity)** Technology based on a low-power radio signal that permits access to the Internet from a laptop computer or smartphone when the user is within range of a base station transmitter ("hotspot"). (15)

**World Trade Organization (WTO)** The successor to the General Agreement on Tariffs and Trade (GATT). (3)

**World Wide Web** Global computer network connecting Internet sites that contain text, graphics, and streaming audio and video resources. (15)

# Author/Name Index

Note: Page numbers with *e, f,* or *t* represent *exhibits, figures,* and *tables* respectively.

## C



## D

## E



## F



## G

## H



## I

## J



## K



## L

## S

## T



## U



## V



## W

## Y



## Z

# Subject/Organization Index

Page numbers with *e*, *f*, or *t* represent *exhibits*, *figures*, and *tables* respectively.

## A

## C

## E

## G

## J

## N

## O



## P

## Q



## R

## T

## U

## V



## W

## X



## Y



## Z